AUSTRALIAN SOLDIERS IN ASIA-PACIFIC IN WORLD WAR II

LACHLAN GRANT is a historian at the Australian War Memorial in Canberra. He has published widely on the Australian prisoner-of-war experience and Australian experiences of the Second World War. He is also a Visiting Fellow at the School of Strategic and Defence Studies at the Australian National University. He is a graduate of Monash University where he completed a PhD (2010) and MA (2005) in history.

AUSTRALIAN SOLDIERS IN ASIA-PACIFIC IN WORLD WAR II

LACHLAN GRANT

NEWSOUTH

A NewSouth book

Published by
NewSouth Publishing
University of New South Wales Press Ltd
University of New South Wales
Sydney NSW 2052
AUSTRALIA
newsouthpublishing.com

© Lachlan Grant 2014
First published 2014

10 9 8 7 6 5 4 3 2 1

National Library of Australia Cataloguing-in-Publication entry
Author: Grant, Lachlan, author.
Title: Australian soldiers in Asia-Pacific in World War II/Lachlan Grant.
ISBN: 9781742231419 (paperback)
       9781742241845 (ePub/Kindle)
       9781742247069 (ePDF)
Subjects: World War, 1939–1945 – Participation, Australian.
          World War, 1939–1945 – Social aspects – South Pacific Ocean.
          World War, 1939–1945 – Social aspects – Southeast Asia.
          World War, 1939–1945 – South Pacific Ocean.
          World War, 1939–1945 – Southeast Asia.
          Australia – History, Military – 1939–1945.
Dewey Number: 940.5426

Design Josephine Pajor-Markus
Front cover image Members of the 2/19th Battalion march past a rickshaw puller in Kluang, Malaya. Australian War Memorial P00102.035
Back cover image Members of the 2/27th Battalion trade with locals at Makassar in September 1945. Australian War Memorial 120834
Maps Keith Mitchell
Printer Everbest, China

This project has been assisted by the Australian Academy of the Humanities.

CONTENTS

ACKNOWLEDGMENTS

Many years of research and writing have gone into the production of this work, which would not have been completed without the assistance and support of many people. At the Australian War Memorial I acknowledge the support of my colleagues in the Military History Section: Steven Bullard, Peter Burness, Emma Campbell, Ashley Ekins, Meleah Hampton, Karl James, Michael Kelly, Aaron Pegram, Juliet Schyvens, Haruki Yoshida, and editors Christina Zissis, Robert Nichols and Andrew McDonald. I also thank the head of publications at the Memorial, Mark Small. From Monash University I thank Christina Twomey and Ian Copland, who were the supervisors for the original research upon which this book is based. I also thank my former colleagues at Monash for their support, in particular Bain Attwood, Johnny Bell, David Garrioch, Michael Hau, Meighen Katz, Mark Peel, Richard Scully, Simon Sleight and Alistair Thomson. I acknowledge my colleagues at the Australian National University, in particular Joan Beaumont and Rhys Crawley. From Nanyang Technological University, Singapore, Kevin Blackburn – who was an examiner of the original thesis – has been a great supporter of this work, as has Peter Stanley at the University of New South Wales, Canberra.

I would like to acknowledge, too, the invaluable advice and comments from my examiners, NTU's Kevin Blackburn, and Stuart Ward at the University of Copenhagen, as well as the comments from readers for NewSouth and referees for the *Australian Journal of*

Politics and History. I also pay tribute to the late Hank Nelson from the Australian National University, whose pioneering research on prisoners of war in the 1980s first raised the importance of the questions upon which this study has been built. My thanks to staff at the Australian War Memorial Research Centre, State Library of Victoria and Monash University Library rare books section. At NewSouth I thank Phillipa McGuinness for her enthusiastic support and vision for this book, as well as Uthpala Gunethilake and Elspeth Menzies. This work would not have been possible without the funding and support provided by an Australian Post-graduate Award by the Monash Research Graduate School and the former School of Historical Studies and Faculty of Arts at Monash University. The research for chapter 6 was supported by an Australian Army History Unit Research Grant, for which I am grateful. I am also grateful for the generosity of the Australian Academy of the Humanities, who assisted the publication of this book with an award from their Publication Subsidy Scheme.

Of a much more personal nature, I thank my family: my Mum and Dad, Andrew, Megan, Henry and Freddie, and my friends Jonathan Jackson and Derryn Schoenborn. They have all been there with me through the journey. Also, this book may not have been completed if not for the professionalism and dedication of staff at the oncology department at Canberra Hospital. Last of all, to the most important person in my life, my partner, best friend, fiancée and inspiration: Amanda Kate Wescombe, this book would not have been possible without your continual enthusiasm and encouragement. I hope we share the same fun and enjoyment on all our future journeys as we did on this one. Words alone cannot express my gratitude.

This book is dedicated to my grandfathers Jack (John) E.F. Grant (VX6009) and Christopher J. Lee (VX148193). It was hearing their stories when I was young that first introduced me to the concept that experiences of war could enhance and broaden individual outlooks toward other peoples and cultures.

MAPS

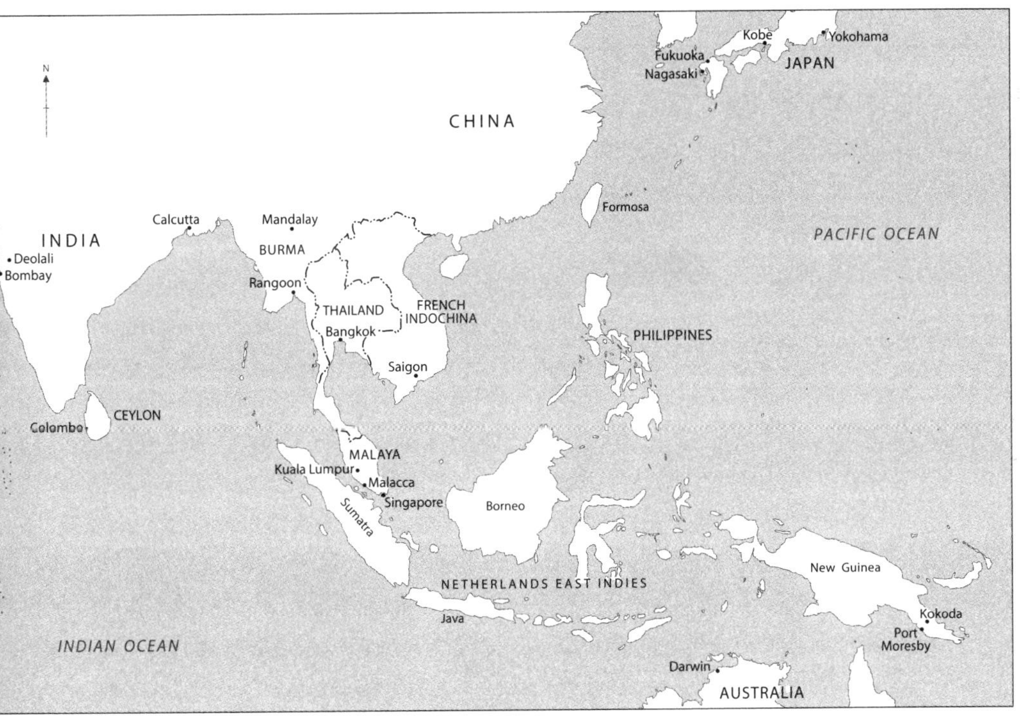

Asia and the Pacific

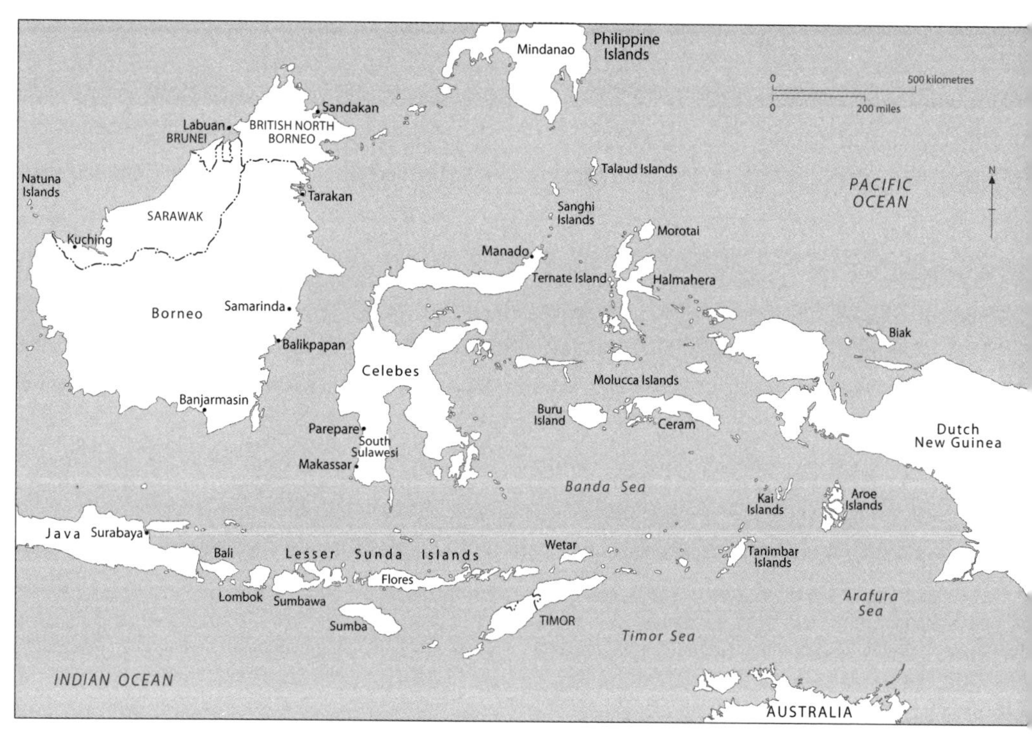

Eastern Netherlands East Indies

INTRODUCTION

In some ways Charles Alvin Kelly at first appears a typical Australian soldier. From rural Victoria, he answered the call and volunteered for the Second Australian Imperial Force (AIF), enlisting in his hometown in April 1940. Posted to the 2/7th Battalion, Private Kelly kept a small diary during his overseas service. He saw action in Greece in April 1941 and during the evacuation he survived the sinking of the *Costa Rica*. Saved by a destroyer, he was among the survivors taken to Crete. There, he became a prisoner of war of the Germans, but escaped from the prison compound, evaded recapture and was rescued by the submarine HMS *Torbay*. Returning to Australia following Japan's entry into the war, Kelly's battalion was diverted to Ceylon, where it became part of the island's garrison. Here Kelly's story diverges.

Seeing the folly of the Greek campaign and having experienced miserable conditions as a prisoner, Kelly became critical of world powers and their empires, whom he blamed for the war. In Ceylon, he befriended the locals and became inquisitive and curious about their conditions, culture and beliefs. Intrigued by Buddhist teachings, he entered heated debates with an army chaplain who criticised Kelly for dabbling in what the chaplain considered heathen texts. But Kelly found comfort in his discovery and became a Buddhist. His diary concludes with his return to Australia in 1942 and he was discharged from the AIF in 1943. What became of Kelly once he re-entered civilian life is somewhat of a mystery. He may have begun his career as an ordinary Australian soldier, but Kelly's story is anything but typical. His tale and outlook were certainly unusual, and highlight the diverse and complex experiences of Australian soldiers' Second World War encounters with Asia and empire.

Evocative of a green hell of mud and blood, they are place names that roll off the tongue: Kokoda, Milne Bay, Buna. Each has become representative of the hard jungle fighting and a snapshot of Australian experiences of the war in the Pacific. Similarly, the extraordinary prison camp at Changi and the brutal enslavement of prisoners of war on the Burma–Thailand Railway – many of whom laboured to their deaths – are experiences indelibly ingrained in the Australian wartime narrative. While these images are evocative and disturbing, Australian experiences of the war in Asia and the Pacific are also rich and complex. The battlefield, the prison camp and the work party formed only part of the soldier's narrative. Australians entering Asia and the Pacific during the Second World War encountered a new world: a world of different peoples, cultures, languages and religions, and a world of empire, dominance and white man's rule. As part of a larger story, these are experiences full of colour, drama and personal contact.

This book provides an insight into the lives, attitudes and experiences of Australian soldiers in Asia and the Pacific during the Second World War. Tales of friendship, woe, spiritual awakening, advantage, frustration, deceit, rebellion, souvenir hunting and sex are all part of the story. In forming relations with local communities, Australian troops caused controversy – whether intentionally or unwittingly – as they challenged or upset the established colonial order. While some soldiers asserted their place in the racial hierarchy, others were sympathetic toward the plight of the colonised. Some were highly inquisitive and wanted to learn something of and from the Asian cultures, languages and religions that they found themselves immersed in.

At the outbreak of the Second World War, Australia had a

population of approximately seven million. The half-a-million soldiers, sailors, airmen and nurses of the Australian military forces who served overseas represent an extraordinary group, encountering in their travels a region enveloped in conflict, political turmoil and social upheaval. They constitute the largest single group of Australians to enter Asia and the Pacific at that point in history, and the absence of their stories from the wider historiography is glaring. Today, more than 70 years after the event, it may be difficult – particularly for younger generations – to imagine or identify with the colonial world into which the men of the Second AIF descended from the gangplanks of the *Queen Mary* as it docked at Singapore in February 1941. These were predominantly white Australian young men who had volunteered to defend the might of the British Empire. They came from a generation of Australians who at that time still considered themselves equally British and Australian. They entered Singapore and Malaya believing that they were equal partners within the empire – Australians side by side with other Britons. But the society based on race and class within the British colonial world of Southeast Asia proved confronting for Australian troops. They were scenes repeated in various locations throughout the Second World War as Australian soldiers' encounters with empire in Asia and the Pacific challenged understandings of Australia's place in the region and the world.

This is a particularly pertinent topic given the importance placed upon the Second World War as a turning point in Australian history. As a consequence of the outbreak of war against Japan, Australia challenged the principle of 'imperial defence' and forged a more independent path in world affairs. These political and diplomatic affairs have captured the attention of historians, but what of the views on such matters by troops on the ground? Certainly, Australian soldiers' interactions with Asian communities were wide and varied. Ultimately, the level of interaction depended on the individual. Nevertheless, shortly after the arrival of Australian troops an Australian newsreel reporting the 1941 Anzac Day services in Singapore and Kuala Lumpur exclaimed, 'The Malayan dawn that comes up like thunder brought a rising sun, and a young Australia quickly became part of the Malayan scene.'[1] The homage to Rudyard Kipling's famous poem *Mandalay* would not have been lost on Australian cinema audiences of 1940, nor would the nationalistic rhetoric about a young Australia. Within their own writing – in the forms of diaries and letters home – we can see that Australian soldiers were imbued with the literary culture of the British Empire, with perennial reference to Kipling and his famous poem. While proud of the empire they had come to defend, as representatives of a 'young' nation they also brought with them a certain naivety about the outside world. But, having traditionally accepted a strong identification with Britain pre-war, how did Australian soldiers react and behave on encountering the colonies of Malaya, Singapore, Burma, India and Ceylon? For some soldiers, views could be reconfirmed by their experiences. For others, like Kelly, the encounter was eye-opening, and could challenge and change outlooks.

What contrasts existed, if any, between those entering the old European colonies of Asia and those in the Australian territories of Papua and New Guinea? In Papua and New Guinea it was the Australians rather than the British who were the colonial 'mastas', the upholders of the white man's prestige. Here, where Australian troops were instructed by fellow Australians to uphold the 'attitude of superiority', and where they were told that they were 'superior beings', how did the different colonial structures in place affect their behaviour and attitudes? The emergence of the myth of the legendary Papuan stretcher-bearers – colloquially known as 'fuzzy wuzzy angels' – comfortably encapsulates the finer aspects of friendship and co-operation between Australians and Papuans. However, the myth has overshadowed the darker and more insidious aspects of Australian colonialism. Few Australians today may realise that Papuans and New Guineans were forcibly recruited to work for the Australian military. Press-ganged, beaten and mistreated, the local inhabitants were treated in ways that most Australians would consider – both at the time and now – unjust and unfair. Certainly, the carriers won great admiration among Australians both during the war and since; and deservedly so. The enduring legend of the 'fuzzy wuzzy angel' is testament to this. However, the story of Papuans loyally volunteering to assist Australians in a friendly partnership is only one piece of the jigsaw.

Existing histories of Australian participation in the Pacific War have generally focused on the military experiences of combat, campaigns and grand strategy. The pioneering work of Hank Nelson first identified the importance of Australia's Second World War encounter with Asia in his landmark study on the experiences of Australian prisoners of the Japanese. It was Nelson's view that the importance of the prisoner-of-war experience in Australian national history was that the men of the 8th Division were the largest single group of Australians to enter Asia en masse. For Australian soldiers in the Middle East and North Africa, attitudes toward Allies and locals have been the subject of recent work by Mark Johnston; however, a quarter of a century after Nelson's findings, there has yet to be a single-volume study focused solely on the face-to-face encounters between Australians and their near neighbours during the Second World War.[2]

The Pacific War was an imperial war, fought between colonial powers over colonised regions, and its historiography has been heavily shaped by issues of culture and imperialism. Historians have long demonstrated the ways in which concepts of race and racism shaped affairs at diplomatic and political levels, as well as how they influenced ordinary soldiers on the ground as they came face to face with the enemy. But, rather than documenting the experience of battle and contact with the Japanese, what of the interactions and cross-cultural contacts between soldiers and the peoples who inhabited the lands in which the war in Asia and the Pacific was fought? Experiences engaging with local populations form one of the most common components of Australian writing on fighting wars in foreign locales and, as a cross-section of the Australian community, the writings of these soldiers form an important chapter in understanding ordinary Australian attitudes and outlooks.

Complicating matters is the widely held view that Australian participation in the Pacific War saw a continuation, even a strengthening, of Australian fears of the so-called 'yellow peril'. Returning veterans – and publications by ex-prisoner-of-war authors Rohan Rivett and Russell Braddon – have often been cited, as has the rhetoric of Returned and Services League (RSL) leadership, as evidence for continuing 'anti-Asian' sentiment. However, the diversity of the veteran community shows that this is a problematic practice leading to an unreasonably skewed perspective. For example, the peak of RSL membership in the 1950s (which included many First World War veterans) numbered less than half of the total returned Second World War veterans. Some veterans had refused to join the organisation for political reasons. It is important to consider here, also, that 'anti-Asian' and 'anti-Japanese' can mean quite different things. A prisoner or soldier who may have held an untoward view of his Japanese adversary may at the same time have formed strong bonds with Chinese, Thais, Indians or Indonesians. In addition, the ex-prisoner as the source of anti-Japanese sentiment in post-war Australia has become something of a standard typecast, yet even prisoners of war who were sent to Japan forged a range of outlooks. Overall, as a cross-section of the Australian community, the diversity of soldiers' views regarding Asia and Australia's place and role in the region is a topic unaddressed by historians, who have generally not looked beyond the aforementioned usual suspects when considering those who engaged and interacted with the people of the region. Whose voices and what kinds of stories have, therefore, remained unheard?

Certainly, much has been written by historians on Australian–Asian relations during the periods before and after the Second

World War, but the focus has traditionally been on the attitudes and relations at a political, diplomatic, cultural and business level.[3] By documenting the attitudes and outlooks of politicians, academics, businessmen, writers and journalists – citizens who may be classified as 'social elites' – this body of work overlooks the views of ordinary Australian soldiers, nurses, sailors and airmen and their face-to-face encounters with the people and cultures of Asia. Their unique, diverse and complex voices and views on these matters – a soldier such as Charles Kelly is just a single, albeit unusual, example – have gone unheralded.

1

AUSTRALIA, THE WAR, AND THE WORLD

In Australian history, the Second World War has been clearly identified as a time when Australia diverged from a national path closely tied to Britain and empire to one in which it became more independent in international affairs and more confident in its own identity. Despite the formation of the Commonwealth government nearly four decades before the war, Australians possessed a dual nationality whereby they were considered British subjects in an international context. Unquestionably, an Australian from this period could regard themselves as both British and Australian. Such feelings were cemented in both blood ties and national policy. The White Australia policy had ensured that by the 1933 census approximately 97 per cent of the population had been born in Australia or the British Isles and that Australians were 'fundamentally British in race and nationality', possessing the 'essential characteristics of their British ancestors'.[1] Furthermore, Australian citizenship was not introduced until the *Nationality and Citizenship Act 1948*. Before this, Australians were British citizens. Further evidence of the power of Australia's identification with Britain is seen in the sharp surge in recruitment in the months following the fall of France and at the height of Britain's crisis; mid-1940 saw enlistments in the AIF peak as 102,000 volunteers fronted up to recruiting stations between June and August.[2]

Furthermore, Australia remained inherently tied to Britain

through trade and diplomacy. British products dominated Australian imports as tariffs were raised on non-British goods. Moreover, Australia relied on Britain for foreign diplomacy until 1940, when the government made its own consular appointments, and on the BBC for news regarding overseas developments, having no political outlet pre-war in which to shape an Australian perspective on world affairs. Furthermore, the majority of overseas news published in Australian newspapers came from abroad – about 85 per cent through London, 12 per cent through New York, and 2–3 per cent through the rest of the world. Very little of it concerned Asian or Pacific affairs, as the news was selected by representatives of British news agencies on account of its interest to the British public. Such factors ensured that Australia had a blinkered view of the world, and was seeing world affairs through British eyes.[3] Furthermore, if Australians did not view Britain as a superior and the centre of empire during this period, then many saw Australia – along with Canada and New Zealand – as Britain's partner in the empire; Australia equal with Britain.[4] For the men of the AIF, such sentiments were tested by their encounters with the British colonies of Asia.

The Second Australian Imperial Force was formed following the outbreak of war in Europe. As opposed to the Citizens' Military Force (or Militia), the AIF was an expeditionary force designed for overseas service, to be made up entirely of volunteers. Motivations for enlistments varied. Barrett, in his survey of veterans, showed that volunteers were motivated by a range of factors, including a sense of civic duty to Australia and to the British Empire.[5]

The letters, diaries and memoirs featured in this book are drawn from a range of Australian military units which encountered Asia and the Pacific during the Second World War. From the four AIF divisions raised during the war, contingents of the 6th, 7th and 9th divisions first encountered Asia en route to battlefields in North Africa and the Mediterranean. Albeit briefly,

the troop ships of these convoys stopped for leave at the regular
ports of call of Bombay and Colombo, and experiences during
these stopovers could have a lasting impression. In Southeast Asia
and the Pacific strategic planning was founded on the assumption that Singapore was the key to security in the region, and
from February 1941 elements of the 8th Division began arriving
in Singapore and moving into camps in Malaya. By the time of
the Japanese attack on Pearl Harbor on 7 December and the syn-
chronised attack on Malaya (8 December on the opposite side
of the International Date Line) two brigades of the 8th Division
were located in Malaya and the division's third brigade had elements scattered south-eastward along the island chains to Australia's north and north-west on Ambon, Timor and New Britain.
After fierce resistance the entire 8th Division was captured following a series of defeats on Rabaul (23 January 1942), Ambon (3
February) and Timor (20 February), and the surrender of all Allied
forces on Singapore (15 February). On 12 March units of the 7th
Division on Java – known as Blackforce – also surrendered. In just
a seven-week period, 22,000 Australians had become prisoners of
the Japanese.

In Malaya in July 1941 a handful of Australian soldiers were
requisitioned from their units in the 8th Division to train in guerrilla tactics at the Bush Warfare School in Burma and form part
of what was known as the British 204 Military Mission to China.
They entered China, where they were to train Chinese forces, via
the Burma Road in January of 1942. Following increasing illness
and a mixed response by the Chinese the group was eventually
withdrawn to Calcutta the following October before returning to
Australia.

Following Japan's entry into the war, preparations were made
for the recall and eventual return of the Australian divisions in
the Middle East and North Africa. On return they once again
disembarked for leave in Bombay and Colombo. Two brigades
of the 6th Division were diverted to Ceylon when it was threat-

ened with Japanese invasion, and there they remained until the middle of 1942. From then, Australian forces were fighting the Japanese in New Guinea and would be involved in a series of campaigns there and on neighbouring islands until the end of the war. Launched from Morotai, the 7th and 9th divisions were engaged in May, June and July 1945 in the amphibious landings at Tarakan, North Borneo, and Balikpapan, where they remained involved until war's end in August 1945. The Royal Australian Navy (RAN) was involved in all Allied naval campaigns throughout the Pacific War. Like the navy, members of the Royal Australian Air Force (RAAF) took part in all the major Allied campaigns during the war. Serving with Australian squadrons, or through the Empire Air Training Scheme on attachment to the Royal Air Force, Australian airmen saw action in Europe, the Mediterranean, North Africa, Asia and the Pacific.

By war's end Australian prisoners of the Japanese were scattered in prison camps across the entire region. From mid-1942 the Japanese began moving prisoners from the main camps on Singapore and Java to destinations throughout Asia. Prisoners were transported to Burma, Formosa, Thailand, Borneo and Japan. By mid-1943 over 12,000 Australian prisoners of war were scattered between Thailand and Burma, slaving on the construction of a 420-kilometre railway between Thanbyuzayat in Burma and Ban Pong in Thailand. By 1945, Australian prisoners of the Japanese were located throughout the region: at Rabaul, on Ambon, and in Java, Sumatra, Borneo, the Philippines, Singapore, Malaya, Thailand, Burma, French-Indochina, Hainan, Manchuria, Korea and Japan.

The very thought of Asia and the Pacific may have provoked a variety of responses among Australians in 1941; fear and apprehension, certainly, but also ambition and aspiration for those who recognised the potential of the Asian market. Before the outbreak of war Australia remained committed to the White Australia policy (which restricted Asian immigration to Australia), and respective governments remained unwavering in this view during the course of the war. The Australian–New Zealand agreement of 1944 in fact reinforced Australia's and New Zealand's respective rights to determine their own immigration policies. Further strengthening this point of view at the 1945 United Nations conference in San Francisco, Australian Minister for External Affairs Dr H.V. Evatt successfully defended individual states' rights to decide domestic policies within their jurisdictions and without UN interference.[6] Public attitudes, however, were softening on the White Australia policy during the war. While nine out of ten people surveyed in a 1943 Gallup poll favoured the resumption of white immigration after the war, 40 per cent favoured 'limited' non-white immigration. While there are no polls before the war with which to draw comparisons, there was goodwill shown in Australia towards China's resistance to Japan. For example, a Department of Information pamphlet asked whether Chinese immigration to the Northern Territory would threaten Australian standards of living. Another pamphlet posed the question of Asian migration, citing the mixed races of the United States that were currently fighting side by side. There is evidence that in the early 1940s different sections of the Australian community began campaigning for change. Church groups led such discussions; concerned with both Christian and humanitarian principles they were among the first in Australia to publicly declare that the term 'white' (in the context of the term 'White Australia') was racially offensive.[7] Groups favouring closer relations with Asia lobbied the government, and support was also found amongst prominent individuals such as newspaper editor Keith Murdoch, who proclaimed: 'what is called our White Australia policy is an absolute bar against such peaceful relationships'.[8] The Second World War introduced changes in Australian attitudes to such matters, yet historians have placed little focus on the ways Australian soldiers may have identified with such issues.

By and large, Australian perceptions of their region were largely constructed by a long European literary tradition. With profound ignorance, most Australians were uninterested in, or possessed little knowledge of Asia before the Second World War.[9] For Australian military travellers in the 1940s, this lack of genuine knowledge about Asia and the Pacific was made up for by knowledge gained from colonial literature, films and the media, which emphasised the romantic and exotic nature of the region. Despite their geographic proximity to Asia, Australians adopted a European – and particularly British – view of Asia and the Pacific. Influenced by colonial literature, in particular Rudyard Kipling, as well as by Hollywood genre films of the period, Australian ideas and perceptions of Asia were unrealistically romantic. According to the literature, Asian and Pacific locations were fertile, exotic places of adventure. Asia had provided the backdrop for a variety of works that formed the basis of an imperial culture that captured European colonialism in Asia within a romantic genre for white adventures. The new frontier of the East was mystical, a world of extremes, making adventure possible in order to attest the merit of the English race.[10] Australian soldiers embraced this concept with a naïve sense of enthusiasm. Grasping this sense of adventure, the act of travelling abroad enticed many men and women serving within the Australian military to adopt the language and style of colonial writers in their diaries, letters and memoirs.

Beginning with influential scientific works such as Charles Darwin's *Journal of Researches into the Geology and Natural History of the Various Countries Visited During the Voyage of H.M.S. Beagle*, Alexander Von Humbolt's *Cosmos*, and Alfred Russell Wallace's *The Malay Archipelago*, the tropical landscapes of Southeast Asia and the Pacific were portrayed as a naturalist's paradise of breathtaking beauty abundant in riches. Such scientific studies coincided with and preceded the Romantic movement in Europe, paving the way for literary works that depicted and enhanced the Western image of Southeast Asia and the Pacific as wonderful and exotic. Beginning with authors such as Jean-Jacques Rousseau and his portrayal of the noble savages in the Pacific Islands, such views were furthered by the concept of the romantic tropical orient that filtered through in the writings, novels and poems of authors such as Joseph Conrad, Rudyard Kipling and Somerset Maugham, who based their writings partly on personal experiences living and travelling within the region.[11]

Australian perceptions of Southeast Asia were largely a product of this pre-established genre of colonial literature. Australians entering Asia on the verge of war in 1941 carried with them pre-conceived ideas based on this strong literary background. Historians such as Broinowski, Vickers, Walker and Dixon have all established the influence British colonial literature had on Australian writers.[12] With an ode to the British 'boys' own' genre, including titles such as *Chums*, *Boys' Own*, *Kim*, *The Jungle Book* and *King Solomon's Mines*, from the early 20th century a series of Australian authors produced fiction giving an authority of Asia as an adventure zone for white men.[13] Interest in New Guinea and the Pacific was shown by Australian film-makers, particularly Frank Hurley, and Australian writers during the 1920s and 1930s adopted themes from British colonial fiction and reconfirmed for Australian audiences their colonial responsibilities in the region as inheritors of their very own 'white man's burden'.[14] Instilled with imperial culture, Australians serving abroad took with them images of Asia constructed from this literature and wrote home with reference to a variety of literary works, reflecting their sense of empire nationalism. But in what ways would such cultural baggage affect their behaviour and outlooks once settled in the colonies?

British historian John MacKenzie has shown how juvenile literature and school textbooks in Britain promoted empire patriotism.[15] These sources also played an important role in shaping Australian views of the world, as a didactic imperialism predominated.[16] Textbooks and children's literature provide some of the most explicit examples of imperial popular culture in Australia. One textbook used by students in Victoria was *The Pictorial History of the British Empire*, the title page of which outlines the contents as containing a 'full and instructive account of the most remarkable customs of our forefathers, accurate pen and pencil sketches of the most remarkable places in the empire, and lives of the most distinguished heroes of our race in peaceful and warlike achievements'.[17] The soldiers who served in the Second World War grew up in the 1920s and 1930s with school readings littered with such adventurous tales of empire emphasising the advancement of the British 'race'.[18] Further imperial cultural affiliations were effected through organisations such as the Boy Scout movement, as well as via the popularity of English music and dancehall productions within Australia before the war.[19]

At a political level, the outbreak of the Second World War sowed the seeds to improve Australia's diplomatic representation abroad and Australian knowledge of the region. In a statement on foreign policy in 1939 the leader of the United Australia Party and Prime Minister of Australia, Robert Menzies, outlined his wish for Australia to become a 'principal' in Pacific affairs and to increase its diplomatic contact with the United States, China, Japan, the Netherlands East Indies and 'other countries which fringe the Pacific'. However, Menzies did not mean that Australia was to act in the Pacific 'as if we are a completely separate Power', but that it 'must, of course, act as an integral part of the British Empire. We must have full consultation and co-operation with Great Britain, South Africa, New Zealand and Canada'.[20] The first independent consular appointments to Washington, Ottawa and Tokyo in 1940, and to Chungking (the provisional capital of Chiang Kai-sheck's nationalist government) the following year, were evidence of the commitment to this policy.

At the outbreak of war in the Pacific in December 1941 the conservative Menzies had been replaced as prime minister by the Australian Labor Party's John Curtin, who during the course of the war made decisions which dynamically altered the way in which Australia viewed and placed itself in relation to the Great Powers. During the tumultuous period of stunning Japanese victories in the early months of the war, such changes were dramatically symbolised by Curtin's memorandum to British Prime Minister Winston Churchill, in which he alleged that the evacuation of Singapore would be regarded as an 'inexcusable betrayal', and Curtin's 1941 New Year's address – published in the Melbourne *Herald* – in which he proclaimed: 'Without any inhibitions of any kind, I make it clear that Australia looks to America, free of any pangs as to our traditional links or kinship with the United Kingdom.'[21] Relations between Churchill and the Labor government were severely tested during this period over policies regarding the defence of Singapore and, later, by Curtin's insistence upon the direct return of AIF divisions from the Middle East to Australia to confront the Japanese threat (without informing the Australian Prime Minister, Churchill had attempted to divert part of the 7th Division to Burma). Churchill's prejudice towards Australians was clear in his response that Australians were from 'bad stock', though when Churchill later published his multi-volume history of the war he was far more sympathetic toward Curtin's predicament. From the Australian perspective, the 'beat Hitler first' policy agreed between Churchill and President of the United States Franklin D. Roosevelt, without Australian knowledge or consultation, reflected the unevenness of the Australian–British relationship in terms of empire membership and big decisions regarding the course of the war and imperial defence.[22]

Much debate and discussion by historians have continued regarding the sensibilities of Curtin's statements, fuelled in particular by the politics of former Australian Prime Minister Paul Keating. Keating attempted to reorientate Australian commemoration and remembrance from a focus on the First World War to one on the Second World War to suit his 'big picture' of Australia in Asia and his republican agenda. Most historians agree that the political crises of 1942 awakened Australia to its responsibilities as an independent nation within the British Commonwealth. While a turn to the United States during 1942–45 was one of convenience – and Australia, in fact, reinforced ties with Britain in the postwar decade – Australia became more assertive in foreign policy matters, acquiring its own overseas representation. This saw the expansion of the Department of External Affairs, and the creation and development of policies to deal with Asia in the postwar period.[23]

Furthermore, it is important to emphasise that the changes that took place during the war were not due to anti-British or anti-imperialist sentiments. Nor were they a reflection of Australian republican sentiments among Australian politicians of this time. Within the ruling party, radical anti-British nationalists were marginalised; a majority of significant Labor government figures preferred to build upon the strength of the British attachment. Importantly, successive Australian governments were just as determined as the British government to protect colonialism in Asia. Rather than a rejection of the past, the important changes that took place within Australian nationalism represented reforms that reorientated Australia's relationship with Britain.[24]

Wartime debate on future foreign policy revolved around a number of key issues regarding how to achieve peace, stability, security and prosperity for Australia and the region. Following the fall of Singapore in 1942 Australian leaders determined that Australia be set on a political course that instrumented an independent approach to Australian foreign policy. The threat created by the Japanese successes of 1942 confirmed that new solutions were required to solve the problem of Australian security, all faith for which had previously been put in the Singapore Strategy (the plan that Singapore would be constructed as an impregnable fortress, the cornerstone of British Empire defence in the East). Central to this change in foreign policy was the view that the United States would be the influential power in the region, and this view was exemplified by Prime Minister Curtin's proclamation in *The Herald*.

This change in direction was particularly fostered by the Minister for External Affairs, Dr H.V. Evatt, and was ratified by Australia's signing of the *Statute of Westminster Adoption Act 1942*, which formally adopted a 1931 act of the British Imperial Parliament granting the parliaments and governments of dominions the power to act independently of the British parliament and government. In his determination to reform Australian relations with Britain and the United States, Evatt attempted to create new regional and global forums that could advance Australian interests. An important initiative in this regard was the Australian–New Zealand Agreement 1944 (or Anzac agreement). This agreement claimed Australia and New Zealand the right to be parties to peace talks and demanded an international conference on Pacific affairs prior to a peace settlement. Additionally, the agreement called for a zone of regional defence based on Australia and New Zealand in the south and south-west Pacific. Furthermore, the agreement refused to recognise any change of sovereignty due to the establishment of military bases in the region during the war (a statement clearly directed at the United States, which had played a leading role in driving Japanese forces from the region). The agreement was therefore significant in outlining Australian designs for Papua and New Guinea, raising questions of Australian imperial ambitions. Days after signing the agreement, Evatt sent a message to London proposing a postwar role for Australia of full responsibility for policing Portuguese Timor, Australian New Guinea and the British Solomon Islands Protectorate, as well as a share in the responsibility policing the Netherlands East Indies. Needless to say, the Americans, British and Dutch were not impressed by the assertiveness of the Australian government on this matter.[25]

The view that the days of European colonial presence in Asia were numbered, the recognition that social hardships among populations of the world were fundamental causes of conflict, and the need to regulate relations between states in order to prevent conflict (as outlined within the Atlantic Charter and United Nations Charter) compromised Australian commitment to the White Australia policy. Also complicating matters was that while Australia supported the emergence of self-reliant states in Asia and the Pacific (as outlined in the charters), its stance was somewhat contradictory given that it believed that it was too early for the European powers to abandon their colonies (in the interests of stability and security), and supported the continuation of the trustee-style mandate system of the League of Nations. But there was no bipartisan support for the policies advocated by Evatt either within the ruling Labor Party – which from July 1945 was led by Ben Chifley, who had succeeded Curtin as prime minister following Curtin's untimely death – or among the opposition. Australia's haphazard and inconsistent approach to such matters was evident during the postwar period, in which it publicly proclaimed support for the independence of India and the republican movement in Indonesia in 1947 and 1948, while at the same time supporting the continuation of French colonial rule in Indochina and British rule in Singapore and Malaya. Meanwhile, within Australia's own major dependency of Papua and New Guinea, independence was not foreseen as a possibility.[26]

While these changes in outlook at a political and diplomatic level have been well documented by historians, the focus here will be on what the encounter with Asia and the Pacific meant for soldiers on the front lines, those who were engaging with Asia and empire at an individual, face-to-face level. While such political battles were taking place in Canberra and London, eventually resulting in an overall change of national perspective, the diaries and letters of the men and women of the Australian military forces preparing for the defence of the empire in Southeast Asia during 1941 reveal a process by which the soldiers themselves had already begun to formulate their own opinions. A group ignored in historical discussion on such matters, some soldiers were more forthright (though far less public) in their views than the Australian government under prime ministers Curtin and Chifley – a government that by war's end in 1945 still did not fully support the idea of a 'free' Asia.

2

THE NEW WORLD
Arriving in British Asia

A colourful atmosphere greeted the *Queen Mary* as it berthed at Singapore's naval docks on 18 February 1941. Aboard, troops of the 22nd Brigade of the 8th Australian Division were in a boisterous mood. Greeting them on the dock were a brass band and an official party of dignitaries, including the Governor of the Straits Settlements, Sir Shenton Thomas. In the broadcast that followed, the governor described the division's arrival as 'one more proof of the unity of Empire, one more recognition of the fact that we stand or fall together'.[1] For Australian soldiers, however, the unity of empire was soon tested. Here they found a 'new world', a world full of fascination, a world to explore. But they also found a world of hierarchy and of class and racial divisions. It was a world in which individual understandings of Australia's place in the empire were not matched by the treatment the Australians received by the British ruling classes.

Much has been made by scholars, going back to the exploits of the First AIF, of the Australian soldier-tourist analogy. The lure of travel that may have enticed volunteers, the issuing of guidebooks by the military, the ocean voyage and stops at the ports of call have all been duly noted. Australian soldiers in the First World War quickly gained a reputation as 'six-bob-a-day tourists'. Leave and downtime for soldiers often meant sightseeing, which became a major feature of letters and diaries as authors were essentially writing for audiences at home.[2] One needs to be careful, however, not to simplistically confine the experiences of

A contingent of the 8th Division arrives in Singapore in August 1941. A dockworker stands in the foreground holding out his hat to catch coins thrown by Australian troops awaiting disembarkation. The arrival of the 8th Division signalled a major encounter between large numbers of Australians and the people and cultures of Asia.
Australian War Memorial 009249/13

Australians at war to one of travel and tourism. Soldiers were not tourists and had no say in their destination abroad. Their experiences of military life mostly consisted of long hours of boredom or monotonous routine. While the opportunity to sightsee on leave may have been a highlight, experiences of battle – brief as they may be – or the endurance of long years of imprisonment defined the war for most servicemen and servicewomen. However, military service did offer many Australians who would not have been able to afford overseas travel the opportunity to see something of the world. As one soldier wrote aboard *Aquitania* en route to Singapore, 'I am seeing part of the world which it has long been my wish to see and instead of being an expensive holiday cruise am being paid to see it. Is that any good?'[3] Once in Malaya, the troops described themselves as the 'so called tourists of Malaya' and many wrote home of the excitement and 'glamours attached to arriving in a strange country'.[4] Importantly – as the historian Hank Nelson has championed – the 8th Division was the first and largest single group of Australians to enter Asia, giving their experiences a unique place in Australian national history.

Significantly, descriptions of the voyage to Singapore and of sightseeing in Asia illustrate empire patriotism of the era, demonstrating a sense of knowledge, belonging, and pride in symbols of British prestige. This process began with the embarkation upon (pre-war luxury) ocean liners from companies such as P&O and Cunard White Star that had been requisitioned by the British government for the transportation of Allied soldiers. Following the Washington Naval Treaty (1922), which limited naval construction, the ocean liner rivalled the battleship as a symbol of national naval prowess during the interwar period. Rivalries were contested for the speed record across the Atlantic, with the fastest ship recognised by the unofficial awarding of the Blue Riband. While this had been contested since the late 19th century it took on more importance in the interwar period. As an example of how these ocean liners became symbolic of national pride, a 1936 article in the *Times* spoke of how the *Queen Mary* – the 'pride of [British] craftsmanship' – aimed 'to re-establish British naval supremacy in the North Atlantic' (this it would do in record-breaking runs across the Atlantic).[5]

For Australian soldiers in the Second World War, boarding the 'crack Atlantic' liners, with such familiar names as *Queen Mary*, *Aquitania*, *Mauritania*, *Ile de France*, *Queen Elizabeth*, *Nieuw Amsterdam* and *Queen of Bermuda*, immediately conjured images of opulence and adventure and reconfirmed notions of British seafaring prowess.[6] 'We had a grand sea trip over', noted one soldier, adding that 'being on board the *Queen Mary* made the voyage all the more appealing'.[7] Such a journey upon the famous liner – a journey that few of the volunteers of the AIF would have been able to afford during peacetime – added to the thrill and novelty of the overseas travel experience. Never having thought he would set foot on the *Queen Mary*, Walter Bills – a Melbourne city clerk from Hawthorn – glowed when describing not only the enormity of the occasion but also the ship, with its 'shopping centre that rivals Bourke Street'.[8] One soldier who missed out on passage aboard the *Queen Mary* – though he still wrote of delight at boarding the 'marvellous' *Aquitania* – felt 'swindled'. For men and women who had been nurtured on tales of empire, the size and power of the *Queen Mary* was a glowing exhibition of Britain's technical know-how and its mastery of the seas. Decades later, veterans still described the *Queen Mary*'s powerful manoeuvre in which she left the convoy bound solo for Singapore as a 'sight never to be forgotten'.[9]

Further reinforcing the way in which men and women of the AIF were imbued with imperial culture is the citation of well-known works of colonial literature within their writing. Imagining the entering and discovering of a 'new world' already familiar to them through fiction, troops drew upon their knowledge of colonial literature and similarly described their new surrounds as luxurious, romantic and exotic. As one soldier preparing 'for the great adventure' of his first leave to Singapore reminisced: 'we had read so much about the East, more or less, and were avid to learn something of the romantic colour and oriental mysticism peculiar to all Eastern countries'.[10] The Australian worldview at this time was British by default. Within the letters and diaries of soldiers, sailors, airmen and nurses, references to colonial literature are numerous and varied, incorporating the likes of Rudyard Kipling, W. Somerset Maugham, Joseph Conrad, George Orwell, Siegfried Sassoon, Edgar Wallace, P.G. Wodehouse, Rupert Brooke, John Buchan, Beatrice Grimshaw and R.M. Ballantyne.

Foremost of these writers was Kipling. Popular among Australians during this period, Kipling greatly influenced a generation of Australian writers.[11] In particular, Kipling's *Mandalay* was made even more famous in Australia during the 1930s when it was popularised by the song version – 'On the Road to Mandalay' – recorded by the famous Australian baritone Peter Dawson. This was a point made by William Noonan, a member of 'Tulip Force'; a group of Australian commandos who entered China via the Burma Road in 1942. Burma, wrote Noonan, was virtually unknown to Australians except for a few 'picturesque lines' from the unofficial poet laureate of the British Empire.[12]

Though he left a mark on Australian novelists, less noted is the influence of Kipling on Australian soldiers. This is clearly reflected within their letters, diaries and memoirs. By far he is the most often-cited author within the writing of Australian servicemen and servicewomen encountering Asia during the Second World War. It seems few Australians writing from Southeast Asia in 1941 failed to embellish their writing with reference to or quotes from Kipling.[13] The impulsive pull of British imperial culture of the era is emphasised by the reverence given to this pre-existing canon of literature by the AIF troops writing shortly after their arrival in Asia.

But just as those in Burma wrote of the error in Kipling's geography (in which he set China 'across the bay'), the ingrained imperial culture failed to prepare them for the sights, the sounds and the smells upon experiencing Asia firsthand.[14] Everything was new and exotic. One description of Singapore read:

> My curiosity whetted by so strange a contrast to that
> of my homeland, I wended my way through Singapore,
> to be amused and initiated in the bizarre atmosphere of
> its shopping centre. Chinese richsha pullers, grinning,
> gesticulating, babbling in their native tongue importuned
> me, hounding and obstructing my uncertain progress
> through the densely crowded thoroughfares. Snake
> charmers, peddlers, fortune tellers and street entertainers,
> all clamouring with hungry persistency, wore down my
> 'sales resistance' and my capital.[15]

Another soldier described a market in Malacca in a similar manner, with 'one gentleman insisting that he was "the man with a radio mind"', and young children performing tricks for money.[16] Even the local currency, baffling as it was in the words of one soldier, was a novelty. With its dollars and cents and colourful paper notes, it conjured an illusion of riches. With his pockets full, the Australian soldier felt he carried enough money to 'own the world'.[17]

Across the entire region soldiers, sailors, airmen and nurses described their surrounds romantically. Their writing conjured enduring images and enhanced perceptions – and delivered to those at home confirmation – of British colonial treasure. The Australian troops were well aware, for example, that Malaya 'contained most of the world's rubber and tin, and much of its quinine and oil', and with its strategic geographic location understood that it 'should be securely held'.[18] Men such as Private Frank Williams of the 4th Reserve Motor Transport Company – a farmer from Swan Hill who would later die on the Burma–Thailand Railway – cited the figures for the average acreage and yield of the rubber plantations in letters home.[19] Wanting a slice of the riches, some were even on the lookout for postwar business opportunities.[20]

From Ceylon, Private Arthur Wallin – a Jolimont railway worker from Richmond – wrote of the low housing costs and the possibilities for capitalising on the lack of exports if he were to open the first fruit cannery in the colony.[21] Paraphernalia for visiting troops reinforced the word. Emphasis on land size and mineral and agricultural wealth, for example, are notable features within soldier guidebooks such as the one published in India for visiting Australian soldiers by the Wills tobacco company.[22] And it was not only private companies in on the act; later guidebooks published by the Australian military for New Guinea, Java and Borneo were also littered with such trivia.

Like Western travellers writing from Asia before them, military personnel in Asia and the Pacific, too, could imagine the surrounding landscapes as promised lands or paradises. The brilliant greens of the coconut and banana palms, rubber plantations and lush jungle enforced an image of Malaya as being a fertile Arcadia or 'garden of Eden'. Approaching Singapore aboard the *Queen Mary*, Noonan was struck by: 'the luxuriant growth, familiar to us through fiction' but which 'was soon an imposing reality in its many rich shades of green'. The plantations, he wrote, were 'rich luxurious and moist', 'a Garden of Eden where most things will grow and man's wants are easily supplied'.[23] The sporting fields of Malaya were impeccable: 'the best in the world', wrote another soldier to his council-worker father, where 'the grass grows like wildfire ... there is no doubt they leave the Sydney showgrounds in the shade'.[24]

Even the drinking water was 'rich', according to Adele Shelton-Smith, correspondent for the *Women's Weekly*; it was 'so soft' that the men would surely return home with better complexions than their girlfriends.[25] Such was the fertility of the Orient that Driver Tom Jacobi of Queensland was convinced that the rainwater was curing his baldness. Accordingly, he is said to have exhibited his new curls proudly. Not only was there a seeming abundance of game and food in Malaya but animal specimens appeared larger than life. A warrant-officer from Coogee told a correspondent, 'There are snails like ice-cream cones and scorpions like lobsters. Everything is huge in this country.'[26]

In reconstructing the language and myths of a popular colonial literary tradition and by referring to the literature, these soldiers were overwhelmingly emphasising their pride in Britain's colonial possessions. The descriptions of landscapes within the British Empire as luxuriant and opulent Edens, emphasising the richness and value of the colonies, reflect the kind of empire nationalism that led many troops to volunteer for the AIF. Furthermore, it shows the way in which everyday Australians of the period saw the world largely through 'British' eyes.

Furthermore, an underlying notion of imperial culture in the soldiers' writing also exists in their tales and descriptions of colonial pastimes in the Far East. One notion in particular that Australians associated with the idealised colonial lifestyle was the regal sport of wild-game hunting. Known as *shikar* in colonial India, it is more commonly known by the African word *safari*. Vivid descriptions of the killing of animals and colourful documentation of flora and fauna are common in letters, diaries and memoirs. Amid the jungles of Southeast Asia – home to jaguars, panthers, wild elephants and tigers – the allure of this quintessential image of empire inspired theatrical descriptions in soldiers' writing. In Ceylon, Charles Kelly of the 2/7th Battalion wrote of the *Boys' Own*-style adventure of exploring unmapped areas and being on the lookout for wild game. It was, according to Kelly, a 'little safari'.[27]

By far the animal most associated with this colonial image within British Asia was the tiger, and many soldiers wrote in their diaries and letters of tiger sightings and shootings, and of being generally alert to the perceived threat of the biggest of the cat species. In Burma a set of tiger tracks by a lake prompted a group of soldiers from Tulip Force to purchase a goat, which they tied to a sapling in a nearby clearing and waited high in the branches of an overlooking tree with rifles at the ready.[28] There were no tigers on this occasion, but the pursuit and killing of wild game had significant ideological overtones in the culture of imperialism – the hunt became a symbolic activity of global dominance.[29] It was a practice that became inseparable from colonialism, and in kind the men of the AIF deliberately shot wild animals for fun. Even the official history documented the occasion of an elephant hunt in Malaya in May 1941.[30] That Australian soldiers identified the practice with imperial culture is apparent within a photograph of men posing proudly beside a slain tiger in Malaya. Evoking enduring images of the British Raj, the scene reinforces the sense of adventure inspired by arrival in the colonies, and emphasises a familiarity with symbolic images of empire.[31]

As an aside, if all the reports of slain tigers by men of the AIF are to be believed – and if they are not all tall tales of adventure in the colonies – then the tiger population of the Malayan peninsula was quite possibly decimated by the presence of the 8th Division. However, some wanton acts were less refined than the regal pursuit of *shikar*. This was the case when a transport carrying Australian troops across the Indian Ocean spotted a large whale; machine-guns were mounted on deck and the graceful marine mammal was mercilessly killed.[32]

Another travel pastime, the search to acquire valuable souvenirs, was also an aspect of imperial culture; the desire to collect, document and display the conquered world. From Ceylon to the popular Change Alley in Singapore – where it was said anything could be purchased, from a small pin to a ship of the line – soldiers were on the lookout for quality mementoes. On account of the extra business that soldiers brought, at one camp stalls made from plaited palm leaves were erected everywhere Australians frequented, and even lined the roadside toward the camp.[33] Many men – perhaps naively – expressed frustration at not being able to find quality mementoes or 'treasure' on the cheap. The desire for quality mementoes was so strong that the soldiers placed great value upon those collected. In Malaya during the fighting in early 1942 a captain at a casualty clearing station with the sombre job of sorting through the kit bags of casualties was astounded to find men reluctant to abandon their prizes – they had, extraordinarily, carried their souvenirs into battle. 'It is astonishing the queer articles some carry', he wrote, 'trophies that have been collected throughout Malaya'. He found, among other items, exotic hunting knives, silks, a hall clock, and ladies shoes – 'some of extravagant design'.[34] Even a prisoner of war, on his death bed on the Burma end of the railway in 1943, continued to cling to a souvenir purchased some two years earlier made from polished brass and weighing ten pounds. This prized possession had been lugged through the Malayan campaign and was kept – at the expense of any other items of value, which he had jettisoned – on the long march to imprisonment at Changi. It went with him to Thailand and was carried on the horrific march into the mountains to the railway and beyond into Burma. With death upon him, he was reportedly asked why he had not thrown away this valueless millstone. His reply: 'Stuff like this is hard to come by back home.'[35]

Ideas and affirmations of Australian nationalism are not absent from the narratives, but they tend to co-exist alongside empire nationalism. For example, a fundamental aspect within the writing of soldiers encountering Asia for the first time was the discussion of skin colour. Extremely common within the correspondence of Australians abroad in Asia and the Pacific is mention of sunbathing during spare time. A correspondent from the *Women's Weekly* reported on the Australian accents and laughter that could be heard about swimming pools in Malaya and Singapore, with 'bronzed figures sunbathing' among the 'tropical palms and tropical flowers'.[36] After two months in Malaya, one soldier wrote in a letter home: 'We are all fairly brown here. Most of the time we get around in shorts and boots and socks.'[37] New arrivals could become quite self-conscious about their own skin colour. A nurse with 'rosy cheeks and fair skin' felt she clearly stood out as a new arrival. Such was her self-consciousness about her whiteness and her desire to fit in that she sunbathed in her spare time until covered by 'an almost black suntan'.[38]

However, sunbathing was not restricted as a leisurely pursuit. Many soldiers went about their duties shirtless, even in combat. In Malaya, gunners manning an artillery battery – stripped to the waist – had to face the additional hazard of hot shell cases ejected from the breech burning their bare skin.[39] Officialdom frowned upon such indulgences, no less because the uncovered body increased the risks of malaria, and so, much to the chagrin of the men, orders were handed out through Asia and the Pacific either restricting the time of day or banning altogether the practice of going shirtless.[40]

Consciousness of skin colour saturates the letters and diaries of Australian military personnel. Australians sunning themselves on board an RAN vessel were said to 'vary in colour / From near-pink to nigger'.[41] A commando in China similarly described his often shirtless colleagues as having been as 'brown as niggers'.[42] Such was the class consciousness and its fixation on skin colour within British colonies during the era that on an occasion when the Viceroy of India Lord Curzon visited Hong Kong he commented on a group of British soldiers swimming at a communal pool, confessing that he never knew that the working classes had such white skins. The assumption that subordinate classes were not 'white', at least in the same way as their 'betters', highlighted the cycle of class biases and racial prejudices in British society.[43] The British ruling classes were less pale than – or not as white as – the working classes, but it is safe to say that Australian soldiers were not working on tans so as to further their social status within a racial hierarchy partly based on the colour of one's skin.

Despite one digger being concerned that the Malayan sun did not tan his skin bronze but instead turned it a 'yellow sort of colour' – an apprehension towards conscious racial prejudices within the British colony and an unwillingness to appear the colour of a racial subordinate – for Australian soldiers the desire to acquire a suntan was down to their own view of themselves as Australians. This was done by associating themselves with one of the classically influenced qualities inherent in the myth of Anzac: that of the bronzed warrior.[44] As a myth born from British race patriotism, the Anzac legend reflected the idea that Australians had, as *The Age* newspaper reported in 1926: 'proved themselves worthy of the highest traditions of the British race'.[45] Anzac literature portrayed the Australian soldier as belonging to a new, vigorous race. Physically hardened from generations battling the Australian bush – or so the legend described – Australian soldiers were tall, tough and suntanned.[46] A gunner in Malaya expressed such an attitude. Even as the Malayan campaign intensified and soldiers were on full alert, men of his artillery battery persisted in wearing little. He noted that 'as usual we were stripped to the waist – real, sun-bronzed Anzacs'.[47]

The general appearance of the men of the 8th Division was commented upon even by local white residents. A *Straits Times* reporter, observing the arrival of the *Queen Mary*, commented that 'usually undemonstrative' Malayan dock workers joined in the cheering, realising, it seemed, 'that these bronzed carefree "orang puteh" [white people]' had come to defend their homes.[48] The Governor of the Straits Settlements, Shenton Thomas, proclaimed, 'Every one of them is bronzed and lean and fighting fit.'[49] They were, as a Singapore resident wrote in the *Women's Weekly*, 'superb specimens'.[50] In colonial societies in which skin colour partly determined the social order, 'bronze' was seemingly far more complimentary and suggestive of strength, fitness and good health than 'yellow' and its association with the subjugated Asian populace (and separate connotations to illness and cowardice). In Australian parlance, 'bronze' distinguished them from other whites within Malayan society.

The Australian soldiers also indulged in such descriptions.

One of the earliest publications on the Malayan campaign by an Australian soldier proclaimed:

> Their physique was impressive, more so as they displayed the novel habit of marching without shirts. It was a usual sight in many small towns in the early morning, as soon as the sun had begun to chase away the mist, to see their bronzed bodies swinging along in column of three.

Within soldiers' writing the importance of skin colour as a component of the Anzac legend and their identity as Australian soldiers is evident. Descriptions from Malaya mark a clear attempt to include the men of the 8th Division within the broader story of Anzac. As Duffy wrote: 'Brothers and kin of the men who had held Tobruk, the morning mists parted before them and the sun gleamed golden on their bare swinging arms.'[51]

The recreation of patriotic images from imperial culture within early written accounts by soldiers shortly after their arrival in the colonies shows the way in which Australian soldiers identified with being 'British'. These men entered the region believing that they were equal partners in empire. Therefore, they were unprepared for the kind of discrimination that Other Ranks were to receive within British colonial society and, to their surprise, relations with other whites proved most difficult. This would cause Australian troops to wonder if they were genuine partners in empire or simply subordinates in the eyes of the British.

Certainly, Australian soldiers had come across this kind of class-based discrimination in previous encounters with British society. Men of the First AIF visiting Britain during the Great War also found that the country did not match the myths they knew from school readings. They, too, were struck by the class consciousness, which they saw as a sign of English snobbery, and were dismayed by the filth and poverty of London. The English, on the other hand, saw the Australians as arrogant.[52] But despite these previous occurrences it remained something new for individuals of the Second AIF to discover in Asia. With great expectations at stake, such encounters remained raw for the uninitiated. Importantly, in Malaya, Singapore and elsewhere in Asia, Australian soldiers' reactions to their relations with local whites would lead to assertions that Australians were more friendly and easygoing in their relationships with Asians (genuine or not, this will be under question in the following chapter). But before looking at Australian–Asian interactions, let us first consider the reception provided to Australian troops by the colonial whites.

A prickly issue facing garrison troops was the cool reception they received from the white resident communities. One of the few places where Australian soldiers had any contact with Australian women in Malaya was the Anzac Club in Singapore, and the efforts of these volunteers were greatly appreciated. Relations with non-Australians, however, were cordial at best. 'Englishwomen were inclined to treat Australians, especially the other ranks, with quiet reserve and considerable caution', noted the unit history of the 2/15th Field Artillery Regiment, adding rather sympathetically that, 'They did not appear to notice the British garrison troops at all.'[53] While rank-and-file British troops were treated similarly, with many sharing much the same outlook towards the colonial society they had been sent to defend, the Australians felt particularly aggrieved. Where this matter differed for Australian troops was in their expectation – and the subsequent reality of – British colonial society. The Australian volunteers expected, perhaps naively, that the doors of society would be open to them. The voluntary nature of the AIF brought with it for many men – whether entitled or not – a sense of individual independence. On the other hand, British troops in Singapore were mostly either professional soldiers or national service conscripts and, although they may have disliked it, they were perhaps more accustomed to their second-class status in a class-based society.[54] As the Australian force was made up of citizens who had volunteered for the duration of the war, Australian soldiers expected that they would be welcomed and treated as equals while on leave. Therefore, prejudice towards soldiers by civic and non-military establishments – based on rank rather than character – did not sit well with the rank and file.

Further issues arose in encounters with other European garrison troops as the arrival of the Australians caused resentment among British forces in Malaya. The relations between Australian and British troops in Singapore, particularly men of the 2nd Battalion, Argyll and Sutherland Highlanders, caused alarm among the 8th Division command.[55] This was fuelled by a series of incidents between the Scots and members of the AIF and RAAF, including a violent confrontation at the Union Jack Club. The professional soldiers of the 2nd Argyll and Sutherland Highlanders Battalion, the garrison force on the island since 1939, jealously defended what was considered 'Scottish turf', and were disgruntled to see the local press glamorise the raw recruits from 'down under'. The Australian soldiers also received more pay than their British counterparts. An uncompromising warning to all Australians advising them not to encroach on Scottish territory was – according to Russell Braddon, a gunner with the 2/15th Field Regiment – all that was required for every free Australian on the island to go into the city on the first day of leave. 'There they were met by every free Argyll, and great and bloody were the battles – until the Provosts arrived, whereupon both sides, furious at this gratuitous display of officious intervention, ceased battle and fell upon a common foe.'[56] The ensuing 'battle for Lavender Street' and 'battle for the Union Jack Club' were public relations nightmares for Malaya Command and tested imperial solidarity.

The British Military Police also caused tension between Australian and British forces in Malaya. Whereas the provosts of the 8th Division had taken a pragmatic and tolerant approach to policing Australian soldiers, causing few clashes with troops, the British Red Caps – as the provosts were known – were seen as inflexible, intolerant and unreasonably harsh. Rightly or wrongly, the heavy-handedness and over-officious nature of the British provosts in Malaya was seen as provocation and is said to have brought out the worst in the Australians. So incensed were the latter that one particular incident near the Union Jack Club, in which a drunken member of the 4th Anti-Tank Regiment had been violently assaulted by Red Caps after he had given some cheek, almost caused a riot. It has been claimed that, on hearing news of the incident, men grabbed rifles and bayonets to take umbrage with the Red Caps, and the situation failed to escalate only because the British provosts were wisely warned off. Whether or not this episode occurred as described, tensions certainly existed. As a result, Major General Gordon Bennett ruled, as was the standard policy of the Australian army at the time – and much to the annoyance of the British – that the AIF was to be policed only by Australian provosts.[57]

Aside from their relations with British soldiers, establishing friendly relations with the trading civilians and planters from England, according to Braddon, 'turned out to be impossible'. First, Other Ranks were barred from European clubs and places of imperial prestige such as Raffles Hotel. Second, to address a European anywhere in Singapore, even if simply to ask for directions while lost, 'was to incur the most calculated snob'. While men did not expect gratitude for having been posted in Malaya – although for Braddon, homesickness caused such a longing – they did expect a certain degree of civility. Foremost, they expected to be treated with respect and as equals. When Braddon asked a British planter why 'this vicious policy of ignoring and ostracising the ordinary soldier had grown up' he was told it was because 'you chaps were always hanging around the brothels'. However, Braddon notes, since Other Ranks were barred from socialising at white clubs there were few other places for them to go.[58]

The institutional treatment of 'poor whites' in Singapore humiliated ordinary Australian soldiers as the white citizens they had been sent to defend made it clear they did not want to know

    Australian Soldiers in Asia-Pacific in World War II

Members of the 2/19th Battalion march past a rickshaw puller in Kluang, Malaya. Members of the 8th Division began arriving in Malaya in February 1941. For many their first contact with Asia and the British Empire was an eye-opening experience.
Australian War Memorial
P00102.035

them socially.[59] Ostracised and made to feel unwelcome, such behaviour by local whites came as a shock to the AIF volunteers. There was an undercurrent of hostility which was made apparent by the non-admittance of Other Ranks within prestigious hotels and clubs such as the Selangor 'Spotted Dog' Club in Kuala Lumpur and the Sungei Ujong Club at Seremban. This caused further grievances amongst the AIF as there were many privates who were respected members of exclusive Australian clubs and carried with them letters of introduction to the secretaries of the affiliated clubs in Malaya. Even so, and despite protests by the Australian clubs on behalf of their members, these men continued to be refused entry based on military rank. There were further grievances, and a growing sense that Australians were being singled out, as clubs continued to entertain guests who held the rank of private in the Malayan Volunteer Defence Force.[60] Even former Australian residents of Singapore with local club memberships were denied entry to their clubs if wearing their Australian uniform.[61] As Gilbert Mant – who served in Malaya with the 2/19th Battalion before later covering the campaign as a war correspondent – wrote, 'blame it on the climate … but unquestionably there was an acute class consciousness and a moral flabbiness' among the white residents which, due to a colonial lifestyle that revolved around leisure and clubs, created a 'moral looseness'. Completing the humiliation was that when the troops took to the bars of Lavender Street, or attended clubs of Indian, Chinese or Malayan patronage, they faced accusations and were despised for lowering white prestige.[62] As an authoritative account of the Malayan campaign by leading historians has noted, because race and rank decided which doors were open and which were firmly barred, was it not surprising that 'when the going got tough' some soldiers questioned why they should die for an outpost of empire that made little provisions to make them welcome?[63]

Upon arrival, reputations could at first be enhanced. As one soldier wrote, 'visiting Singapore itself merely strengthened my impression. When one sees such fine buildings as the Cathay, "Raffles", and the Singapore Airport hotel, and then wanders off into Chinatown, or even only just off the main streets, the contrast is apt to leave him gasping'.[64] While at first the Australians were clearly impressed by these establishments, diaries and letters home show that these first impressions did not necessarily last. Once apparent that ordinary soldiers were barred from such fine places of imperial prestige and forced to socialise in the less attractive streets with the 'lesser breeds', such discrimination stung their sense of belonging.

Similar issues were faced by soldiers in other parts of the region. Like their compatriots in Singapore, soldiers in Colombo learned with disappointment that the Galle Face Hotel – 'that house of international popularity' – was out of bounds to all ranks.[65] Exclusion from institutions such as this – a symbol of empire and colonial opulence – resulted in troops questioning whether they were truly equals in the empire that they had volunteered to defend. It demonstrated in no uncertain way to these individuals that the British Empire was one of privilege. This was a concept that went against the grain of Australian popular understandings of equality, egalitarianism and fairness conceptualised through terms such as: 'fair go' and 'mateship'. It is important to emphasise that these ill feelings did not lead to anti-British sentiments. Such attitudes were rare among Australians at the time and reserved for a radical minority. Perhaps these men were simply naïve to the wider outside world, but whatever the case, as with the 1932–33 Ashes 'bodyline' series in test cricket, it was the seemingly 'un-British' nature of such behaviour that concerned these soldiers the most.

For the small group attending training at the Bush Warfare School in Burma, the reception they received from white residents there was similarly cold. Fears that the 'common soldiers' would wreck homes, along with misunderstandings regarding the voluntary make-up of the Australian force (which ultimately led to questions of why men had given up 'good jobs to join the army'), caused tension between the groups. There were exceptions, however, such as the Australian mining engineer who treated the soldiers 'royally' and an Australian community in a mining town of northern Burma who 'treated the lads to a large quantity of the contents of the club cellar' and opened their tennis courts and golf course to the men. But in these cases the emphasis has been made on the hospitality being provided by Australian residents in Burma, not by the British.[66]

In Bombay the hospitality committee stressed within a guide-book issued to visiting troops that 'citizens are very anxious to ensure that you enjoy yourselves'.[67] In reality, like elsewhere, troops felt little was done to make them welcome. Here, Noonan was again struck by the class-consciousness of the British. When answering an enquiry about servants in Australia and informing his hosts that there was no servant problem in Australia because there were no servants, and that the housewife did her own housework, he was staggered by the responding view that Australia seemed an undesirable destination.[68] An Australian officer with the Royal Navy's HMS *Panther* was also stunned by what he considered the discourteous behaviour of the English at a YMCA dance in Bombay, ironically organised in honour of the men of the visiting destroyers HMS *Panther* and *Paladin*. None of the English women would agree to dance. 'No, thank you,' 'I'd rather not, it's far too hot,' and 'I think I'd rather sit down,' met the sailor's requests. Never had 'a more "frigid" dance in terms of sociability' been attended, according to the officer: 'It seemed obvious that sailors, as a group, were far from popular with the local girls, so I gave up trying to be sociable and returned aboard for an early night.'[69] But, with so few Western women in places such as Bombay, Singapore and Colombo, girls looking for a date could take their pick from the plentiful supply of officers. Rank-and-file soldiers (and even junior-ranking officers, as the aforementioned anecdote suggests) were unlikely to get a look in. Put simply, they were an unlikely match for the daughters of colonial civil servants or businessmen.[70] The profession a soldier, sailor or airman may have had in their civilian life – and there were privates and NCOs in the AIF with high social and professional standings – did not enter the equation. British soldiers would attest that such feelings did not afflict only Australian servicemen, but for the Australians, all of whom were volunteers, it created a feeling that they were not welcome, which undermined their sense of being equal partners in an empire of which they were naturally proud.

Much resentment was therefore aimed toward the residential white communities of the region. Within Malaya Australian troops were highly critical of the lack of preparedness of the local white community. As the entire AIF in Malaya was on high alert and had gone to action stations before 7–8 December 1941, it did not go unnoticed 'that the rest of the world didn't seem to think there was a war on'.[71] An officer arriving with reinforcements in Singapore toward the end of the crisis wondered why his soldiers were equipped for war when the first sights that met the troops were officers in mess dress and fashionable women in evening dress. 'It was not incongruous, it was wrong. Either we were crazy, or they were crazy. Either there was danger, or there was no danger.'[72] The Australian official history was diplomatically less critical of the civilians in Singapore, suggesting that the Australian soldier, away from home and daily domestic life, was much more able to be ready and fully prepared without outside distractions and, therefore, more likely to be critical toward the carrying on of normal daily life in light of the inherent danger.[73] For example, one report from an artillery crew setting up a gun in Singapore suggests that some civil servants did not fully comprehend the seriousness of the military situation. One resident who stopped to chat with the gunners began to contemplate evacuating his family only after he was assured that the Japanese were 'really on the Island'.[74] Such was the unreality of what was occurring, and it was a reflection on the lack of preparedness and continuation of normal life that Captain James Bryant – a veteran of

the First AIF and Military Medal recipient who had stood alongside Leslie Morshead in the trench at Lone Pine in the famous
Gallipoli photograph – casually documented within his diary a
night at the Cathay Theatre followed by drinks at Raffles the next
evening. This entry was written on 2–3 February 1942, only days
before the battle for Singapore commenced.[75]

Another factor that highlighted for soldiers the apparent lack
of commitment to the war effort was the charging of Australian
military forces, or individual military personnel, for damages to
private property in Malaya. This proved especially problematic
when considering that much of the fighting took place amid
plantations across the region. Soldiers in Malaya were disheart-
ened by orders that 'troops billeted in or carrying out training in
rubber estates will be careful to avoid damage to rubber trees'.
This included scratches, damage to bark, the downing of limbs,
damage to roots by vehicles, or cutting of roots by digging.[76]
Another routine order expressed that rubber trees should be cut
down only for 'essential military purposes' – such as clearing firing
lines for artillery – as this would involve 'heavy claims for compensation as well as trouble and delay'.[77] One gunner felt that by
imposing a fine of $5 (Malayan) for any soldier who damaged a
rubber tree – however slightly, and even though the damage may
have been caused in the pursuit of training – 'nothing could have
been more calculated to interfere with mobility and efficiency' in
these predominantly rubber-growing areas.[78] Having to pay compensation for damage caused to private plantations raised alarming questions among the troops about exactly on whose behalf
they were defending Malaya.

In contrast, personal views of officers – who were not barred
from high-end establishments and therefore socialised with the
white community – could understandably differ to those of Other
Ranks. Major General Bennett believed the British administration
in Malaya had been the most successful colonial regime in Southeast Asia. Defending the European community in Malaya in his

book *Why Singapore Fell* (presumably from critics such as the many rank-and-file soldiers under his command), he argued that while in Malaya the administration certainly worked:

> the plantations managed by these men of England were models of efficiency. Of course they made money out of the country. Is that a crime? Is it any different from earning a living in America or England? Are we not making money out of the country in which we work? They earned their money. They gave lucrative employment to the millions of natives and enabled them to live in comfort and according to the standard they are accustomed to. The fact that the natives in Malaya are happier and healthier than those in many neighbouring countries shows that the development by British brains with the aid of British capital was beneficial to all concerned.[79]

Similar sentiments could be shared by individual soldiers, though different conclusions were drawn. While one soldier felt that the British had brought material benefits and built fine infrastructure to better the lives of the Malayan, he doubted that the average Malayan was 'intrinsically happier than in the days when he lived in his kampong [village] and was a fierce fighting man'. In closing, he felt it was 'impossible to escape the conclusion that the Europeans in Malaya led preposterously spoilt, artificial existences. Life was a terrible round of leisured boredom. They lived in an outdated atmosphere of Kipling, and nobody was wise enough to see the coming tragedy that was to engulf them'.[80]

While many measures were taken to make the Australians feel comfortable, and friendships were maintained throughout the community, including with English men and women, there were certainly many within the imperial establishment who believed 'the prestige of the white man' was best maintained by remaining aloof from the 'natives'. Such people, as the official historian Wigmore notes, frowned upon the Australians because of their 'easy-going' ways with Asians.[81] While many of the Australians had been instructed on appropriate behaviour in the colonies – for example, amid lectures on tropical diseases on the voyage to Singapore were those on the importance of maintaining 'British prestige' in foreign places – some of the behaviour of the Australians shocked the British establishment and their sense of colonial order.[82]

In particular, the Australians' supposed casual attitudes and behaviour caused unease among the colonial elite. For example, whereas on the occasion when the Australian *Women's Weekly*'s Adele Shelton-Smith reported on the diggers' escapades in Singapore as an example of Aussie larrikin behaviour, the white residential community viewed such actions as an insidious undermining of local norms. Reporting that rickshaw drivers made small fortunes from the diggers but worked hard, Shelton-Smith wrote: 'Rickshaw races were frequent, with two Australians in each Rickshaw urging the runner on. As compensation the runner would often be given a ride in his own rickshaw, with an AIF man doing the work.' A photographic spread of the race accompanied the article, showing an Australian soldier – easily identifiable in his slouch hat – pulling one of the rickshaws.[83] While Australians might have dismissed such incidents as a bit of fun or 'a gag for the camera', the 'Burra Sahibs' – the colonial masters – frowned on such acts.[84]

And it was not just these casual acquaintances on the streets of colonial cities in Asia that caused concern among the ruling elite. Friendships, close relationships, and even the attendance of clubs of Indian and Malayan patronage led to accusations that the AIF were lowering British prestige. In all parts of Malaya, it was noted, the 'cultured class of Indians and Chinese had first-rate clubs of their own', and Australian soldiers were soon made welcome and friendships were established. This educated group of Indians and Chinese, according to Mant, were especially aware that they were treated as outsiders (even though, he adds, some were Oxford and Cambridge graduates). To them, membership of the British Commonwealth of Nations was hypocrisy. The Australians, 'raw to the intricacies of Imperialism, could not but feel sympathy for them'.[85] It was not only that the Australians attended clubs patronised by Malayans, Chinese and Indians but also that while on leave in Singapore they were inclined to visit places such as the New World and Great World amusement parks, nightly playgrounds frequented by peoples from all of Singapore's Asian communities. They were not, however, places usually frequented by Singapore's Europeans.[86]

The warmth of the relationship between Asians and Australians, notes Braddon, was 'partly compensated for, and partly arose out of, the fact that it was the only social relationship open'.[87] Partly because of this interaction with communities within Southeast Asia, the British authorities criticised the men of the AIF for lowering white prestige.[88] Such a scenario faced Corporal Alan Barnes of No. 1 Squadron, RAAF, and Leading Aircraftman Bruce Bowley of No. 21 Squadron, RAAF, who represented a local team in the Malayan cricket season alongside teammates from mixed backgrounds. When their team played at the Singapore Cricket Club, the pair emerged from the change rooms only to be admonished by a British major. Tomorrow, the major told them, they were to change in the Europeans-only changing room. It had not occurred to the RAAF cricketers that there would be separate change rooms for Europeans and non-Europeans. From their perspective they had simply arrived at the game and prepared alongside their fellow teammates. The following day, in defiance of the British major, they again changed in the same rooms in an act of solidarity toward their friends and teammates. Because of their sporting prowess, Barnes and Bowley were awarded honorary membership to the Singapore Cricket Club. Not usually admitted because of their rank, they were already well aware of the elitist snobbery of the institution and were even further disillusioned by its whites-only policy and the racial discrimination shown towards their

Asian and Eurasian teammates. Both made a point of not attending the club. They felt more welcome and enjoyed the camaraderie, warmth and mutual respect when their Asian teammates hosted them in the Chinese, Indian and Malayan clubs.[89]

Another aspect of the Australian soldiers' defiance toward local norms was their disregard for the heat of the tropics, exemplified by their habit of working through the middle-part of the day. Guidebooks such as the one issued to soldiers visiting Bombay warned against exposure to the sun before 4 pm.[90] However, as Wigmore noted, 'As often occurred when Australians and British troops were together in the tropics, the British considered that the Australians had too little respect for the heat of the midday sun, and the Australians considered that the British had too much respect for it.' Local planters thought the Australians crazy for their persistence at hard physical jungle training in the tropical midday heat. At first some soldiers felt the siesta hour ate into their opportunity to 'see the world', or saw themselves as having a superior work ethic. However, the contempt Australians held for the siesta hour when they arrived abated rapidly, and they, too, adopted the custom. Looking back, it is striking to consider that in the months following the disaster of the Singapore surrender siesta hours between 12 noon and 4.30 pm were still maintained – at least informally – by some Australian soldiers in Ceylon.[91]

One particular incident in which the AIF pulled rank and broke with local customs was following the arrival at Port Swettenham of a ship packed with 800 tons of frozen meat and motor vehicles for the AIF. The frozen meat obviously had to be unpacked hastily in the tropical heat and, having worked the wharf labourers hard for six long hours, the Australian officers in command decided to employ Australian soldiers to take over, 'despite the fact it was not considered desirable politically or medically to employ white labourers in Malaya'. The ship was emptied in record time as the Australians worked at three times the rate of the poorly nourished 'coolies'.[92] While Wigmore painted this episode as an AIF achievement, such acts were seen as disruptive to normal European–Asian relations in the eyes of local whites.

The ostracism of ordinary rank-and-file troops from white colonial society upset Australian troops' understandings of equality among the white citizens of the empire. The contact between men of the AIF and the white communities of Asia likewise challenged Australian soldiers' notions of egalitarianism as it became clear that Australians were not considered equal partners in the empire. If this was not evident in 1941, it would become clear before long, for when in December 1943 the godsend of Red Cross consignments from the Swiss consulate addressed to 'British P.O.W.' arrived at a camp in Thailand the English officers refused to share the packages with Australian prisoners. For the commander of 'A Force', the highly respected Brigadier Arthur Varley, who was committed to the care of all men under his command regardless of nationality, this was a very 'un-British' sentiment.[93] Such factors ate at the soldiers' very conceptions of what they believed was fair and right. As historian Hank Nelson has noted, though proud of their membership of the empire the men of the 8th Division in Malaya and Singapore found 'they did not like Empires of privilege, particularly when the lords of empire classified Australians with the lesser breeds'.[94]

Entering the region immersed in imperial culture, the men of the AIF were initially proud and thrilled to be visiting the opulent British colonies. Having volunteered to defend this empire, it did not take long before they soon became confronted by the social barriers within British colonial society. By positioning and creating, perhaps subconsciously, an image of themselves as victims of Singapore's reputation there emerged a desire to respond to their exclusion from British colonial society with an outlook that led – as we shall see in the following chapter – to pronouncements that Australian soldiers were more egalitarian and easygoing in their relations with Asians.

3

MAKING FRIENDS
First encounters with Asia

Shortly after the 8th Division's arrival in Malaya, headlines back home proclaimed that the Australian soldiers were 'making friends with all races and creeds'. Indeed, press reports from the period, and later the Australian official histories series, commonly described the troops of the AIF as being fresh, casual, and different (ostensibly from the British) in their outlook towards others. An important question remains: was this reporting – which exists also in the diaries and letters of soldiers and nurses – a response to the unanticipated discrimination they had received at the hands of the British? Did the encounter with white colonial societies shape the supposed egalitarian digger's attitudes toward Asia? An aside to this question – neglected by military historians of the campaign – is the effect such attitudes, and more generally the experience of Asia, might have had upon the 8th Division when following months of idleness in Malaya they were called upon to defend the peninsula from the Japanese.

Certainly, as one historian has noted, colourful descriptions of the local cultures provided reporters with 'a mechanism for lauding the virtues of the Australian soldiers'. These men were depicted as being naturally adaptable to new environments, with no preconceived ideas of race or colour and with an egalitarian attitude that people were to be judged on their merits. While racial attitudes were ambiguous within such narratives, it has been said that during the early stages of the war the Australians' 'natural friendliness provided correspondents with an irresistible opportunity to emphasise their distinctiveness as soldiers'.[1] Certainly, Gavin Long, the general editor of the official history series, described the first contact between the Second AIF and Asia in just such a way:

> For all but a few it was their first experience of Asia and of
> a city crowded with dark-skinned people. The arrival of
> the Australians and New Zealanders in an Eastern country
> on this and later occasions caused some anxiety to both
> the local authorities and their own officers. The European
> soldier, coming from countries where class distinctions are
> more rigid, and the American, brought up in the presence
> of a Negro population, are conditioned to accept the
> castes and poverty of the East more easily than does the
> Australian, who habitually treats the Asiatic in a friendly
> and jocular style. To the end of the war most Australian
> soldiers had not acquired that remote and autocratic manner
> towards Asians then considered essential to the maintenance
> of European prestige in the East – a manner imitated by
> Europeans from that adopted by Asian people of rank and
> wealth towards their inferiors.[2]

Then followed an anecdote relating how 'the Australians handed their haversack lunches to importunate native beggars'. Such descriptions set the tone for subsequent volumes in the official histories with regard to Asian–Australian relations. Historians such as Nelson have also described how the egalitarian traditions of Australian soldiers made them refreshingly casual and curious in their meetings with local peoples and that the men of the AIF had a 'naive desire' to be well liked by the people of the world they encountered.[3]

The contact between so many Australians and Asians during the Second World War raises important questions regarding the way men and women of the AIF wished to represent themselves in their correspondence. There was a determination within the press, the official histories, and the correspondence of some men to represent a fresh 'Australian' outlook when it came to relations with Asians by depicting Australian behaviour and encounters in a certain way. In opposition to the British, Australian soldiers wanted to be seen as more open and casual in their encounters with others. But to what degree are such descriptions genuine? Were they real, merely pastiche, or another story of the self-promoting prowess of the famed AIF?

According to press reports from the period, the arrival of the AIF in Malaya made quite an impression on the locals. With their custom of bestowing titles and nicknames the Malayans, according to the *Women's Weekly*, were quick to call the men of the AIF the 'laughing soldiers' or the '*tid apa* boys' (meaning 'why worry' or 'why bother').[4] It was also reported that, according to the Malayans, the night-time blooming of the moonflower shortly after the AIF's arrival was a lucky omen for friendship.[5] Similarly, the Deputy Chief of the Australian General Staff noted while passing through Malaya: 'in every town I went through I saw a digger with three or four native boys round him. The Digger would have a book and the native boys were teaching him the language. It was always a friendly laughing group'.[6] Australian soldiers, said Wigmore in his volume of the official history series, 'soon showed themselves to be in the main the sort of individuals to whom children take an instant liking, and whose relationships with others were on a man-to-man basis in which human values were of far more concern than rank, riches, race, creed and colour'.[7] This self-promotion by the press and official historians strongly reflected the conscious desire and established tradition for AIF writers to big-note themselves. Rather than portraying their battlefield prowess in such imagery, in this case they were embracing the egalitarian concept of the Anzac legend for the self-serving purpose of depicting themselves as refreshingly different from the British.

MAKING FRIENDS with all races and all creeds

AUSTRALIAN PADRE takes the children of Chinese friends for a Sunday morning stroll. Pictures from our photographer in Malaya prove how completely false were malicious foreign reports that our troops in Malaya were not on friendly terms with the population. Adele Shelton Smith cables from Malaya, "Their friends are legion and include all nationalities. They have been lavishly entertained and helped in both work and play."

DEVOUT MOHAMMEDAN reads his Koran at the doorway of a mosque while a Digger coaxes some native children to take him in with them.

"ALL PRESENT AND CORRECT, SIR." One of the native youngsters tries out a bit of parade ground smartness on a friendly Digger sentry.

This spread in the *Australian Women's Weekly* demonstrates the way in which Australian soldiers were promoted in media reports from Malaya as easygoing, fun-loving and good humoured.

National Library of Australia

Individual authors expressed similar views in private correspondence. For example, Chinese and Indian people invited Australian soldiers into their homes for refreshments, or even to listen
to the English news broadcasts if they had a wireless.[8] Some of
the luckier troops would receive invitations from local Chinese
chambers of commerce for social occasions.[9] Strong English language skills and a formal education were, however, seen by some
as a prerequisite for friendly relations. An RAAF nurse wrote of
her meeting with a group of Indian and Burmese girls at a dance in

Australian soldiers join a funeral parade in Malaya. In some cases the soldiers had been
friends with the deceased and attended such events upon invitation, though on other
occasions Australian troops joined such parades uninvited.
Australian War Memorial 009350

Bangkok: 'They are most interesting conversationalists and highly educated of course.'[10] Nevertheless, the curious and enquiring nature of the men ensured that soon they were attending funerals and weddings – occasionally by invitation – and getting guided tours of mosques and temples. Indeed, collections of diaries or letters that are accompanied by photographs often show men participating in wedding or funeral processions. The 'fun loving', 'good humoured' and 'easy-going' nature of the AIF in Malaya is accentuated throughout the Australian War Memorial's photographic collection, giving some indication of the general acceptance of this version of events. However, so little is known about the other side of these encounters, or of the motivations for initiating them, that it is difficult to ascertain the equality of these meetings and whether the Australians were intruding or truly welcome.

Nevertheless, from the writing of a small group of soldiers we do know that genuine friendships were formed. 'There is no doubt the hospitality extended by the people here to the Australians is simply amazing!' wrote Walter Bills – a Melbourne city clerk from Hawthorn and member of the AASC – singling out 'the Chinese in particular' who 'have been untiring in trying to make our stay pleasant'. Bills considered the Chinese residents very polite, writing that 'it's really quite a pleasure to speak with them', and he often spent evenings chatting with new acquaintances. Bills met one English-speaking acquaintance on several occasions, referring to him as his 'friend'.[11] The use of the term by soldiers such as Bills is significant, as its usage is often quite selective. Furthermore, the term 'friend' expresses a level of equality and mutual respect in the relationship. It is not a word that is often used to describe a relationship such as one between a master and a servant, for example, and it is not a term easily compatible with derogatory racist language.

Close relations were also formed on sporting fields across Malaya. Regular soccer, hockey and tennis matches took place between AIF teams and local Chinese and Malayan teams. For example, Williams often wrote in his letters of the regular soccer matches against Malayan teams, including the team made up of members of the local constabulary.[12] Likewise, Bills spoke in his letters home of tennis matches against Malayan opponents. Although their opponents were too strong – and 'literally danced' around the court – he felt the hospitality extended to them would be unseen in any other country. On top of this, drinks were brought out to them at the end of every set.[13] Sporting competition was therefore an important aspect in the formation of relations between the AIF and Asian communities of a certain class. Some Australian servicemen – such as Barnes and Bowley – joined local teams, playing alongside teammates of different races for the first time. There was genuine affection for some of their new teammates, and friendships were fostered that lasted decades after the war was over.[14]

Relationships were also reported to have been formed between the AIF and local children wherever they travelled. One news pictorial featuring Australian servicemen in a variety of countries declared that the 'Digger is king of the kids everywhere'.[15] Why soldiers formed such strong relationships with children is intriguing. One historian has noted, firstly, how the age groups of enlisted soldiers meant that many young fathers were in the services, and the sight of children prompted bouts of homesickness (this may have been true, too, for those who had younger siblings). Secondly, in a conflict between races, nations and ethnic groups, children reminded the soldiers of the basic humanitarian notion that all people were much the same the world over. Furthermore, in a world built around racial hierarchies, it has been suggested that children carried less prejudice and were therefore more forthcoming and friendly with foreign newcomers.[16] But are children really immune to concepts and ideologies promoted through nationalism and propaganda? Whatever the case, it is claimed that, where propaganda promoting the fighting prowess of the AIF adversely affected relations in the early days after their arrival, children – unlike their anxious parents – approached the Australians innocently and without alarm. Wherever the Australians travelled in Malaya, it was reported in the press, they were followed by children yelling 'Hullo, Joe'; a greeting which they had learned from the Australians.[17] The troops interacted with the children on other levels, too. They played games and, as Williams noted, even helped them fishing in nearby channels.[18] Furthermore, it is claimed that the interaction with children led local communities to respond to what they saw as loneliness among the young men separated from their own families.[19] Relations with children, therefore, may have been important in the breaking down of racial barriers and the forming of friendships. Certainly, reports that the Australian soldier was 'king of the kids' were an important way in which the press demonstrated the purported easygoing nature and friendliness of the Australians. And, as we know little about the other side of these relations, it is worth considering why men of the AIF placed such importance on these descriptions.

Feelings of sympathy and compassion toward the colonised are certainly not rare within the letters and diaries held in Australian archives. Scenes from Malaya of hardworking, 'weak-eyed emaciated boys and girls' drew compassion.[20] As Bills wrote of labourers loading his truck at a petrol dump:

> This was quite a new experience as hitherto we've always had
> to do our own loading. When one sees them sweating and
> straining at their work one feels like helping but the foreman
> told us not to. Apparently they were quite happy, chatting
> incessantly amongst themselves as they worked. Nevertheless
> it doesn't seem right that these natives should work their
> fingers off to the bone for a few cents a day, whilst the white
> men look on. But the problem of 'the workers' is world-
> wide and from what I gather these natives are treated fairly
> well, according of course to their standard of living. Having

known nothing else but hard manual labour all their lives,
they seem resigned to a life of toil from early childhood.[21]

Later, after consulting a Chinese friend, Bills noted the low wages (70–80 Malayan cents per day, a dollar for the Chinese) and the difficulties a man had in providing an existence for his family (estimated to cost around 50 cents per day). Asians could afford few luxuries if they were to survive, he noted; life was a long and continual struggle. Exhausted as they were after a day's work, Bills observed that the working classes did not appear to indulge in recreation; rather they just sat outside their shops and homes thinking.[22]

Clearly concerned by the conditions of Asian workers in Malaya and Singapore, soldiers wrote home of their support on a range of matters such as fairer working hours, higher wages or the abolishment of rickshaws. As a symbol of colonial cities such as Singapore – and featured within many postcards from the era – the rickshaw represented a disjunction between the glamour of high society and the colonial order with the poverty and reality of working life on the streets.[23] A number of AIF writers wrote of their unease with the occupation. It was 'about time this human slavery was done away with in my opinion', wrote Bills, as 'a man engaged in this kind of work although earning more than the average labourer has a short life; the strenuous work being more than the human constitution can stand'.[24] Emphasising his feelings on the matter he later recalled, whilst strolling through China-town, 'a rickshaw man, his expression that of a beaten dog, looks at me with pleading eyes'. Another wrote: 'Perhaps my most vivid first impression, really, was the awful, hopeless, and dead look in the eyes of the rickshaw coolies. Dead men walking!'[25]

In similar vein to these men writing from Malaya, drawings by Roy Hodgkinson of Australian sailors in Colombo reflect a certain degree of pity toward hardworking Ceylonese. Hodgkinson's drawings and paintings often take a humanistic approach to

Lowly rickshaw pullers were a stark contrast to surrounding colonial opulence in Malaya and Singapore. Here a group of Australian soldiers enjoy a rickshaw ride outside the Federated Malay States Railways building in Kuala Lumpur, February 1941.
Australian War Memorial 005977

While the RAAF officers pictured here in Calcutta in 1945 know it's just a 'gag for the camera', the 'Burra Sahibs' (white colonialists) frowned on such antics. Such acts upset the usual arrangement in the British colonies of an Asian at the service of the white man.
Australian War Memorial SEA0146

Where some found rickshaws a source of entertainment, others felt the practice undignified and were sympathetic to the plight of the pullers. In this drawing by Roy Hodgkinson, the strain of the rickshaw puller is clear.
Australian War Memorial ART22775

covering Australian military forces abroad by showing the strain and strength of men struggling amid adverse situations. However, in a drawing of RAN sailors in Ceylon, it is the Ceylonese who are shown as the battlers rather than Australian servicemen. In an illustration of sailors in rickshaws, immediate attention is drawn to the emaciated rickshaw puller. With ribcage showing, his muscles strain upon his lean frame as he bends to lift the rickshaw. In the foreground, two older men look just as weathered, and their grim looks of determination reflect the daily struggle. Similar depictions of the Ceylonese are featured in further drawings; one of RAN souvenir hunters in a market scene, the other of dock workers straining on ropes as HMAS *Napier* docks.[26]

Others wrote home of the harsh conditions facing the lives of Australia's regional neighbours. In a letter to his young daughter, Walter Ross provided what he believed to be a worldly lesson on the good fortune of growing up in Australia: 'You think you are hard done by when Mother and I used to ask you to do a little work to help your Mother but you don't know that little girls no bigger and older than you have to do the work of a man,' wrote Ross. 'I see them every day carrying two full petrol tins of water long distances on hooks and a stick across the shoulders. I have seen them doing that all day long week in and week out.' He added that 'the little children never see toys like you children do'. Women unloading ships, their clothes dripping with perspiration, were not an uncommon sight while out on the road. The 'houses that the working class live in are terrible', he noted, and 'they don't seem to have any other life … so see Nancy you have so much to be thankful for in dear old Australia, so do all you can to keep it and help Mother'.[27]

An incident of note that caused problems for the 8th Division in Malaya and strongly reflected Australian attitudes toward Asian working conditions was an issue over a plantation strike. In May 1941 the governor requested Major General Bennett send a contingent of Australian troops to quash a strike by plantation workers.

Bennett refused; pointing out that such an action contravened Australian principles and Australian policy. When sent an order from Malaya Command stating that the AIF troops were legally bound to obey the request, Bennett reported the incident to the Australian government, which then cabled Malaya Command confirming that the AIF was not to be used as strike-breakers. When other troops were sent in to quash the strike instead blood was spilt and a number of workers were killed. Furthermore, as the workers were seeking a daily pay increase of 10 cents (equal to about 3 pence in Australian money of the time) for males and 5 cents for females on top of the daily rates of 50 cents and 45 cents respectively, a number of Australian soldiers sympathised with the strikers, making the potential involvement of the AIF problematic. Bennett later found out that India had also objected.[28] Not long afterward the British commander of Allied forces in the region, General Sir Archibald Wavell, expressed in an order to the troops his expectancy that Australian troops would prove the fighting spirit that won and maintained the empire. Wavell had himself only recently commanded Australian troops in Libya and Greece and seen them do just that. However, he may have sensed they were up against it in Malaya. By this time the cynicism developing among the men of the AIF in Malaya about such an empire of privilege was clear. As one Australian soldier made his feelings known: 'Bugger the bloody British Empire.'[29]

There is little doubt that the experiences of Australians serving abroad during the war influenced their attitudes to empire and imperialism, as the 2/7th Battalion's Private Charles Kelly, a veteran of the calamitous Greece and Crete campaigns and an escaped prisoner of war, made clear on his return from the Mediterranean. Speaking to a Dutch sailor aboard his troopship, he 'got a little dope on German colonies versus English colonies, and am afraid I must agree with the Dutchmen that the English are no better than the Hun'. His experiences as a soldier seemingly influenced his dislike for the colonial powers. While serving as a member of the Ceylon garrison in early 1942 Kelly became sympathetic toward the plight of the Ceylonese under the yoke of British colonialism. 'Each day I grow to like the Singhalese people more and more and find some very interesting and very elevating company among these people', he wrote in his diary. Having immersed himself in the Buddhist religion during his stay, Kelly marked each day in his diary with a new Buddhist proverb. One day's quotation, 'there is no darkness like ignorance', seemed to be aimed at fellow members of the AIF, of whom he could be very critical over their relations with others:

> The more I see of the Singhalese people, the more I like
> them. I regret to see the way some of our men treat them,
> because they are very sensitive to insult, and are of very fine
> intelligence. Some of the lower class of our men are apt to
> regard them as coolies, which is a very wrong idea to adopt.
> Their average intelligence is higher than that of our rank
> and file, and definitely finer.

In solidarity with the Ceylonese lower classes, he later decided not to go drinking with his mates whilst on leave, explaining: 'I am afraid I cannot see the wisdom in paying 2Rs [rupees] 25cts, about 4/6 a bottle, for beer that is produced by slave labour. The fellow who serves this stuff looks sheepish as he holds out his hand for money.'[30]

More so than expressing feelings of sympathy, empathy, compassion or friendship, there were some soldiers who developed more peculiar, enlightened and tolerant views. These men formed friendships with locals, yearned for knowledge about the peoples and cultures they were encountering, and educated themselves in the languages, religions, cultures and customs of the area. A thirst for knowledge in the new environment was clearly evident among soldiers who purchased guides such as *The Handbook to British Malaya* and *Malay for Beginners*. Bills, a critic of fellow soldiers who loitered around the camp and slept through their spare time, was determined to see and learn as much as possible during his time abroad. 'Although one's job may be monotonous and repulsive (to me)', he wrote, 'one has a wonderful opportunity to study a new land and a "new" people'.[31]

As many troops were enthusiastic sightseers, particular interest was paid to the temples and shrines of the various religions throughout the landscape. For many it was the first time they had encountered an Eastern religion. William Noonan not only dedicated pages to the description of the architecture of Buddhist, Islamic, Taoist and Hindu temples in his travels throughout Malaya, Burma, China and India but also provided detailed description of each faith's system of beliefs and customs.[32] Recognising the diversity of Asia, Noonan later recalled that one of the things he learnt quickly was that you could not generalise about people and that 'any specific judgement had to be about a particular person' rather than a group of people as a whole.[33] Others also wrote about the Eastern religions. Voyages offered time for men to indulge in educational activities. Captain Donald Lyndon of the 2/6th Battalion, for example, wrote about 'Mohamedanism' after one particularly interesting lecture on board ship.[34] It was also common for men to write about local people and many sent home postcards featuring traditional Malayan village scenes. Others wrote about local customs. For example, Bills documented in detail a range of matters, from the difference in wedding arrangements and ceremony to relations between the different groups of Asians in Malaya. All this was learnt through personal observations and conversations with local acquaintances.[35]

Encountering these 'new' religions for the very first time could have a profound effect on the Australians. Shortly after his arrival on Ceylon, Kelly visited a local Buddhist temple near his camp. There, one of the monks who spoke English talked about the volumes of work dedicated to his religion. Intrigued, Kelly returned later that evening – which happened to be on a national day of prayer – to listen to the priest make a speech (a Ceylonese friend interpreted for him). The priest spoke of how anxious he was for peace and freedom for all people. For Kelly, already a veteran of campaigns in Greece and Crete, the priest's words struck a chord. Soon Kelly had acquired books on the religion from Ceylonese friends. To him, Buddhism seemed far more logical and simple, yet more comprehensive, than the teachings of Christ. Critical of missionaries trying to 'take away from these people such a wonderful teaching', he frequently argued and debated with an AIF Roman Catholic padre who had noticed that he was read-ing works on Buddhism. Spending most of his days engrossed in religious books, he was soon debating Singhalese Christians who tried to discourage his curiosity. Soon he became 'more than ever convinced' that Buddhism was 'the true teaching' and took to wearing a sarong in the evenings. He even became critical of aspects of Ceylonese culture that merged 'native' customs that were not consistent with Buddhist teaching.[36]

On reflection, an important factor in Kelly's conversion seems to be his cynicism toward imperialism, the war and the role of the Great Powers. Furthermore, his feelings toward Buddhism show that for some Australians serving abroad certain aspects of Asian cultures could appear as worthy as those they had inherited at home. He was also determined that he was going to write a book upon his return to introduce an Australian audience to Buddhism. The book was to be titled *The Bodhi-Tree*, after the tree under which Buddha attained his nirvana. Kelly did survive the war and return to Australia, but what legacy his flirtation with Buddhism had on his life remains unknown. For a soldier like Kelly, a seemingly ordinary Australian citizen-soldier from rural Victoria, the Second World War encounter with Asia and empire proved a dramatic and eye-opening period of his life.

While the insights provided by soldiers such as Kelly are unique, other descriptions of the friendly and easygoing ways of Australians appear to be more 'good-news stories' for the press, especially when considering some of the more common and private views that describe contacts with Asia. In reality, as Leonard Woolf had written during his time in the Ceylon Civil Service at the beginning of the 20th century, many Australians behaved 'in many astonishing ways like characters in a Kipling story'. Just as Woolf could not make up his mind one way or the other as to whether Kipling had 'moulded his characters accurately in the image' of white colonial society, or whether white colonial society was moulding its character 'accurately in the image of a Kipling story', Australian soldiers' interactions with Asian communities are open for interpretation.[37]

Similar to the observations made by Woolf in Ceylon, in 1941 the Australian press also promoted what may be described as the Australian soldiers' imitation or adoption of certain facets of a colonial lifestyle. Such descriptions, of course, bring into question the reporting of friendships and Australian egalitarianism. While Malays and Chinese may well have liked the Australians more than the British, we simply cannot make that judgment from the Australian records. Perhaps Australian soldiers were friendlier. Perhaps they were liked simply because they had more money to spend and tipped generously compared with their lower-paid British comrades. Whatever the case, there remained significant inequalities in the relations between Australians and Asians based on an innate sense of white superiority. In the main, the nature of the contact and relations between Australian soldiers and Asians reflects the inherent racism within both Australian and colonial society of the period.

Many Australian soldiers and nurses found themselves asserting their position in the racial hierarchy by imitating aspects of colonial society. In this way they were 'discovering' their own whiteness and the power it conferred over others. Despite what we have seen within the press and official histories, most diaries and letters reveal that, in terms of the egalitarian traditions of the AIF, Asians were not necessarily viewed as equal to the white citizens of the empire. Nor did the AIF's sense of egalitarianism and mateship mean that friendships were immediately struck between Asians and Australians. It seems that men of the AIF were egalitarian in the sense that they were curious in their encounters with others, but most were not necessarily embracing the otherness by striking friendships or treating others as equals. Certainly, when it came to notions of egalitarianism and mateship Australian soldiers were rather inward-looking. As one historian notes, while occasionally depicted in a 'matey' way – which could be interpreted as 'rather harmless paternalism' – the diggers emerge as mostly condescending or patronising, exhibiting a smugness that acts as 'a veneer to more vicious racial imperialism'.[38]

Descriptions of sightseeing and other touristic pursuits – some of the most common ways in which Australians first came into contact with Asians – demonstrate the way in which troops on leave imposed themselves within the colonial order and demonstrated their wealth and power over others. This is most clearly demonstrated by the behaviour of Australian troops amid the pomp and ceremony surrounding the arrival of AIF troops in Singapore. When *Queen Mary* berthed at Singapore naval docks, in imitation of the behavioural standards set by their forefathers of the First AIF in Colombo a generation previous, the soldiers rained coins upon the Asian dock workers. Amused by the chaotic scenes that ensued, the troops yelled 'encouragement' at the mad scramble below. Adding to their amusement, some men even heated the coins with cigarette lighters first.[39] As a form of entertainment, it demonstrated the sense of racial superiority by the newly arrived troops keen to assert their wealth, power and domination over a racial other. The *Straits Times* diplomatically described the showering of coins as a generous gift; as 'souvenirs'. When the men sighted the arrival of the official welcoming party, which included the governor and the high naval, army, and air officers, coins started raining in their direction, too. Again, the *Straits Times* reported tactfully that the official party picked up the coins as souvenirs.[40] 'Unused to such bonhomie, the elite, under a barrage of remarks and good-humoured barracking, tried, oh, so very hard to unbend and show that they were enjoying themselves', wrote one author shortly after the episode. 'This only made their awkwardness more apparent.'[41] While Nelson has described the episode as 'raucous and racist', noting that – in reference to the Australians' egalitarianism – at least their 'larrikinism and ill-disciplined irreverence was democratic', this overshadows the way in which such acts asserted the Australians' sense of power over the Asian population.[42] The latter frequently featured as the unwilling victims of soldiers' larrikin behaviour. In this way attitudes to race undermine egalitarian notions.

Asians also found themselves the victims of the poor behaviour of intoxicated Australian troops on leave. Part of the blame was placed on the strength of the local alcohol, which caused a nuisance for the AIF command. 'Those of them who drink behave disgracefully on leave,' wrote Captain Donald Lyndon of the 2/6th Battalion. In Colombo, Lyndon had great difficulty controlling the revelry:

> Getting them back on the ship is a nightmare. Only about
> half turn up at the proper time and then squabbling and half
> drunk. I've had to commandeer a wheelbarrow to get them
> on to the wharf. They have bottles in all pockets and stuck
> down their pants and I have to go in amongst them and say
> 'Gimme that', and take it and throw it overboard.

This is in stark contrast to views of the official historian, who made a point of the good behaviour of the troops in Ceylon, obviously reflecting the way in which attempts were made to protect the reputation of the AIF within such publications.[43]

In Malaya the 8th Division's War Diary noted: 'only offences of substance have in every case been associated with the excessive consumption of alcohol. In some cases this has been aggravated by the vicious effect of native liquors'.[44] Singaporean beer was also stronger than Australian brews, and this had an extra effect on dehydrated soldiers not acclimatised to the heat and humidity of Singapore. A driver from the 2/20th Battalion wrote in a letter to his brother that if he were to get drunk on the local beer he would have a 'beauty' of a hangover, 'as it is liquid dynamite and it has appropriate names like *Anchor* and *Tiger*'.[45] One particular incident was that of a gunner from the 2/10th Field Regiment who, in a drunken act of vandalism, smashed in a Chinese shopkeeper's window. Nelson has described such vandalism as a re-creation of drunken antics at home in Australia, citing a diarist: 'two feeds of steak and eggs at Cabaret get full. [Two diggers] break streetlights, a good night'.[46] Whether or not troops were indeed re-enacting good times at home, in Malaya, Singapore and elsewhere visited by Australian troops it was locals, mostly Asians and their property, who bore the brunt of such larrikin antics.

Again, members of the Asian community were often victims of the potential chaos caused by the inquisitive Australian soldiers' penchant for sightseeing and touring, anecdotes of which are scattered within battalion histories. Such was the case during the 2/16th Battalion's stay in India. While stationed at the British barracks at Deolali, 240 kilometres north-east of Bombay, orders were posted that the nearby holy city of Nasik was to remain out of bounds. Malcom Uren, author of the battalion's official history, observes:

> That notice read like a pressing invitation to visit the place
> and the Battalion went there almost to a man. In their zest
> for sightseeing and their ignorance of local customs and
> behaviour, the visiting troops unknowingly violated the
> mosques and made such bold errors as joining a religious
> procession in the mistaken belief it was some kind of local
> entertainment.[47]

The population of Nasik was reported to be anti-British and, following the escapades of the marauding sightseers, 'soon showed itself to be anti-Australian [as well] by massing in large crowds and demonstrating noisily against the sightseeing tourists'. And the drama did not end there. As the scene began to turn ugly, the men returned quickly 'in tight order' to where the taxis were waiting to take them back to Deolali, only to find that the taxi drivers had suddenly doubled their fares for the return journey. The soldiers were not impressed. 'That kind of blackmail was dealt with vigorously', noted Uren, 'and it might be true that some of the taxi drivers were unfortunately left behind when the taxis returned to Deolali'.[48]

The more intrepid sightseers amid the ranks, unsatisfied with the usual tourist trail, felt determined to see the 'real Asia'. Such was the resignation of Bills, who feared that what may have been his only chance to visit Singapore was going to be in the nature of a 'Cook's Conducted Tour'. With two dozen taxi-loads signed up he feared it would be 'Singapore and sights for two dollars!'[49] For Australian soldiers and nurses the authentic experience of Asia was to be found distant from the tourist trail. Australians were curious and enthusiastic to visit and explore the slums of Asian cities. While such an attraction to viewing the wretched living conditions of the Asian masses may have been an attempt to authenticate their travel experience, descriptions of the inherent and confronting poverty encountered were taken as part and parcel of the exotic and mystical East in an apparent desire to discover the 'real' Orient, as if it were cunningly concealed from the tourist's gaze.[50] In dependencies and colonies of empire during the 19th and 20th centuries, palatial hotels, restaurants and even rickshaws expressed and reinforced hierarchical racial distinctions.[51]

The desire to view the squalor and poverty was a way of confirming in the eyes of soldiers their place within the racial hierarchy. This is reflected in the correspondence of an AIF driver who expressed in a letter his disappointment that his organised tour of

Men of the AIF sightseeing shortly after their arrival in Singapore and Malaya in February 1941. Some soldiers who had participated in organised tours of Singapore were disappointed that their excursion did not take in the city's slums.
Australian War Memorial 005971

Singapore did not take in the city's slums.[52] This was not a problem for a nurse on leave in Bombay, who wrote in a letter home: 'we passed through different areas, Hindus and Mohammedan and also the Untouchable quarter, you've never seen or smelt anything like it or imagined anything so awful, South Melbourne, Carlton or even Dudley Flats are palaces compared to these, how they live and eat and sleep there beats me'.[53] Likewise, an RAAF nurse, having observed the desperation of young children selling wares in the gutters of Bangkok, described the scene in a letter to a friend as a 'highlight', adding: 'what an amazing place and how differently we all seem to eke out an existence'.[54] In addition, a description from the nurse in Bombay of the beggars' 'repulsive twisted limbs' contained no sympathy for the poor beings and she obviously felt that such circumstance was the choice of the beggar: 'it is, of course, a profession and they've been brought up to it from childhood'.[55] Such lack of sympathy for the ailing and impoverished confirms that the local populaces were peripheral to the touristic experience of sightseeing, and that Asians were a sight to be gawked at. Indeed, one soldier's photo album includes a snap of the poor sleeping in a Colombo park.[56] In one sense Australians were reinforcing their position in the racial hierarchy by emphasising the backwardness, squalor and poverty of others. Comparisons to conditions in poor urban areas within Australia were, in addition, a subtle way of declaring aspects of Australian society as better than those found elsewhere in the empire.[57]

Travel to Asia prior to the Second World War confirmed for many Australians their preconceptions of the region.[58] Travellers, too, have habitually complained about food, lack of hygiene and, most of all, the idleness and dishonesty of 'natives', who were seen as disconnected from the 'glorious past' that enhanced the exoticness of a destination.[59] These views are also expressed within the writing of Australian soldiers in the 1940s. Whereas the landscape was often described in a romantic or luxurious fashion, the local populations were generally depicted as quite separate and disconnected from the world they inhabited. As seen through the window of colonial literature, Asia and the Pacific were places for the adventures of white men. 'Natives' were peripheral. They were marginal within the grand adventure and, with their 'colourful native costumes', were described as if extras in an epic Hollywood production.[60]

Such a view was concisely expressed by one anonymous Australian soldier. When asked by an Australian reporter what he thought of Singapore, the Digger answered: 'It's nice, very nice, but there are many foreigners about.'[61] 'Everything is so green. Bar the people, they are as black as Bocker's hair', wrote another in a letter to his wife.[62] An able seaman from the destroyer HMAS *Napier* was more forthright in his views, writing in his diary: 'I think Bombay is a marvellous place. The only thing wrong with it, is the wogs who live here.'[63] Such prejudices were widespread, a reflection of common attitudes of the period. If Australian military personnel could be attracted by the visual appeal of environment and landscapes, they could just as easily be repelled by the apparent 'backwardness' of Indigenous cultures and people.

Australians encountering Asia for the very first time were faced with the confronting squalor, poverty and low living standards of the Asian populations. As historian Mark Johnston has noted, the men of the AIF had lived through the Great Depression, and many of the troops had come from those sections of society most affected.[64] Even so, few had encountered people living in such poverty, and it created in diaries and letters a contrasting vision towards the region. While Asia could be described as lush and exotic it was, on the other hand, repulsive. Singapore, for example, was as likely to be described as 'the sewer of the Pacific' as a luxurious symbol of British colonial prestige.[65] Opulent buildings reflective of wealth and power could be juxtaposed with the shocking sight of beggars starving in the gutters.[66] Such contrasts proved confounding. On the one hand there was glamour, luxury and empire; on the other there was poverty, squalor, stench and miserable masses.[67] On one side Singapore was 'beautiful', while 'on the other lay miserable hovels'.[68] Some soldiers were so disappointed with what they found that they returned to their camp or ship even before their leave had expired.[69]

Australian troops glimpsed the living conditions that Asians endured firsthand. They provided commentary in their diaries and letters on the squalor and conditions of houses and homes.[70] Such ethnographic observations could border on the voyeuristic or be insidious in nature. As an officer in Singapore wrote in his diary: 'Interesting looking into Chinese flats from our balcony. Only six feet wide, they do not seem to mind us watching their domestic relations.'[71] Not only did members of the AIF seek out the slums to experience the 'real' Asia while sightseeing in Singapore but when travelling up and down the Malayan peninsula rank-and-file members of the AIF also had to make their way through a number of first-class carriages 'which yawned luxury' to the 'filthy coolie carriages' which were 'packed sardine-tight' at the back of the train.[72] In Bombay Skinner wrote of the terrible sight of a woman, baby in her arms, falling headlong into the gutter, too weak to move from hunger: 'It is a sight I can't forget easily, but this sort of thing goes on every day in the streets.'[73] Even more confronting for *Napier's* crew was the sight of dead bodies floating down the river as they approached Chittagong (in current-day Bangladesh).[74]

In the eyes of these soldiers, the confronting living standards endured by the communities in Asia seemingly reconfirmed racial stereotypes that had long been documented within Western writing on the Orient and Far East. It evoked images of laziness, unhygienic practices and backwardness. These recurring commentaries on smell and cleanliness reflect the imprint of an Australian upbringing filled with reminders about the importance of hygiene. One digger, for example, was stunned to see a 'villainous' Chinese dentist re-arranging his dirty instruments in the gutter, while soldiers wrote home to warn relatives to wash and sterilise souvenirs sent home.[75] Such fixation on hygiene combined with the personal appearance of local peoples assisted in confirming the perceived characteristics and behaviour of certain 'types'.

The living conditions of Asian people across the region also rekindled negative stereotypes regarding the perceived 'laziness' of non-European peoples.[76] Braddon observed Singapore wharf labourers 'who managed, with a maximum of shouting and gesticulation, to do a minimum of work'.[77] Others described the Malayans as 'indolent people'.[78] In Burma, Rivett noted 'the amount of time everybody seems to find, at all hours of the day, to sit out on the verandas of their huts and shops doing precisely nothing'. Sarcastically, he added: 'I suppose the men do work at times, but you have to be smart to catch them at it.'[79]

Perhaps the main contact between Australians and Asians was between troops and shopkeepers. Within descriptions of souvenir-hunting an emphasis is placed on the supposed dishonesty of the shopkeepers. Of Singapore's Change Alley, one wrote: 'how quick the change from stately Raffles Place to this multi-coloured scene of robbers, scoundrels, sycophants and thieves. Change Alley! The refuge of every oily-tongued Indian and easily-lying salesman'.[80] Official warnings about spurious items and extravagant prices assisted in reinforcing common stereotypes of Asians in the minds of Australian troops by highlighting perceived cunning and dishonesty. A pamphlet issued to troops visiting Colombo warned: 'make your purchases from shops of standing. Special precautions should be made in purchasing Jewellery and Stones. Beware of spurious imitations offered at tempting prices'.[81] A guide to Bombay recommended troops heading to the bazaar first visit an exhibit of selected 'curios' displaying correct prices at the Jehangir Building canteen so as not to be 'stung' by vendors. Soldiers also became dismayed when 'everything had doubled or trebled normal prices' upon news that the AIF brigades in Ceylon were not just passing through but staying as part of the island's garrison.[82] Such doubts over the authenticity of souvenirs – determining the 'jade from the not-so-jade' – and the opportunism of local shopkeepers apparently confirmed long-held stereotypes of Asians as unscrupulous, deviant and dishonest.[83] No matter what the agreed-upon price, some felt certain that the shopkeepers were 'having a dry chuckle at these stupid white men'.[84]

Certainly, many Australian soldiers were aware of the diverse national groups represented within Asia. As a member of the 8th Division Signals wrote home to his friend from Malaya: 'The population is of course very mixed and Malays, Chinese, Indians, Siamese, Singhalese, Eurasians, Japs and Europeans can be seen in a day's jaunt. The habits of such a mixed community are varied and amusing.'[85] While some had difficulty distinguishing between the various groups following their arrival, other soldiers classed foreign races of people into different 'types', recording the similarities and differences associated with each.[86] A private from the

2/7th Battalion noted in his diary from Ceylon that the Singhalese were 'a different type of native from the Palestinian Wogs. All very clean looking, and not all screaming for *backsheesh*'.[87] Some were less subtle in their commentary and their racism. After a bombing raid during the Malayan campaign, one signaller wrote in a letter home that 'there were a few native casualties but they are so numerous they will never be missed'.[88] Of the Ceylonese, one wrote: 'They are a small race of men in comparison with the Aussie and there is a vast difference to see the Aussie walking erect and up the street and the native running about in a stooping sort of position. They remind one of a lot of monkeys.'[89]

A reflection of broader Australian society of the era, Australian soldiers largely viewed Asians and Pacific Islanders in racial terms, and their encounter seemed to confirm in their own eyes the long-held racial stereotypes generationally ingrained in Western society and thought. Troops found in the colonies of Asia a class structure based upon strict racial lines and many were quite willing to assert their place within the racial pecking order. Such actions again undermine the self-promoting notion that the Australians' 'easygoing' and 'casual' ways with Asians reflected a sense of Australian egalitarianism. In reality, race and power shaped most relations between Australian soldiers and Asians. Upon the arrival of the first detachment in Singapore in 1941 it was reported:

> already the Malays are the willing slaves of the Diggers.
> When one train load of soldiers was getting underway a
> tall, good-looking boy strolled onto the station ahead with
> no fewer than four Malayans carrying his kit and fussing
> around their tanned Tuan (master) as though they had been
> his servants for years.[90]

Such reporting, however, was not the exclusive domain of the press; many Australian military personnel wrote home with enthusiasm of the newfound novelties and privileges that could be enjoyed by people of European descent in the tropics. For the first time, many Australians discovered their own 'whiteness', and were quick to exploit the privileges this could entail. The experience of being waited on hand and foot by a personal servant was an exotic novelty, and the treatment of people of other races was something completely foreign to many who made up the ranks of the Second AIF.

The participation in such practices was not necessarily deliberate, and could be afforded to the soldiers quite naturally due to local customs and traditions within colonial societies. With the arrival in late 1940 of the 2/16th Battalion at Deolali, a military encampment near Bombay, it was documented:

> The first surprise came shortly after dawn of the first day in Munro Barracks. Big brown men appeared in the sleeping tents carrying hot water, razors, brushes and soap, and a little stove on which they brewed coffee. Lounging in bed the troops were shaved with all the attention associated with the luxury of a first-class hotel. Some of the more attentive of these wallahs also polished boots and swept the tents.[91]

A photograph of an RAAF crew arriving in India is similarly telling. The airmen are walking into camp followed by a line of Indians, the latter loaded up with kit bags upon their shoulders.[92] Indeed, such behaviour was endorsed by a guidebook for soldiers arriving in India, including a list of useful sentences. With a total absence of 'please' or 'thank you', the list reads very much like the tasks and commands a master might set for his servant.[93]

Even before arriving in Asia or the Middle East some officers had Indian servants attending them during the voyage.[94] One nurse in Singapore felt quite comfortable with the arrangement, writing home to her husband that 'our half day servants are so efficient that it does help such a lot actually for ourselves we do

New RAAF arrivals in India have immediately obtained the services of locals to carry their gear.
Australian War Memorial P02491.099

not lift a hand'. She adds: 'Boots cleaned and every other imaginable thing is done for us. Only wish I could stow a few boys in my trunk for you Dear.'[95] But it was not just officers who shared in the privilege, as some Other Ranks actively sought the employment of personal servants. As a private in Burma wrote home: 'We are living more like kings than soldiers. Right now I have a black boy to clean my boots, make my bed, and do the odd jobs.'[96] So widespread was the custom, the 2/15th Field Regiment even noted in its history that upon arrival in Malaya 'smiling Indian boys offered their services as batmen. We had our beds made, our tents tidied, our boots cleaned for a few shillings a week'.[97] In Ceylon, Kelly even employed four servants to serve out minor punishments he had received, such as cleaning the barracks, while he ate dinner. What makes this anecdote significant is that Kelly's diaries demonstrate a sympathetic, open and tolerant approach toward the colonised subjects of the British Empire, reflecting the way in which new arrivals could easily become seduced and empowered within colonial society.[98]

Concerned by the practice, the military authorities attempted to restrict the employment of 'Asiatic labour'. In September 1941 the 8th Division ordered that servants could be employed only as cleaners of 'drains, latrines and camp areas and similar work' and as cooks at 'hospitals, camp reception stations and similar medical units'. Applications were required for permission to employ a servant and it was mandatory that payment was to be equal to that of the going rate.[99] Such orders were perhaps required to ensure that the Australians did not upset local standards. At Deolali, soldiers had been so impressed by the special attentions they received that they paid a rupee per man (about Australian 1s. 11d.). This was a substantial sum of money for an Indian worker in the 1940s. As Uren explained:

> The attendants were delighted. Here was richness for them,
> richness from the extraordinary generous Sahibs from
> Australia. The ignorance of the Australian of economic
> conditions, especially the value of such personal services
> in India, resulted in many such gross over-payments. The
> Australian completely upset the standards of the Tommies
> who were required to remain in Deolali.[100]

A further financial consequence of the steady stream of new troops stepping off the transports was reflected in the situation that developed in Malaya, whereby the spending of the new arrivals saw an increase in prices which indirectly caused hard-

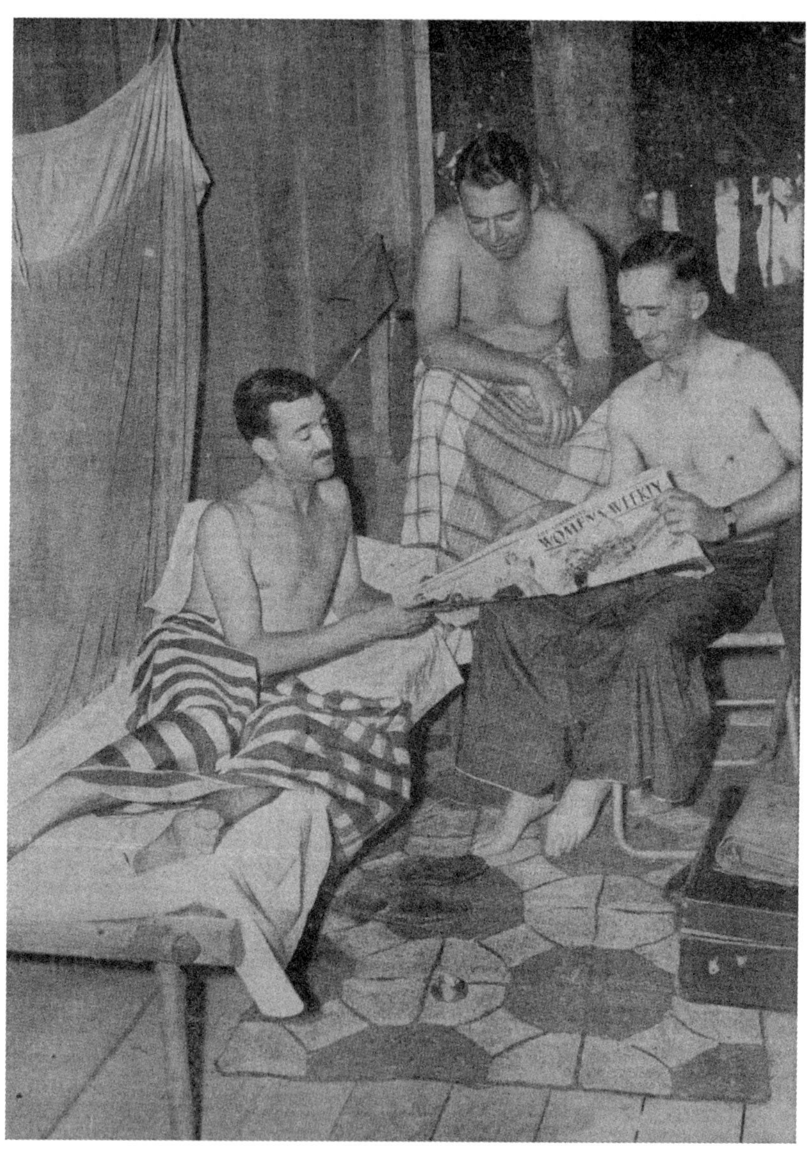

Tales of the colonial lifestyle, including the employment of personal servants, and the reported adoption of siesta hours, as highlighted in this article, 'Sarong siesta', from the *Australian Women's Weekly,* damaged the image of troops stationed in the British colonies.
National Library of Australia

ship amongst rubber tappers and ordinary workers whose meagre wages did not keep up with inflation.[101]

Perhaps nowhere within colonial society was the uneven relationship between Europeans and Asians more evident and symbolic than in the profession of the rickshaw puller. Finding rickshaws one of the great novelties of the region, it was common for soldiers to send home postcards or photographs of themselves from Colombo, Calcutta or Singapore riding the conveyances.[102] For many, the rickshaw evidently reflected the correct relationships between whites and others in colonial society.[103] Indeed, some correspondents found them a source of entertainment. As a nurse wrote with unease following her first rickshaw ride in Singapore: 'I felt more than a little guilty, sitting up and being pulled by the poorest specimen on two legs I have ever seen, but still he enjoyed the novelty almost as much as myself.'[104] Others wrote of the hilarity with which they met the profession. 'You could not help laughing at these blacks and Chinese', a soldier from the 2/29th Battalion wrote in a letter to his wife, amused that the men pulled the carts themselves 'instead of having a horse to drive'.[105] Similarly diverted, a member of the 2/20th Battalion wrote:

It is the funniest sight imaginable to see a couple of 15 stone soldiers in a rickshaw with the poor coolies dragging them along. The boys have races in town with them, you see about six rickshaws tearing down the street with the boys egging them on to go faster but they never go any faster.[106]

Possibly in response to such foolhardiness, a pamphlet issued to visiting troops in Colombo advised that rickshaws were 'built to carry one person only'.[107] While the majority of troops appear to have been well behaved, there were soldiers who behaved disrespectfully toward rickshaw drivers and shopkeepers. Various anecdotes tell of verbal abuse, violence and even the refusal to pay for services provided. Such stories from Malaya include that of drunken Australian troops chasing a local Chinese man with a meat cleaver, or of brandishing knives on rickshaw drivers reluctant to take them to 'number one girl'.[108] In Bombay there were reports of assaults not only on taxi drivers but also on members of the local constabulary.

A racist attitude is clearly inherent in these correspondences by the nature of contact between Australians and Asians and the unevenness of the master–servant relationship. Emphasising the insular nature of white Australian society of the period, Plante wrote of her discomfort in Bombay. It was not the privilege of being white in India that caused her unease, but the close proximity of a racial other: 'I'm getting used to being waited on by natives, though it still seems unusual to have a black hand come over your shoulder.' Such feelings were further exemplified when Plante wrote of her fears that a local swimming pool they were to visit would not be segregated (to her relief the pool turned out to be 'whites only').[109] It appears Plante was not the only one concerned, as guides to Bombay made clear in their listings which swimming baths were exclusively European.[110]

Self-promoting tales of sightseeing, leave to Singapore, servants, siestas and safaris drew strong criticism at the time. The conduct by men and women of the AIF in Malaya, and the perceived emulation of a colonial lifestyle as it was reported in Australian newspapers and magazines, caused much resentment among Australians serving concurrently on the front lines in North Africa, Greece, Crete and the Middle East throughout 1941. Ray Parkin, a veteran from service in the Mediterranean aboard the cruiser HMAS *Perth* and later a prisoner of war alongside members of the 7th Division captured on Java (themselves veterans of the Middle East campaigns), wrote of the unfortunate feelings between men of the 7th and 8th divisions during their captivity: 'From the point of view of the 7th, they think the 8th were soft, pampered and over-publicised'. Much to the chagrin of the 7th, while engaged

The reporting within the Australian press of the AIF in Malaya, particularly by the *Australian Women's Weekly*'s Adele Shelton-Smith (depicted here), led to much anger among the men of the 8th Division.
The Nineteenth: The Magazine of the 2/19th Battalion AIF Malaya

Again, Shelton-Smith is the subject of this drawing by S.J. McAlister of the 2/19th Battalion. This cartoon features quotations from Shelton-Smith's articles from the *Australian Women's Weekly*.
The Nineteenth: The Magazine of the 2/19th Battalion AIF Malaya

in a bitter and bloody struggle with the Vichy French in Syria in 1941, they picked up copies of the *Australian Women's Weekly* and 'read the glamorising articles on the 8th and their excellent conditions. They read of the 8th having sheets and servants, while they were shaking sand and scorpions from their blankets'. In the confines of captivity following the early Japanese victories, these tensions were magnified under the desperation of the conditions imposed upon prisoners of war in the region.[111] British troops in Asia were similarly charged with being 'softer' because of their engagement in and enjoyment of the luxuries afforded to white men in the colonies.[112] As Parkin makes clear, this was certainly a view other members of the AIF held towards the 8th Division.

The soldiers themselves, quite unsurprisingly, refuted such claims. Shelton-Smith's reports for the *Women's Weekly* attracted extensive criticism for what was considered a disproportionate emphasis on leisure rather than work. Shelton-Smith had tried to report accurately on the troops' training as well as on their recreational activities, spending considerable time interviewing soldiers returning from manoeuvres while at the same time attempting to show readers, including concerned family, that the men were well and in high morale. Her reports, combined with the photographs by the *Women's Weekly*'s photographer Bill Brindle, tended to emphasise a holiday camp atmosphere that consequently provoked comment from loved ones at home and outraged the men in Malaya. Writing particularly for a female audience, less attention was paid to military manoeuvres in favour of more leisurely aspects of their lives.[113]

While soldiers were highly critical of Shelton-Smith, such images were nevertheless projected by the men within their own writing. Furthermore, although training in the jungle was indeed tough, and the boredom and monotony of camp life tedious, soldiers evidently preferred to document their leisure time in letters home. Due to wartime censors they were also limited in what they could say about military matters, and descriptions of sightseeing were considered more suitable. Inevitably, they were also sight-seeing for those at home, hence the detailed descriptions within letters. However, there are certain truths to the stories, and the soldiers and nurses who wrote home from Malaya and Singapore are as much to blame for the creation of the perceived pampering of the 8th Division as Shelton-Smith. As Sister Pat Gunter admitted in her memoir, 'letters from sisters in the Middle East embarrassed me when I compared my life of ease with theirs'.[114]

Through their writing, troops in Malaya had unwillingly and unwittingly constructed an image of a summer camp. This was in keeping with the first impression by an arriving RAAF airman that the Selatar airfield at Singapore was 'a vast country club'.[115] Another soldier wrote glowingly from Malaya of daily visits to an AIF camp by an ice-cream vendor.[116] Such images are further emphasised through aforementioned tales of sightseeing, servants, siesta hours, rickshaws and the enjoyment of the benefits that could be afforded by the white race within European colonial society in Asia. These were reinforced by descriptions with accompanying photos in the *Women's Weekly* of soldiers at leisure on beaches, climbing palm trees, attending dances, and lounging by the swimming pool of a Chinese millionaire's seaside mansion.[117]

The reporting of such behaviour in the press caused considerable angst among the members of the 8th Division. These feelings were particularly aggravated by remarks in letters from wives, girlfriends, family and friends referencing newspaper and magazine articles published in Australia that gave the impression that the AIF was leading 'exotic lives in the tropics'. Even the official history of the Malayan campaign comments on this issue. 'Sometimes a wife or girl would add that she too knew how to have a gay time', noted Wigmore. The ignoring of the rigorous training undertaken in the enervating heat of the Malayan jungles, as well as the monotony and tedium of daily camp life in what at the time was a non-combat zone, upset the troops.[118] Such grievances were noted among many AIF writers, as the soldiers soon got sick of the publicity. Back to 'thousands of homes' around Australia 'went whinging tales of parties given for the troops by wealthy planters or miners and even by Sultans. Lonely girlfriends brooded darkly on tales of beer and cabarets, of Chinese dancing partners and Lamour modelled, sarong-draped natives'. The men of the 8th Division 'were going to have a hard time explaining someday that the glamorised parties, few and far between, were simple tea parties paid for by an occasional philanthropist, that the cabarets of Singapore, Kuala Lumpur or Seremban, with their 20-cents-a-time shuffle, were tawdry refuges from the monotony of army routine'.[119]

One soldier reflected upon the episode: 'Imagine the Digger's delight when certain journals produced glowing articles describing the Malayan picnic', including 'the Digger's penchant for taxi girls, of sumptuous parties given by the Sultan of Johore, of hilarious leaves in Singapore'. He added that 'wives wrote to husbands saying if that was the way things were, they too would have their fling'.[120] Photos in the *Women's Weekly* of soldiers at a local dance hall waltzing with taxi-girls led to protestations that 'wives, girlfriends, sisters and mothers' should not be forgotten. Anyhow, the price for a taxi-dancer – a professional dancer with whom a ticket could be purchased in return for a dance and who was often escorted home by her parents – was 'above the means of any private', according to one soldier. Certainly, he proclaimed, the soldiers did 'not make brutes of ourselves in the dark drab parts of Singapore'.[121] As British historians Bayly and Harper have noted, troops of the AIF believed 'they were innocent victims of Singapore's reputation' for leisure and colonial opulence. Some soldiers were even sent white feathers.[122]

The resentment and disgust held toward the Australian press by the 8th Division lingered long after the completion of the war. Published in 2006, the history of the 2/19th Battalion, for example, still included several cartoons drawn by its members in 1941 to express their anger towards the *Women's Weekly* reporter. Most confronting is the imagined retaliatory physical violence toward Shelton-Smith depicted in these cartoons, highlighting the soldiers' ongoing dislike. In one cartoon Shelton-Smith is being strangled by a muscular digger, in another she is being stabbed by a group of Diggers with bayonets.[123] Regardless of the furore over Shelton-Smith's reports about army life in Malaya, it remains clear that certain aspects of the 8th Division's experience in Malaya in 1941 reveal how troops could be seduced by the colonial lifestyle. One aspect of the Malayan campaign and the catastrophic fall of Singapore largely neglected by military historians is the way these cultural and social aspects of soldiers' lives in Malaya shaped the perception and performance of the 8th Division as a fighting force.

The perceived friendliness, easygoing and egalitarian nature of Australian troops provided a means for depicting Australian attitudes as unique among the countries of the empire. Such reporting was in part a critique as well as a desire to paint the Australian visitors as different to the white British residents of colonial Southeast Asia. As opposed to the old-world British view, the Australian soldier's refreshingly casual outlook was highlighted within the media, by the official historians, and within battalion histories. Certainly, in the writing of published AIF authors such as Noonan, and in letters and diaries by men such as Bills, Wallin and Kelly, there is a clear expression of a middle-class outlook and sense of moral righteousness. Without judgment, these men were quite open in their encounters and at times sympathetic towards the colonised. And while these authors are not necessarily representative of the majority, their views are not uncommon. In the main, however, relations between Australians and Asians were not equal. Self-promoting tales of the Australians' congenial behaviour towards Asians is undermined by anecdotes of servants and raucous sightseeing in which the uneven relationship between the two is apparent. Australians may well have been more casual and easygoing in their encounters than British troops, but their egalitarian ideal was not necessarily all-encompassing toward members of other races. Racism remained, and many of the Australians' actions toward – and treatment of – Asians were little or no different to the ways in which they had been treated by the British.

4

'NOTHING LIKE DOROTHY LAMOUR'

Perceptions of Asian women

The Second AIF's encounters with, relations with and attitudes toward Asian shopkeepers and rickshaw drivers was one matter; attitudes towards members of the opposite sex in the region was another. Did Australian soldiers have an ingrained perception of Asian women, and was this challenged by the experience of travel? For the young men of the AIF the possibility of an encounter with an exotic foreign woman could be both enticing and exciting. As one soldier swooned amid his new surrounds, Malacca 'is noted for its many beautiful Eurasian girls'.[1] Likewise, a gunner with the 2/15th Field Regiment in Malaya described 'a dozen erect young Malayan women' wandering down the road past the camp to the local village. They were, the gunner noted, 'young, shapely and shyly very much aware that we were men'.[2] In Asia and the Pacific, the newly arrived looked for signs of confirmation of the existence of the enchanting and exotic myths so alluringly captured within many tales of the tropics. Their expectations were shaped by a long European literary tradition and contemporary Hollywood genre films about the mystical Orient and exotic South Seas; these had constructed an image of the region as a place for a white man's adventures.

Of particular note were the many references – from Malaya, Singapore and later New Guinea – to the Hollywood starlet Dorothy Lamour. By the outbreak of the Second World War, Lamour had become famous for her starring role in a number of Hollywood adventures set in Asia and the Pacific. A popular sex symbol of the era, Lamour was a white American who notably played the role of a 'native' girl.[3] She became famous as the 'sarong girl' because of her trademark garment, first worn in her breakthrough role in *The Jungle Princess* (1936), set in Malaya. She also starred in *The Road to Singapore* (1940), but is most associated with her roles in films set in the South Seas, such as *The Hurricane* (1938) and *Her Jungle Love* (1938). In their writing home, Australian soldiers were quick to point out – and had been told so by locals – that Lamour wore her sarong in a fashion which no Malayan, Indonesian or Polynesian ever would.[4] As one soldier wryly observed, 'I don't suppose they [the locals] have the legs to show off like she does.'[5] Such was the popularity of Lamour's films that Australian soldiers bought what they called sarongs, but which were in fact 'not very Dorothy Lamourish' saris, to send home to girlfriends and wives. This inspired the *Australian Women's Weekly* to publish a step-by-step guide on how to wear the garment.[6] Indeed, comments from across the region such as 'nothing like Dorothy Lamour' were not just reflections on the appearance of local women but symbolic of a wider rejection of the cultural baggage that had enhanced the Australians' initial expectations of the region.

Such awareness in fact predated Hollywood. During the 19th century the mystical Orient became associated with escapism and fantasy, in sharp juxtaposition with the increasingly institutionalised European attitudes of the era.[7] Therefore, it has been proclaimed, in the 19th and early 20th centuries sojourners looked for a more libertine attitude abroad and for a sexual experience unobtainable at home. Certainly, these encounters were shaped by power, race and class.[8] For Australian authors in the first half of the 20th century, with a world outlook seen through British eyes, perceptions of Asia as a sexual paradise and a place of carnal delight were adopted and replicated within the works of Australian artists and writers, who would depict Asian women as beautiful and report on Geishas and the bare-breasted girls of Bali.[9] As for military travellers, as historian Alison Broinowski has noted, everywhere a soldier went in wartime became an 'illicit space' owing to the reputation of soldiers as frequenters of red-light districts. Significantly, however, Broinowski has noted that the sexual conquests of the AIF – as reported within Australian war writing – were confined to the Middle East and Europe. Whereas men have spoken openly about affairs with 'Greek, Jewish, and English women, and even with a French–Egyptian', the literature was 'uneasy about Asian lovers'.[10] How, then, did Australian soldiers in Asia and the Pacific during the Second World War describe their encounters with the opposite sex?

Exaggerations regarding the fertility of the region combined with fears of overpopulation and suspicions of the 'Asiatic hordes' cast upon the Asian other a dubious image of exaggerated potency. It was an exotic image that persisted during the Second World War. American GIs, historians have noted, were seduced by a 'romantic mythology of women who were attractive, lustful and available'. In reality, however, the very qualities of otherness associated with the women of Asia and the Pacific created obstacles for American soldiers that proved troublesome and complicated to resolve.[11] Similar attitudes affected the insights of Australian soldiers regarding their experiences in the region. Inspired by their absence from home and bombarded with enticing images of exotic women based on literary tradition and Hollywood genre films of the period, the men of the Second AIF found encounters and relations with the women of Asia and the Pacific both complex and frustrating. Upon contact with Asian women, certain myths proved confounding and their authenticity became questionable.

While some stereotypes were rejected, a variety of myths that Westerners associated with Asians persisted among Australian servicemen who entered Asia and the Pacific during the war. For example, some Australian soldiers thought that Asian women possessed an inherited elegance that was missing in Western women. At the New World amusement park in Singapore, where Noonan and his friends had attended a cabaret in order to 'get an eyeful of the taxi girls', he described a scene in which, apart from a couple of Australians dancing with taxi-girls, the rest were 'Asiatics who could execute Western dance steps with a grace that is beyond [us] Occidentals'. An avid observer and describer of the female sex during his wartime travels, Noonan seemed convinced that Asian women had an inherent poise.[12]

Some descriptions were more voyeuristic. Observing a group of women washing by the roadside in Burma, he wrote:

> Their frequent ablutions are an open-air job for all to see.
> Clad only in their longyis, which are adequate, they tip
> large quantities of water over themselves with dippers.
> Their skilful movements in changing from wet longyi to dry
> one are accomplished with a tantalizing and disappointing
> display of modesty. We thought so anyway.[13]

Prisoners of war in Thailand described similar displays of modesty. As a large group of Australian prisoners rested by a river, Ray Parkin recounted the scene of a young Thai mother bathing beside a river barge on the opposite bank. Tantalisingly, he wrote, a few of the men saw the woman's 'well-formed breasts' as she leaned forward.[14] Such observances of daily life by men bereft of female companionship within the military forces reaffirmed the sensuous mystique supposedly possessed by Oriental women.

Understandably, the military authorities wished to restrict relations between soldiers and foreign women in order to limit the potential spread of venereal disease (VD), and to ensure good relations between the military and the local population. Guidebooks and pamphlets were issued to Australian soldiers that specifically warned against sexual relations with women in Asia and the Pacific. A major concern was that domestic interference could inhibit co-operation between Allied military forces and the Indigenous populations. Such concerns are highlighted in an article on life in Malaya within *Salt*, a fortnightly periodical published and distributed widely by the Army's Educational Service. The article warned that 'all Asiatic races resent Europeans taking notice of their womenfolk, and any familiarity will cause trouble'.[15] Similarly, the guidebook to Borneo warned: 'You may think that some of the womenfolk in Borneo are not unattractive, but don't think because they are native women you can take liberties with them.' It added: 'The men in Borneo are as sensitive about their own women folk as you are.'[16] The servicemen's guidebook to Java was more expressive: 'Above all, avoid the slightest suggestion of familiarity with their womenfolk. They would resent it passionately – and might quite possibly express that resentment with a *kris* [a ceremonial knife].'[17]

For the military authorities, more weight was placed on the importance of co-operation between Indigenous peoples and Allied forces, and the health of their own fighting men, than on the wellbeing of Indigenous women and communities. A significant consideration was that unsavoury incidents involving Australian soldiers – ostensibly domestic interference – could adversely affect local support for the Allied war effort. As the *Borneo Book* outlined: 'the bad reputation which you may earn will spread to your cobbers; indeed to all white soldiers. You have only to think for a moment to realise what bad effects may grow out of that'.[18] Similarly, a guide to New Guinea stated rather more baldly that the 'three golden rules' in any village were 'gardens, pigs and women'. All were 'of basic importance in the lives of New Guinea natives, and interference with them will bring trouble to your mates'. This 1943 guidebook outlined the issues far more clearly than did later publications. It stated that, first: although in some villages women may associate with European men, in others they do not, and in any case 'their menfolk' must be considered. Second: 'If the woman is not consenting, the intercourse is just rape – whether the victim be white or brown.' Third: if the men are not consenting to their women associating with visitors, then 'it is at least a very serious kind of interference'. Fourth: 'an affair with a native woman is not a love-match', but 'a deal' in which payment was expected.[19] Despite wishing to restrict contact, this final point suggests that women were a commodity and might be made available if payment were arranged.[20]

To the military, the physical wellbeing of Australian fighting men was paramount; hence the risks of VD were strongly emphasised in order to discourage sexual liaisons between Australian troops and local women. In response to the large incidence of VD among the AIF in the Middle East, military authorities worked hard to tackle the problem. One measure in the Middle East that attempted to lower infection was the suspension of pay, but this led to fewer men coming forward for diagnosis. More effective was the setting up of special aid-posts, the distribution of information regarding prevention, and the encouragement to seek medical help.[21] An example of the information campaign is the booklet issued to soldiers entering Singapore titled *Venereal Disease in Singapore: And How to Avoid It*. It reflects the attempts by which military authorities discouraged men to seek sexual relations. 'It should be the pride and ambition of every soldier to keep himself as fit and healthy as possible and to do everything in his power to avoid being sick in hospital', the booklet enthused. It proclaimed that VD was rife in the East, as 'practically all prostitutes in Singapore are completely ignorant and illiterate, and have no idea of how to keep themselves clean and free of infection'. Women who were infected were not compelled to seek treatment, as those who exploited sexual workers 'were not willing to lose money for that time'.

To further illustrate the point, *Venereal Disease in Singapore* detailed the effects of VD and the possibility of lingering in hospital for several months. Infection could cause permanent and irreversible damage, and those infected would be invalided out of the service, sent home and required to explain to family and loved ones both why they had come home and why regular visits to and treatment from a doctor were required. 'Continence and abstention' were the only sure preventative measures, though the heavy consumption of alcohol – 'the most powerful ally of Venereal Disease' – was strongly discouraged. 'Keep away from all Prostitutes', the pamphlet strongly concluded. 'They are ALL diseased, however attractive they make themselves look.'[22] Such descriptions prolonged the double-edged representation of Asian women long presented within colonial literature or writing from the East. Certainly, Asian women – if not seen as graceful lilies – could alternatively be depicted as evil dragon ladies within pre-war Australia.[23]

If such pamphlets were not enough to discourage sexual activity by Australian soldiers, further direct warnings were issued to the men. An order posted by the 2/20th Battalion proclaimed upon arrival in Malaya in February 1941 that 'practically the whole female population is infected'.[24] Such orders and warnings are commonly found in the unit war diaries of all divisions, brigades and battalions of the AIF. Publications such as *Salt* also printed frequent articles regarding the menace of VD. It was not just the physical health of Australia's fighting men, however, that was the concern of such publications; it was also the potential spread of sexually transmitted diseases among Australian women following the men's return home from duty.[25] This was a constant message throughout the conflict and by 1945 it had not changed. As the general orders issued by Kuching Force in Borneo attest, the prospect of 'the most violent forms of VD' being passed onto Australian women was very real, with the attendant risk of permanent disability for both mother and child.[26] Furthermore, as had been the case elsewhere, in 1945 fraternisation with locals was banned across the Netherlands East Indies, and any serviceman who contracted VD was threatened with severe disciplinary action.[27] If these warnings were still not enough, in Parepare in October 1945 a parade was held for troops of the 2/14th Battalion for the sole purpose of displaying the effects of VD on local women. The woman put on public display was among a group of prostitutes rounded up by authorities and receiving medical attention from the Australian medical services.[28]

As well as implying that virtually the entire local populace carried disease, the authorities also played upon fears that local diseases were particularly treacherous and harmful to outsiders, who, it was claimed, lacked the immunity which the Indigenous populations had built up over generations.[29] Furthermore, general orders declared that 'VD in these parts is so insidious that normal precautions are often ineffective'. No method or precaution other than abstinence was considered safe.[30] If this was not persuasive, then racial fears could be summoned up in areas that had been under Japanese control by insinuations that enemy soldiers had already 'had their go'. These information campaigns clearly had a strong effect and certainly succeeded in being a deterrent for some.[31] Such was the fear of contamination that — in the eyes of some — even the sight of Asian or Pacific Islander women could be enough to scare anyone off. Such a case could be made for Noonan in his description of a 'pair of languorous Chinese damsels' in Penang. 'They were eying us with sidelong glances from behind some silk hangings', wrote Noonan. '"Come hither" was the same in Chinese, except that the eyes were black and the brows curved upwards. Fearing its insistence and our own frailty, we made a strategic withdrawal from our position.'[32] While Noonan describes his antics in a rather jovial manner, and although in his shyness he indeed draws upon the attractions of the oriental myths, others were more forthright in their concern. Barrett's study on the Second AIF reveals that fear of venereal disease helped strongly in promoting abstinence. For example, one respondent to Barrett's survey noted that in the Celebes he did not find the women in the brothels attractive despite feeling differently toward 'women in the street'. Another told of his fears of 'virulent strains of VD in plague proportions – their own and the Japs'. Indeed, 7th Division orders were deliberately intended to heighten such fears amongst the troops. Operational instructions,

The military attempted to limit relations between soldiers and Asian women; however, provocative images such as this one from an AIF guidebook (with accompanying caption) confused the message.
Java: A Handbook for Servicemen

for example, warn that VD was rife, that 'practically 100%' of the women were believed to be infected and that some of the conditions that the men had become infected with, such as gonorrhoea, had proved unresponsive to penicillin treatment.[33]

Despite the military guides and booklets warning against courting foreign women so as to not interfere in domestic matters or offend cultural mores, or as a measure against sexually transmitted diseases, the very same publications continued to fuel the myth of Asian and Pacific Islander women being exotically beautiful and virtuous. For instance, within the soldiers' guidebook to Java a picture of a smiling young Javanese woman was accompanied by the caption: 'She is often quite attractive, and ... she knows it.'[34] Soldiers who read only the caption accompanying the pictures would be unaware of the full quotation:

The easy-go-lucky method of approach that may go down with the modern white girl won't be accepted in anything

like the same spirit by the average young native women in
Java. She is often quite attractive – and when she is, she
knows it – but she is usually as prim as the Early Victorians,
and she expects to be treated with just as much respect as
they were. There are 'others', of course, in Java as elsewhere.
But association with them won't do you any good with
the rest of the community. Java village society is intensely
respectable. (Note: The incidence of venereal disease is
high).[35]

Again, the contradiction is apparent. On the one hand, women
are described as 'prim and proper', but the accompanying portrait
and its caption, together with the remark that 'the incidence of
venereal disease is high', may imply otherwise.

Similar examples appear in other military publications issued to
soldiers. An article on Javanese irrigation methods in *Salt* included
a photograph of a bare-breasted Balinese girl. The accompanying caption reads: 'Girl from Bali, which neighbours Java. Balinese
women are famed for their beauty.'[36] Similarly, a photograph of
a Javanese girl in an article on New Caledonia in a later edition
was captioned: 'Import: Attractive Awes, one of the thousands
of Javanese brought to New Caledonia as indentured servants.'[37]
Despite official soldier guides and periodicals such as *Salt* encouraging abstinence and non-interference with the women of Asia
and the Pacific, the very same publications still teasingly draw
upon alluring images that recall stereotypical views of Oriental
women. Contradictions and tensions within these texts reflect the
way in which even the authors of official publications found it difficult to fully cast off the stereotype they were trying to debunk.

No doubt this was all very confusing for attentive troops.
Nonetheless, it is unsurprising that men of the Second AIF found
relations – even contact – with local women difficult, complicated
and frustrating. Social mores aside, Australian soldiers found personal contact with females across the region difficult for various

reasons. The reputation of the AIF as a fierce fighting unit often worked against the men's chances. As the various AIF units began deploying around the southern tip of the Malayan peninsula in the early months of 1941 they were initially puzzled by the absence of women and children. It was not unusual in these early months for soldiers to see women hastily departing as they approached: they 'scuttle out of sight every time', wrote Williams in a letter home.[38] Similarly, men of the 2/19th Battalion found the 'local reception chilly' at Seremban. Some shopkeepers boarded up their shops and hardly a woman ventured into the street for at least a week as 'rape, murder and loot were to be expected from these terrible Australians'. Some attributed this to Japanese radio propaganda.[39] However, it was more likely, as the official historian of the Malayan campaign explained, to have been the result of British propaganda 'misguidedly designed to heighten their reputation as warriors'.[40] These descriptions of men of the great warrior race from down under adversely generated a sense of fear toward the Australians among the local populations.

In Ceylon this was further compounded by the unwanted legacy created a generation earlier. As in Malaya, women and children were initially very reluctant to approach Australian soldiers in Ceylon. However, unlike in Malaya, here it was the poor behaviour exhibited by visiting members of the original AIF during the First World War that caused problems for the Second AIF. As Kelly noted in his diary: 'The women are very timid and will not venture too near, and this I believe is due to the "good" name the Australians earned here in the last war, by raping and imposing other indignities on the women.' Misguided ideas that Australian soldiers would 'carry off their women' caused strain between some groups of Australians and the Ceylonese. This was a strange feeling for men who found themselves in such circumstances. 'Personally, I could not imagine myself wishing to molest them, and it is a little disturbing to be looked at as though one were a wild animal.'[41] Furthermore, after previously serving in the Middle

East and Mediterranean, the garrison troops wished nothing more than to return to Australia, which at that time was believed to be seriously threatened by the Japanese advance. Such frustrations were further factors in the forming of cool relations between many of the garrison troops and the Ceylonese.[42] The sight of women fleeing or expressing fear ran counter to the exotic myths of virtuous 'natives' welcoming and embracing new arrivals. Such scenes certainly did not reinforce the stereotype.

One of the more conventional ways in which Australian soldiers came into contact with Asian women in Malaya was through meeting the so-called 'taxi-girls'. Sometimes mistaken for prostitutes, these dancers worked at local dance halls where, for a small fee, a customer could buy a token granting them a dance with an attractive woman. Taxi-girls, noted one soldier, were 'attractive girls ... generally clad in exotic silk dresses and white bridge

Images of soldiers with taxi-dancers, as depicted here in the *Australian Women's Weekly*, were a source of tension between men of the 8th Division and those at home, who perhaps mistook these professional dancers for prostitutes. The dancer pictured on the right is wearing a digger's slouch hat.
National Library of Australia

coats'. However, while they were 'lovely to look upon', the soldier added: 'Their figures did not possess the conventional lines to which Australians were accustomed. They were lithe and fragile and flat-chested as a fourpenny rabbit.' Nevertheless, 'they could certainly "go to town" when the music was hot'. But the Australian soldiers' encounters with taxi-girls fell short of their visions of exotic Asian women. As the same author would later admit, 'Few of the taxi-girls could speak English and were poor company at the best of times.'[43]

Similarly, another digger described a night on the town in a letter to his sister:

> We were bound for a cabaret and the first thing we noticed,
> even before we heard the dance music, was a strong sweet
> scent. It was the powder used by the Chinese girls, and they
> are fairly plastered with it. They are not bad dancers, but
> as they don't speak English it gets a bit tame after a while.
> You buy a ticket for a dollar, and give up a quarter for each
> dance, so it is an expensive way of amusing yourself.[44]

If some men found the taxi-girls frustrating company then sexual gratification could certainly be sought within the red-light districts of the major cities. These areas were declared out-of-bounds for visiting soldiers, though rather than acting as a deterrent such orders were often taken as invitation, and the men visited these districts in droves. Singapore's Lavender Street and Bombay's Grant Road were both infamous and popular destinations for men on leave. Australians became so associated with the Lavender Street area it was claimed that when a member of the AIF chartered a rickshaw he would immediately be taken there no matter which destination had been requested.[45] It must be noted that soldiers who visited these districts did not necessarily go there seeking sexual pleasures. Of these there were some, perhaps many, but more to the point these districts were notorious points on the sightseeing trail; places to tick off the to-do list while passing through. Furthermore, as detailed in previous chapters, since the ordinary rank-and-file troops were not admitted into the white clubs these districts were some of the few places besides comforts funds where soldiers could go to drink and socialise.

One digger who visited the notorious Bombay precinct wrote wryly in his diary: 'Changed money and went on leave. Saw Grant Road – native quarter where all native brothels are. Harlots kept in cages like birds. All of them chew beetle nut and spit red like blood everywhere.' Rather than being disenchanted by the awful conditions, he added rather matter-of-factly: 'Got merry on Shanghai Beer and got friendly with thirteen year old Indian girl. First woman I had since leaving Australia … Saw M.O. [Medical Officer] immediately for treatment.'[46] The blasé reporting of this affair shows that some men were apparently unconcerned by the slave-like conditions and physical age of the women in these areas. It also demonstrates the total disregard some had for the advice printed in guidebooks and pamphlets.

Not all men, however, succumbed to temptation. One visitor to Lavender Street obligingly noted:

> [The girls] were there alright. Dozens of them – some pretty, some not so pretty and others definitely off the record. 'Hi. You come with me, Digger? Very cheap! Very clean!' We had to hand it to them, they were quite frank about shouting their wares to prospective clients. They thought it was a great joke and laughed when we hurried off saying the price was too hot.

In Rangoon the sight of girls no older than ten or 12 offering themselves for 'five rupees' – while confronting – ultimately drew sympathy.[47] Likewise, Grant Road and its 'cages' proved of little interest to men like Noonan. Perhaps disappointed, he wrote that 'most of the crimson women are black', adding that 'most travel writers have something original to say about India's most cele-brated brothel area, but I have nothing'.[48]

Such worldly experiences could have a profound effect on the Australians. For some, the experience of the red-light districts and the treatment of women were clearly disheartening and disturbing. For example, in his 1944 novel *We Were the Rats*, which was partly based on his experiences within the AIF and initially banned in Australia for its realism, journalist Lawson Glassop recorded his experience of Bombay. Visiting Grant Road out of curiosity after a British 'Tommy' had told him about women in cages, he felt the whole scene was 'repugnant': 'Some had their parents and children in the "cages" with them … It was the most degrading thing we had even seen. It shook us.'[49] Others wrote of how fortunate they felt to live in Australia after seeing such a place. Another memoir – entitled *The War, the Whores and the Afrika Corps* – contained a chapter on escapades and experiences in brothels in Egypt and the Middle East where, unlike in India and Singapore, there were European women working in the establishments. Of Grant Road, the author wrote:

> You hear a lot of stories in the army, but I never heard of
> any soldier having sex in Grant Road. In fact we thought
> it was a great experience for young soldiers and I'm sure
> most of us took more notice of our sex and hygiene lectures
> afterwards. From that day on we matured very quickly.[50]

For a variety of factors it is difficult to determine the truth of the matter. Mostly, such episodes – considered private – were not discussed within the soldiers' writing. Still, the incidence of sexual relations with local women appears to have been rarer among the Australian troops who served in Asia and the Pacific than it was among the men who served in the Mediterranean and Middle East. Although the rates of VD reflect the number of serving men diagnosed with infection rather than those who risked infection, it appears that a majority of Australian soldiers – particularly those stationed in Asia and the Pacific – did not place themselves at risk. While VD was a significant problem in the Middle East (where it occurred at a rate of 35.31 per 1000 men in 1940 and 48.46 per 1000 in 1941) and among British and Commonwealth aircrew within Bomber Command in Britain (where incidents occurred at a rate of 34.5 per thousand in 1942, 35.5 in 1943 and 26 in 1944– 45), it posed a far less significant problem for military authorities in Asia and the Pacific. Although Allan Walker's two medical volumes of the Australian official history series indicate that VD 'occurred in disappointingly large numbers' in Ceylon, infections were negligible within Southeast Asia and New Guinea.[51] According- ing to Walker's *Clinical Problems of War*, 'in Malaya there was noth- ing unusual to record about venereal disease'. From February 1941 rates varied according to the arrival of new troops with maximum incidence steady at 4.03 per thousand, reaching a temporary peak of 7.53 per thousand following the arrival of more troops.[52] These figures essentially correspond with RAAF figures for the region. In Singapore VD affected just 1 per cent of the RAAF strength there in 1941–42, and in India, where a total of 1887 Australians served between 1943–45, rates of infection averaged 3.48 per thousand. Placed in perspective, these were much lower than VD rates of 79.89 per thousand for the First AIF in Egypt in 1916.[53]

According to Walker, VD was not a problem in the Pacific Islands owing to the 'lack of opportunity of acquiring infection, and the absence of settled areas where soldiers might spend leave'. Rates in the army for this period of the conflict were 2.33 per thousand men in 1942, 1.06 in 1943, 0.36 in 1944 and 7.96 in 1945. The increased incidence in 1945 was due to campaigns in Borneo, where disease was more common, as was the contact with local populations in towns and small cities, particularly following the end of hostilities and during the occupation period.[54] In fact, these Second World War figures for the AIF in Singapore, Malaya and the Pacific compare with Australian Bureau of Statistics figures for the rate of infection of 3.57 per thousand for the most common form of STD in Australia in 2011.[55] By way of contrast, the rate of infection in the army back home in Australia – 18.93 per thousand in 1942, 16.85 in 1943, 13.18 in 1944 and 17.08 in 1945 – was a much greater cause for concern.[56] Therefore, we may deduce that, if VD rates are taken as a measure, promiscuity was more likely to have been undertaken at home – with white Australian women – rather than abroad in Asia and the Pacific.

These figures correspond with those recorded among American servicemen in the Pacific. Although problems existed on some islands, VD similarly posed few problems for American servicemen in New Guinea and the South West Pacific Area. The history of the US army medical service declares that 'the appearance of the local women' was a major reason, although action taken by authorities to control the spread of disease by placing villages off limits (and because women were also hiding inland) ensured that GIs could not contact any women. Again, like Australian forces, the Americans seemed more concerned by the rates of infection while their troops were stationed in Australia. In May 1942 rates for American forces in Australia peaked at 45.8 per thousand.[57]

It has been argued that there exists a strong counter-narrative of the Pacific War in which the war in the islands has been described as a sexual vacuum. However, historians such as Brawley and Dixon have argued that while men in the Pacific Islands largely went unfulfilled 'their interest in sex did not diminish'.[58] But it is hardly unusual or even noteworthy that young men thought about it, particularly since the majority of Allied soldiers in the Pacific were not front-line soldiers but worked in large rear-area camps in which boredom prevailed. More noteworthy are the instances – or lack thereof – of VD within the armed services both at home and abroad.

Over half of the 3700 veterans surveyed in Barrett's extensive study on Australian soldiers in the Second World War did not believe that army life had furthered their sexual experience. Many men were shy; others stuck by their principles and remained faithful to their loved ones at home. For some there was no sex on leave; it was either not wanted, not available, not tempting, or too risky with regard to disease.[59] Rather than being enticed by the stereotypical image of exotic and lustful women, Australian soldiers were more wary in their encounters. There were those who found the so-called short-arm parade – in which the men stood naked to be inspected by a medical officer – degrading and humiliating, and certainly nobody wanted to be singled out and sent home in such circumstances. For these men the risk – if they were at all tempted – was not worth it. Furthermore, as Schrijvers notes in his study on American GIs, laden as they were with the expectation of deep-rooted Western conventions, soldiers expected more than 'unbridled sexual release in anonymous alleyways'.[60] Yet meaningful and lasting relationships were unlikely given the social mores of the period (succinctly encapsulated by the White Australia policy, which forbade Asian immigration), and besides, many simply found potential partners unattractive.

Of course, incidents of sexual relations between Australian soldiers and local populations did occur and were recorded. Sexual violence and rape by Australian soldiers certainly occurred. In one notorious incident in Borneo in August 1945 a local woman was gang-raped by members of the 2/13th Battalion. In the court martial that followed the leading perpetrator was found guilty and sentenced to a term in prison.[61] Even today, one particular incident haunts a bystander, who feels guilty for failing to intervene when one of his mates committed an act of rape.[62] In Makassar, a member of HMAS *Gascoyne*'s crew had to be physically protected by other sailors after an irate local had returned from a lengthy spell at a Japanese internment camp to find his wife pregnant. While we do not know the full circumstance of this episode, it seems certain to have been – in the parlance of the military guidebooks – a case of domestic interference.[63] Also at Makassar, in February 1946 a soldier wrote in his diary of his disgust at the 'sickening sight' of five soldiers bringing back to ship two local prostitutes with whom they proceeded to have relations in public view of the hundreds of troops on the ship and milling about the wharf.[64] There also exist reports of sexual misconduct by Australian troops in New Guinea, particularly from the Trobriand Islands.[65] However, such instances do not appear to be common, at least on the record. The Second AIF was not a perverse army of pillage and plunder. It had its bad – even criminal – elements, but by and large the almost one million soldiers, sailors, airmen and nurses who served in the Australian forces, and the just over half a million who served overseas, reflected a cross-section of Australian society at that time and many behaved well.

Some men, while they found the women of the Pacific Islands attractive, nevertheless remained respectful of social mores, or did not wish to interfere with domestic relations. Abstinence could also be motivated by the fear of local men, believed to be skilled with bush-knives.[66] Moreover, if long-term or permanent relations were desired, there were men who were realistically aware that these were unlikely or impractical. The desire may have existed, but the impracticality of a more lasting relationship was recognised and understood. Such was the story of an RAN sailor in Tahiti who, like many in the services, was resigned to the fact that he was just passing through.[67]

The men were also conscious of, and perhaps concerned by, the reaction an Asian bride might receive back home in 'white Australia'. This is reflected by the reaction of Australian soldiers to British soldiers who had married local women. 'In a society as averse to coloured races as the English', Noonan wrote from Maymyo in Burma, 'the wives of these men must have great difficulty in finding a niche when their husband's regiment returns to England'.[68] Furthermore, the detestation which Stanton felt for so-called 'half-castes' in New Guinea is a reflection of Australian racial attitudes of the period.[69] Likewise, American servicemen in the Philippines were chary after their liberation from a prisoner-of-war camp at the sight of veterans who had married Filipino women. These men agonised over their return home, knowing that their Filipino families would not be welcomed in small-town USA.[70] For Australia, such issues came to a head during the post-war period when some members of the British Commonwealth Occupation Force married Japanese brides. The government's stance on the matter was made clear by the immigration minister Arthur Calwell in 1948 when he asserted that no Japanese wife or fiancée of an Australian serviceman would be permitted to enter Australia. It was not until 1952 that this ban was relaxed.[71]

In the end, common utterances among soldiers in Malaya after nights on end watching taxi-girls – 'they look whiter by the day' – indicate frustration.[72] Similar feelings were comparable elsewhere; another soldier noted his wish that 'the New Guinea women would turn white and not smell'.[73] Evidently such feelings went both ways, as a driver from the 2/20th Battalion wrote home to his brothers from Malaya of 'some beautiful Chinese girls over here but they are hard to get on with, they won't look at white men'.[74] The internal conflict faced by the Australians was evident. What these soldiers really desired were familiar women; *white* women – a point perhaps emphasised by the higher rates of VD among soldiers stationed in Australia and Britain.

Rather than viewing the women of Asia and the Pacific as exotic oriental beauties, many men saw them as 'beasts of burden', often possessing masculine characteristics. A common image was one painted by the words of a staff sergeant of 8th Division Head-quarters while a prisoner of war in Changi: 'Every morning for the past week on the march out we pass dozens of Chinese women, each carrying a terrific load of firewood. Some of them would be fifty or more yet carry a load that two of us would shirk.'[75] In Kuala Lumpur, Noonan had similarly observed Tamil and Chinese women carrying baskets of stones for the construction of roads, and in Burma he described Kachin women as 'ruddy-skinned' with 'sturdy muscular figures'. Later he wrote: 'Most of the girls are married before they have a chance to mature or bloom into beautiful womanhood, for marriage means a lifetime of hard work in the fields, the home and the village.' Arriving in China, Noonan encountered Yunnanese women whom he described as 'drab', 'bulky creatures'. 'Even the younger women', he mused, 'were most unattractive'.[76] In the eyes of these men such hard labour apparently made Asian women age quicker than Western women. As a prisoner of war in Burma noted, 'some of them, when young, are very attractive, but I believe they are regarded as old women by the time they are thirty'.[77] Some were simply repulsed by what they saw. Right across the region, the appearance of blackened teeth and blood-red mouths and gums from chewing betel only confirmed in their minds distinctions between their own 'civilised' world and that of the other.[78]

Despite the myth of the attractive and alluring women of the Orient – often reinforced through publications specifically produced for the troops – a common thread of disappointment in the physical appeal of the female population of the region runs through men's letters, diaries and memoirs. Like their American counterparts, men raised on tales of enticing women of the South Seas and Far East, not to mention the image created by Hollywood genre films and saronged starlets such as Dorothy Lamour, soon discovered and developed a more realistic outlook.[79] Rather than finding the women of Asia and the Pacific exotically attractive, many Australian soldiers, for a variety of reasons, were uninterested in or disliked what they saw. Indeed, in the words of one soldier in New Guinea, when attending a traditional dance 'one could imagine himself seeing the pages of a popular South Seas novel', but up close it 'brought disillusionment'.[80]

Overall, by focusing on the Australian soldiers' relations with, contact with and attitudes held toward the women of the region we can see how perceived myths can be unwrapped and challenged. In this instance the colonial encounter, mixed with Australian racial prejudice of the period, affected interactions with Asian and Pacific Islander women. Rather than evincing an attachment to the attractive and lustrous image that they envisaged on arrival, more often than not men rejected the myth, one way or another, after encountering women across the region. The imagery and knowledge they had inherited from the long tradition of colonial literature was quickly discarded. This change, evident in letters, diaries and memoirs, perhaps reflects a desire on behalf of the serving men to portray themselves in particular ways – as more broadminded, more worldly, and different in their outlook to the colonial vision in which they had been conditioned. Asia and the Pacific, it would seem, was nothing like a Dorothy Lamour film. Where Australian soldiers in the British colonies of Asia – with their deeply entrenched codes of behaviour – found it easy to draw comparisons and justify their differences, we will see in the next chapter that in New Guinea, with its Australian colonial administration, the AIF did not have a British elite whose outlook they could challenge.

5

MYTH AND MEMORY
Australia's war in New Guinea

The popular image that emerged from the war in Papua and New Guinea of the Australian digger befriending the compassionate and loyal 'fuzzy wuzzy angel' was far from universal. In actuality, soldiers' perceptions were far more dynamic and complex. They developed a range of attitudes regarding an Australian presence in Papua and New Guinea and the role played by the Indigenous inhabitants in the war. When the war arrived in New Guinea on 23 January 1942 with the Japanese invasion of Rabaul it caused a paradox for Australian outlooks on imperialism and colonialism. By this time Australian soldiers stationed in the British colonies of Asia had begun to question the equality of empire. By war's end, they clearly envisaged that the days of European colonialism in Asia were numbered. However, Papua and New Guinea provided a contradiction. In New Guinea, the Australians and not the British were the colonial 'masters'. Here there existed an Australian colonial structure that affected the behaviour and attitudes of troops differently. Here they did not have the British to bounce off. Ultimately, the Australian war in Papua and New Guinea shows the insidious way in which colonial structures affect individuals' reactions to colonial society.

The island of New Guinea was made up of three separate areas of political administration at the beginning of 1942: Dutch New Guinea in the west; the Australian Mandated Territory of New Guinea in the north-east, and the Australian Territory of Papua in the south-east. Following its occupation by Australian forces in

1914, the territory formerly known as German New Guinea was made an Australian external territory (to be held in trust) after Australia was awarded a mandate to administer the area by the League of Nations in 1920. The south-east had previously been known as British New Guinea until it was formally transferred to the Australian Commonwealth in 1906, shortly after Federation, and was henceforth known as Papua. In February 1942 both Australian areas were placed under military administration and two separate military units were created: the Papuan Administrative Unit and the New Guinea Administrative Unit. By April, these amalgamated and became known as the Australian New Guinea Administrative Unit (ANGAU).[1] Just as Australian soldiers had developed a diverse range of attitudes towards the administration within the British Empire, so too would views vary regarding Australia's role and responsibilities toward the islands' inhabitants.

The New Guinea campaigns were unique in the history of the Australian army. Apart from the small foray into and occupation of German New Guinea and Nauru by the Australian Naval and Military Expeditionary Force in 1914, Australian soldiers in both world wars had previously served as junior members of larger allied forces on foreign soil. In New Guinea, the Australian army was both the major Allied force and the body responsible for civilians and the administration of the territories.

The war changed Australians' attitudes towards the Papuans and New Guineans. Pre-war, most Australians thought little of the islands to their nation's north, and were probably mostly aware of its people from Sunday school readings, which presented the Melanesians as grateful converts; from adventure literature mystifying the South Seas; or from newspaper reports of 'lost valleys', gold strikes or volcanic eruptions. By war's end, Australians had popularly accepted an enduring tale of 'fuzzy wuzzy angels' who faithfully assisted Australian wounded with much care and compassion.[2] However, the reality of relations between Papua New Guineans and Australian soldiers was far more complex; far more dynamic. The lives of both groups were dramatically transformed by the war. Furthermore, their experience in Papua and New Guinea reshaped the way Australians came to view their nation's future role in the region.

Popularly remembered within Australian historical narratives for their contribution to the war effort as stretcher-bearers and carriers, Papuans and New Guineans have for a long period been seen in Australia as willing participants in the Allied cause. Since the 1980s, however, several historians have opened our eyes to the complex realities that faced Papua New Guineans during the Second World War. They have demonstrated, for instance, that the popular construction of the 'fuzzy wuzzy angel' as a primitive, detached from the real conflict, ignores the fact that Papuans and New Guineans assessed the situation and chose sides accordingly. They sided with those whom they felt offered the best opportunity for survival for themselves and their families, keeping their own livelihoods safe while also serving the interests of their colonial masters.[3] Complex allegiances, as White and Lindstrom have documented, also saw Papua New Guineans fighting Papua New Guineans. In one incident, Papuans acting under Japanese orders massacred 96 villagers who were suspected of collaboration with the AIF.[4]

Likewise, historians have detailed the poor treatment of Papuan and New Guinean labourers, many of whom were recruited forcibly by Australian, American and Japanese militaries. While things had improved by 1945, in the early years of the conflict, and despite promises to the contrary, Allied forces failed to meet adequate levels of basic welfare for their Papuan and New Guinean labourers by not providing adequate rations, clothing or payment, and by the spread of disease.[5] Furthermore, representations of Papuan and New Guinean wartime history within Australian popular conscience had not been altered by the time of the Australian government's *Australia Remembers* initiative that commemorated the 50th anniversary of the end of the Second World

The success of the campaigns in the South West Pacific Area of operations relied on the muscle of Indigenous labour; however, the treatment and conditions under which they were employed did not meet most Australians' understandings of equality and fairness. Here stretcher-bearers carry a wounded soldier from Shaggy Ridge in 1944.
Australian War Memorial 064244

War in 1995. As Reed demonstrates, Papuan and New Guinean representation within the program remained innately colonial. By representing Papuans and New Guineans as 'fuzzy wuzzy angels', and continuing to include them as such within Australia's national narrative of Anzac remembrance, Australians denied the diverse range of experiences of Papua New Guineans during the Second World War.[6] In addition, recent popular military histories, such as Peter FitzSimons' bestseller *Kokoda*, provide very little detail or discussion of the variety of situations in which the Papuans found themselves.[7]

In order to unwrap and understand the myth of the 'fuzzy wuzzy angel' and Australia's war in New Guinea it is important to look right back to the arrival of the AIF in the territories, beginning when the 2/22nd Battalion (with supporting units that formed Lark Force) docked at Rabaul in April 1941. As in Southeast Asia, newly arrived troops in New Guinea drew upon their knowledge of literature to describe the exotica of their new surrounds. Indeed, the islands in the tropics appeared a novelty to troops, reminding them of works such as Edgar Wallace's *Sanders of the River* or Daniel Defoe's *Robinson Crusoe*.[8] Hollywood genre films of the period also provided a basis for unrealistic expectations, and when war came to the Pacific Islands newly written Australian and American guidebooks specifically warned against these romanticised images. So strong and so deeply rooted in fiction were these visions, notes Schrijvers, that not even the thought of war could dissuade GIs. Not only were such visualisations based in part upon fantasies but they also gave rise to dangerously high expectations that warranted warnings within soldier pamphlets and guidebooks.[9] 'You'll know the South Seas a lot better than when you looked at Dotty Lamour's sarong in the movies back home', proclaimed the *Pocket Guide to New Guinea and the Solomons*. 'Some things are as you expected – coral reefs and coconut palms, green jungles and natives whose clothing doesn't cost much. Some things you won't find, for they never really existed at all outside the imagination of novelists and movie directors. Others the movies never showed – including diseases, smells, and bites.'[10]

The dangers of such unrealistic perceptions were duly noted by the Australian war correspondent Allan Dawes, whose 1943 publication 'Soldier Superb' documented the fighting in New Guinea. 'Every newcomer to the tropics had to be cured of the illusions engendered by "Coral Island", missionary lantern lectures, Beatrice Grimshaw and Dorothy Lamour', he noted, 'to say nothing of the newspaper articles of cruise tourists and the pamphlets of travel salesmen'.[11] Nevertheless, the image of the islands as an exotic and picturesque location for the white man's adventures was emphasised by the way in which men utilised Edenic qualities in writing and sketches.[12] Soldiers habitually noted the 'abundance' of fruits, hibiscus, frangipani and palms.[13] Murray-Smith referred to his surrounds near Wau as an 'Eden among the mountains'.[14] Similar imagery is evident in the title of William Dargie's watercolour *Patrol in Arcadia*.[15]

Intricately tied to these notions of Edens and Arcadias was the popular myth of the 'lost valley' somewhere within the New Guinea interior. Such views were widespread and were inspired by a literary genre that emerged in the late 19th and early 20th centuries in response to discoveries of lost civilisations by archeologists in Egypt, the Mediterranean and the Middle East. By the 1870s the coastline of New Guinea had been only partly charted, and colonial governments had been established from only 1884. Even by the 1940s parts of the New Guinea interior had not been surveyed, and this sense of the unknown fuelled such myths. In places such as the Finisterre Range – literally, 'the ends of the earth' – few Europeans had preceded the thousands of men of the AIF who fought there in 1943.[16] For Australians, New Guinea was a land of mystery and a place of discovery and, just as the James Hilton novel *Lost Horizon* had popularised the mythical Shangri-La in the 1930s, so too the mythical 'lost valley' was popularised through works such as Arthur Conan Doyle's *The Lost World*.

Colonial pioneers in New Guinea before the Second World War had often laid claim to the discovery of a 'lost valley'. Such discoveries were much publicised, and Australian soldiers were alert to this trend. War correspondents Osmar White and George Johnston both picked up the notion; White emphasised the large, unexplored expanses of New Guinea (around 70 per cent of the total), while Johnston wrote excitedly of AIF patrols discovering lost valleys and new tribes.[17] The *Pocket Guide to New Guinea and the Solomons* also stressed the lack of geographic knowledge and perhaps future potential of the islands for enterprising troops: 'Tough government patrol officers and mineral prospectors have covered an amazing amount of this highland area, but there is still much to be explored.'[18]

Such Edenic qualities also caused Australian soldiers to ponder the value of the islands as an Australian colonial possession and the possibilities for postwar employment and riches. Many were inspired by the untapped potential for New Guinea to be for Australia what in the previous generation India had been for Britain, or the East Indies for the Netherlands.[19] Aware of the presence of rich natural resources, and of the profits that could be made, many Australian soldiers were open to the area's potential and the idea of resettlement after the war. For example, in a 1942 report by an ANGAU officer on re-establishing Australian control following the early Japanese victories, particular areas were scouted as being 'very suitable ground for rubber'.[20]

In addition, individuals wrote home of possible future employment. Murray-Smith's chats with 'old hands' of the New Guinea Volunteer Rifles about the country and what people did there were most informative. 'It's hard living, but by no means bad living, and certainly makes one think. Apart from the commercial side of life here there's the opportunities in the administrative service – patrol officers etc. I continue to make enquiries.'[21] Likewise, Wallin noted the rates of pay for indentured labourers with interest:

The natives wage is a few shillings a month. Actually to the Native it is equal to about what ten pounds would be to us. In peace time Plantations owners forms etc. employ them. The native signs a contract of either eighteen months or three years. During that time he is fed, clothed and given medical attention by the employer and at the end of the contract must be transported back to the village from where he came. Their wages are paid in lump sum when the contract terminates.

In addition, Wallin enthused: 'in peacetime a white man could earn anything from thirty pounds upward a month'.[22] Such views are in sharp contrast to those of diggers stationed in Malaya, who, as discussed in earlier chapters, were critical of the low standards of pay and conditions for Asian labourers (and refused to intervene as strike-breakers).

As if to encourage such entrepreneurial activities by Australian soldiers, articles published within *Salt*, such as one on Sumatra entitled 'Wet but wealthy', emphasised that much of the region's natural resources remained 'largely untapped'.[23] It remains without question that in areas of Australian political influence soldiers were particularly aware of the natural resources on offer. These men looked at the big picture benefits of an Australian colonial mission and its responsibility to uphold the 'white man's burden'. 'We have amalgamated the territories of Papua and New Guinea and have called the one territory, Australian New Guinea', wrote W. Brian Molloy of an Australian anti-aircraft battery. 'This one territory has, in its 184,000 square miles, everything that it takes to make a country rich and prosperous. If we don't do it someone else will.' In the course of defending their country, Australians had almost inadvertently discovered in New Guinea 'a tropical storehouse of unknown wealth and riches, an unexplored land of great mountain ranges and great rivers, a land of Australia [*sic*] for us Australians'.[24]

In similar vein Major Cyril Fyfe wrote: 'it is undeniable that the immense resources, and as yet largely untapped wealth of Australian New Guinea, have never been realised in Australia'. He highlighted that New Guinea was:

> A country munificently rich in almost every tropical product; a country with goldmines to arouse the envy of Croesus. There is scarcely a tropical product that cannot be produced, and produced in abundance, in this one territory: copra, rubber, tea, coffee, sugar, cinchona, pyrethrum, cocoa, and innumerable other products come to mind.

Enthused about New Guinea's potential, Fyfe added: 'I visualise this magnificent territory as a second Malaya or Java, contributing its quota to the storehouse of the nations' and predicted it would 'progress and prosper that it will be among the great colonial possessions of the world'.[25] Such views were reinforced by others who had obviously contemplated such manifests. For example, one noted that: 'many Diggers have given thought to prospects in this treasure house "afterwards", and no men could be better suited'.[26]

Soldiers were also aware of the prosperous returns that had been made from the New Guinea goldfields before the war, and it is certain that some had read and 'learnt a lot about the country' from Ion Idriess' popular *Gold-dust and Ashes: A Romantic Story of the New Guinea Goldfields* (published in 1933).[27] Guidebooks issued to the troops also spoke of the 'important deposits of gold and other valuable minerals' that remained 'largely untouched'. New Guinea, it explained, had been first visited by Spanish and Portuguese explorers. One of these, Álvaro de Saavedra Cerón, had given New Guinea the name Isla de Oro, meaning Island of Gold. The neighbouring Solomon Islands, it was explained, was named by Mendaña, 'perhaps thinking them the source of King Solomon's riches'.[28] Furthermore, the reputation of the New Guinea goldfields may have been enhanced by the title given to the AIF newspaper for the region: *Guinea Gold*. With such promotion it is little wonder that troops – particularly those stationed around the Morobe goldfields and the centres of the pre-war gold mining industry such as Wau and Mubo, described in the press of the 1920s as the new El Dorado – were known to prospect in the chance of striking it lucky. Soldiers improvised, fashioning pans from mess tins and helmets.[29] With deposits clearly visible in the mountain streams, Captain Frank Sublet of the 2/16th Battalion was forced to issue orders that forbade men from prospecting and panning during any creek crossing in the Owen Stanley's.[30] One group of Australian soldiers was even tasked with recovering a stash of gold hidden by the miners at Bulalo while fleeing the Japanese advance. In a scene straight out of a dime western, the soldiers first recovered a key from a safe that had to be opened by an oxy-welding torch. This key opened a box, which had been buried in a secret location in the jungle and held around 4000 ounces in gold bars.[31] In today's currency the cache would be valued at $5.5 million. Prospecting, panning and discovering gold provided for troops a genuine vision of New Guinea's potential riches.

By the outbreak of the Pacific War in 1941 few Australians would have referred to the islanders as anything but 'natives', a term with clear implications of white authority and colonial values, as well as reflecting the racist and paternalistic nature of Australia's relations with Papuans and New Guineans. However, knowledge of the correct etiquettes between black and white society in New Guinea was largely unknown and unusual for newly arrived Australian soldiers; particularly those from the southern states. This is emphasised by several pieces within the *Rabaul Times* aimed at newly arrived Australian troops in 1941, warning them how they should behave. Media reports from Malaya of AIF troops mingling with Asians (such as swapping hats, giving rickshaw pullers rides in their own rickshaws) were alarming to white residents in the 'territories'. In response, the Editor of the *Rabaul*

Times, Gordon Thomas, wrote in his column: 'Perhaps officers do not realise how very embarrassing it can be for the white residents in these same countries when they see the troops of their own colour flagrantly disregarding the hard-fought-for recognition of the standing, respect and prestige of a white race in a native country.' Friendly games of cricket played between soldiers and Papuans, and soldiers doing manual labour, had caused concern. Thomas warned that the newly arrived troops of Lark Force had to share the 'white man's burden'. This suggests that the racial divisions that characterised Rabaul colonial society were concepts unknown to many of the soldiers.[32] As a further reminder, orders were issued to troops of the 2/22nd Battalion that forbade fraternisation with locals.[33]

In order to instruct Australian soldiers on the correct etiquette in dealing with the Indigenous population a series of guidebooks and pamphlets were published by the army. Written by the Papuan government anthropologist F.E. Williams in 1942, the instruction manual *You and the Native* placed particular emphasis on what was deemed Australia's moral imperial responsibility, and demonstrated the kind of relationship that was expected between black and white. 'Remember that the New Guinea natives are one of the world's Backward Peoples', it was explained, 'and that Australia undertook to regard their welfare as a "sacred trust"'.[34] Furthermore, the guide encouraged Australian soldiers embarking for New Guinea to uphold 'the attitude of superiority', and proclaimed that:

> The native has always looked up to the White Man. He
> admires him because of the marvellous things that white
> men at large can do ... You may not be marvellous yourself,
> but he will think you are, merely because you are one of the
> white race ... He is also afraid of the White Man ... It is not
> so much to say that he stands in awe of us. He thinks we are
> superior beings ... Always therefore maintain your position

THE ATTITUDE OF SUPERIORITY

11. The native has always looked up to the white man. He admires him because of the marvellous things that white men at large can do—make electric torches, fly in aeroplanes, etc. You may not be marvellous yourself, but he will think you are, merely because you are one of the white race.

12. He is also rather afraid of the white men, with all the power of their civilisation behind them. Therefore he is rather afraid of you.

Worth Acting Up To

13. It is not too much to say that he stands in awe of us. He thinks we are superior beings. We may not all deserve this reputation, but it is worth acting up to.

14. Always therefore maintain your position or pose of superiority, even if you sometimes have doubts about it. It is flattering to the vanity and in the circumstances must pay us well. As for the native, he will not resent it, because he has brought it about himself and he is used to it.

A section of the handbook *You and the Native*, issued to Australian soldiers in Papua and New Guinea.
You and the Native

or pose of superiority, even if you sometimes have doubts about it.

With regard to work, the guide emphasised that 'the native does not expect the White Man to do manual labour'. The Australian soldier, it was explained, was expected to be the 'guardian of the white man's prestige'.[35]

Furthermore, authorities were concerned by the habit of American soldiers of paying higher than the set rates outlined within guidebooks and manuals, and implored troops not to deliberately descend to their level.[36] This was a frequent complaint of the cynical ANGAU officer Eddie Allan Stanton:

How the Americans bugger up the natives. They started
off by handing out packets of cigarettes, then underpants,
singlets, hats and boots. Piles of food were simply thrown
to the poor, stone-axe savages, and just as promptly thrown
away. All the Nig. was interested in was the tins. They
could be used for storing tobacco in. Now our savage
demands 1/- for pawpaw, 1/- for an egg. A fowl, £1-0-0.

Later he would lament that the 'occupying forces have far too long been treating the native like brothers. The result is now evident. When asked to work, they refuse. They want a cigarette first. If they had been correctly handled in the first instance, troubles such as above would not have occurred'. It was not only that Stanton believed American soldiers and airmen were being too friendly with the 'natives' – placing arms around them, lighting cigarettes for them, laughing with them, and conversing on the same level – more shocking was the sight of 'American Negroes teaching them how to box'. He went on, 'It is no wonder that the native has lost his former respect and obedience for the white man.'[37] Concerned with the maintenance of proper hierarchical relations and social distances between white and black, ANGAU officers often confiscated gifts that Papua New Guineans had received from American servicemen, and worried that overpayments would inflate postwar expectations.[38] Here, in Australian administered territories, maintaining 'white prestige' was clearly a concern.

Evidently, there were those new to the territory who enforced such views. War correspondent Osmar White was quite frank about the way he treated the Papuans in his service. He believed Papuans 'were appalled by the indignity' of a 'taubada' carrying cargo, and treated servants in his employment with threats and physical assaults (his servants provided him with clean shirts, socks and underpants daily, cleaned his personal items and equipment, tucked in his mosquito net at night, and even removed his shoes and shirt at the end of the day). Declaring that the native 'had not evolved beyond slavery', he proclaimed: 'I was received like a king. Here I am obeyed like a god.' On occasion he kicked carriers (sometimes in the ribs) for 'malingering', despite his concerns that they were, by European standards, not fit for heavy work. One, dying of exhaustion, was given a lethal dose of heroin by White, presumably out of a warped sense of compassion; he goes on to assure his readers that this was not one of the men he had assaulted.[39] What makes these revelations so astounding is that White's memoir, *Green Armour*, is hardly a hidden or unknown story of Australia's war in New Guinea. It has enjoyed much acclaim as part of Penguin's *Australian War Classics* series and has influenced many popular retellings of the campaign which draw heavily upon it. Yet how could it be that his book has yet to affect a reassessment of Australian popular narratives of the war in New Guinea?

As in Asia, however, there were those who were critical of white colonial society. For example, war correspondent George Johnston wrote in his diary that in the past Papua had been known as the 'Land of Dohori'; *dohori* meaning 'wait a while'. Following the fall of Rabaul, however, there was such urgency that nobody could afford to 'put off until tomorrow what should have been done today'. Much time had been wasted, as in the past it had always been too much trouble to 'do hard work'. While Papuans were put to work, whites worried about their own affairs: golf matches, cocktail parties, bridge fours, and all-night drinking parties. All had been swept away, stated Johnston, when horrified 'civilians in their white linen suits' watched 'young Australian soldiers, stripped to the waist, working on the roads and in the scrub alongside the natives, sweating from dawn to dusk in the steamy heat of a country 10° below the equator, where tradition had said no white man could possibly lift a hand to do real work'. This was a rude awakening for the white residents. The days of *dohori* were over.[40] In a similarly stinging critique, White wrote that the white residents were: 'people who had gravitated to the outskirts of civilization, where they enjoyed higher status and greater privileges than their talents would have demanded at home'.[41]

Soldiers themselves could be equally critical. Like their brethren in Malaya, troops in Papua and New Guinea were dismayed by the claims for compensation from companies, and troubled by the influence of commercial operations in deciding upon locations of military bases. As a member of the Royal Australian Engineers, clearing land and building bases near Milne Bay, John Henry Hawkins noted:

> They are being built where they will be [of] most use to Lever Bros. After the war they own all the plantation and are paid 1.0.0 a tree for every one the army cuts down. This after fighting and driving the Japs out of it. There are about five million trees so what difference does a few thousand make anyway. If the Japs were still here I wonder would they pay for them.[42]

Australian companies were later paid compensation for damages by the Australian government, much to the chagrin of soldiers like Hawkins. Indeed, the history of the prominent Australian company Burns Philip recorded that it 'did quite well out of compensation from the Australian government later for war damage'. The British government, on the other hand, had rejected Burns Philip's claims for compensation in the Solomon and Gilbert islands.[43] Having to pay compensation for damaged rubber and coconut trees raised alarming questions among soldiers stationed both in Southeast Asia and the south-west Pacific as for whom and what reasons they were defending the islands and driving out foreign invaders.

Nevertheless, Australian perceptions of bringing a civilising mission to the islands were reinforced by aspects of the soldier guidebooks, which are also reflective of the kind of racism that was held regarding the perceived 'backwardness' of the Indigenous inhabitants. Guidebooks reminded soldiers that 'the native is a human-being … He is nearly, if not quite, as good a man as you are'. Military publications, however, could be contradictory on such issues. Despite one guide imploring: 'don't believe it when you are told he has the mentality of a child. That is rubbish. An adult native is an adult. He has a grown up mind, grown up feelings, and frowns upon dignity', adding that they 'are mostly gentlemen', another expressed the paternalistic instructions: 'natives like to wear all their clothes always'. They 'should be encouraged to take them off when warm (i.e. generally by day), and put them on when cold (i.e., by night). In this way they have a chance of keeping them dry'.[44] In the main, men such as Johnston displayed concern that the Indigenous populations were only a degree removed from the primeval and could easily revert to their former ways. Australians frowned upon what they termed 'native savagery', and the practice of cannibalism in the Pacific Islands was a prominent example.[45] In the circumstances of war against Japan, however, 'native savagery' could in fact be encouraged. Wallin, for example, wrote of the 'invaluable work' the Royal Papuan Constabulary were doing by 'killing Japs' around Aitape. To the delight of the soldiers, members of the constabulary brought back 40 fingers of the dead as evidence of their work.[46]

Many soldiers were evidently concerned with upholding prestige. Certainly, the visit by Hollywood star John Wayne (who toured the South Pacific theatre with the USO for three months in 1943–44) caused Stanton to reflect upon what he considered the poor behaviour of a group of Australian showgirls who took part in the show. The manner in which the girls 'allowed soldiers to cuddle them in daylight' did not, according to Stanton, 'give the prestige of white women much of a boost in the eyes of the native'.[47] Some soldiers drew upon such themes for motivation. During a gruelling patrol in New Guinea, Wallin proclaimed that his native carrier was his 'inspiration', though this came about not through any sense of mateship or mutual encouragement but in order to maintain his prestige as a white boss. 'Not wishing to give him the satisfaction of seeing me crack first', Wallin wrote, 'I kept going although I would have soon sat down at more frequent intervals and rested the weary body'.[48]

In contrast, Hawkins was bewildered by the emphasis on prestige. Tasked with clearing virgin jungle for base areas and airstrips, Hawkins faced a tough assignment made harder by the increased working hours imposed on the AIF engineers:

> The Yanks only have to put in four months then are relieved but in all ways they get a much better go than we do. Work hours have been increased to 7 am to 5 pm with only half hour break for dinner and every second Sunday off, which puts us on lower level than the natives.

The situation was not only unfair, according to Hawkins; it was insulting:

> The most extraordinary part of it is that the natives who up till now have had every second Sunday off are to have every Sunday as the weather is too hot to work them for more than six days at a stretch and we have had daily hours extended from 7:30 am till 5 pm with half an hour for dinner. I now have no rest day at all. Truly we must be reckoned as super men. Soon we will be having the Boongs for bosses the way we are going on.[49]

It seems few troops paid much attention to the instructions issued within publications such as *You and the Native*, as evidence shows that there were concerns regarding what were considered unsatisfactory relations between service personnel and the Indigenous population.[50] Friendly relations with Papuans moving freely within unit lines, even entering tents and huts and hanging around kitchens; soldiers and Papuans sharing food and eating together; whites bathing in front of Papuans; white and black sharing vehicles; vehicles stopping to give Papuans a lift; Papuans charging exorbitant prices resulting from growing commercialisation; and the employment of personal servants caused much concern among the military administration. Overwhelmingly, as noted by Powell, ordinary troops could not be persuaded to accept and adopt the norms of white colonial society in New Guinea. They shared battlefield experiences, food, tents, bomb shelters and trenches.[51] When outdoor cinemas were established, soldiers and amazed Papuans and New Guineans watched the newsreels and Hollywood features side by side.[52] Indeed, when the men of the 7th Division established their base at Kaiapit in September 1943 they appeared to the locals as different people to the pre-war 'mastas'. The behaviour of the soldiers confirmed this and they called themselves 'Australians', a term adopted by the local people, enabling them to classify them as distinct from the pre-war 'Inggelis' (English). In the main, ANGAU officers – many of whom were 'old hands' – were classified as English rather than Australian.[53]

The thing that really transformed Australian perceptions of Papuans and New Guineans, however, was the yeoman service they provided, initially on the Kokoda Trail, carrying munitions and supplies up to the front and ferrying out wounded soldiers. When Port Moresby was threatened, and a perceived invasion of Australia loomed large in the nation's imagination, 'the lines of barefooted men in lap-laps and leaves', Nelson claims, 'brought mental as well as material support'. The Australian press, which did not have a reputation at the time for its appreciation of other races, played a crucial role in creating the legend of the 'fuzzy wuzzy angels' – a term taken from the title of a poem written by Sapper Bert Beros in October 1942 and published in the Brisbane *Courier-Mail* and *Australian Women's Weekly*. One particular line in the poem – 'To look upon their faces / Would make you think Christ was black' – was a revolutionary or even blasphemous suggestion to readers at the time, according to Nelson.[54]

Just as significant in establishing and creating the image of the 'fuzzy wuzzy angel' were the films of Australian war correspondent Damian Parer and George Silk's photograph of a wounded Private George Whittington being guided by the Papuan Raphael Oimbari, which first appeared in *Life* magazine on 8 March 1943.[55] In the Academy Award-winning *Kokoda Frontline!*, Parer proclaimed that: 'the care and compassion shown for the wounded by the natives has won the complete admiration of the troops. With them, the black-skinned boys are white'.[56] Likewise, the narrator of Parer's *The Road to Kokoda* enthused: 'Indispensable are the Papuan carriers ... the white man needs their help.'[57] Such a theme has been preserved for posterity within Silk's famous image. However, historian Karl James has revealed that when George Silk took the photograph only Whittington's identity was recorded by the photographer. It was not until the 1970s that Raphael Oimbari was identified as the Papuan in the iconic image, and this was only after Whittington's widow, Connie Stieger, who wished to pay tribute to the man who assisted her late husband, began a campaign which gained the support of the Port Moresby *Post Courier*. Evidently, Oimbari's identity was not considered important at the time the photo was taken.[58]

Such declarations in popular public mediums undisputedly enhanced the reputation of the Papuans in Australian eyes. As a member of the 2/2nd Field Ambulance noted: 'No one but the natives could have carried patients for four days over these tracks, and the success of the unit's efforts were largely due to the great care and arduous carries of these simple "boongs"'.[59] By the same token, much emphasis was placed on the role that the Papuans were playing in the 1943 AIF periodical *Khaki and Green*.[60] One soldier wrote:

> He carries the stretchers up hills that are almost impossible
> for a white man to walk up ... some of the earlier settlers

George Silk's iconic image of Private 'Dick' Whittington and Raphael Oimbari at Buna has come to epitomise the relationship between Papuans, New Guineans and Australians. At the time the photo was taken only Whittington's name was documented. It was not until the 1970s that the Papuan in the famous image was identified.
Australian War Memorial 014028

that were here before the war would have the horrors at the way the Aussie soldiers treat him. They know that if they are wounded it will be the 'boong' that will bring him back so they share their cigarettes, tobacco, and biscuits with him, say "Good day Mirrow", to all and generally treat him as an equal or another ally.[61]

They were, in the words of another soldier, 'some of the finest men I've seen … many of the wounded owe their lives to the ability and stamina of the native carriers'.[62] Padre Frank Harly hoped that 'the Australian people recognise the debt we owe them after the war'.[63]

Australian aircrews, too, were grateful, as in the event of a crash landing they relied on the islanders to pluck them from the ocean or jungle, feed them and ensure their safe return to Allied-controlled areas.[64] Downed airmen rescued by Papuans could be back flying with their squadron within 24 hours.[65] While guidebooks stressed that lost soldiers and aircrew would need all their 'bush lore', it was deemed 'extremely unlikely' that they could return to base without the assistance of the Indigenous population.[66] The 'native' represented the 'best, perhaps, only chance of survival'.[67] Indeed, by 1945 the contents of soldier guidebooks were designed to ensure good relations between Australian soldiers and Indigenous populations, with much emphasis placed upon the ability of the Indigenous people to save the lives of Allied servicemen in trouble.[68] However, it was not so much a sense of loyalty to one side or the other that motivated the Indigenous to assist the downed flyers, notes Bergerud, but human compassion.[69]

Importantly, the changing view of the troops toward the locals has been highlighted by Inglis, who discusses the way in which the Australians addressed Papuans and New Guineans. Whereas terms such as 'coon' and 'wog' (the names given by Australian troops to the people of the Middle East) were full of contempt (they could occasionally be genial, but mostly not), and

terms such as 'boong' were ambiguous depending on the circumstance of its use, the adoption of terms such as 'sport' by Australian soldiers when addressing Papuans and New Guineans was
not. 'Sport' – like 'mate' – could be used reciprocally. Furthermore, when used to address a member of a different race, the user,
according to Inglis, is making 'an affirmation about the family of
man'.[70] This important change is reflective of the openness with
which a number of Australian troops engaged Papuans and New
Guineans in their encounters.

Nonetheless, the deification of the Papuan carriers did not
convince everybody, and some remained quite cynical in their
assessments. Defending the hitting of a Papuan medical orderly
for the insolent manner in which he spoke to a sergeant, Stanton criticised 'those simple minded whites who always advocate
"everything for the Fuzzy-wuzzie!"'. In particular, Stanton singled out for reproof the anthropologist Ian Hogbin. 'As if we,
the white man, owe these natives anything', he wrote sneeringly.
'I am convinced they'd go over to the Japanese tomorrow if thcy
thought he [sic] was in the greater number.' Regarding compensation, he added: 'Good Australians will have to foot the bill.' Later,
when holding an investigation into disturbances at the Ukaka
Native Labour Camp, Stanton reported: 'The natives state that
if the white man hit them, they are going to carve up said white
gents. Nice people, the Fuzzy Wuzzy Angels.'[71]

Likewise, war correspondent Allan Dawes emphasised that,
despite the fine service and compassion shown towards the Australians, the Papuans were no angels, but men – and men who
were not far removed from Stone-Age savagery: 'You don't breed
angels from head-hunters and cannibals and tribal murderers.
But take away their incentive for cannibalism and head-hunting
and murder, substitute some other mission in life, then scratch
the kanaka and you will find a man.'[72] The *Pacific Island Monthly*,
perhaps concerned with the changes taking place by 1943,
reminded its readers: 'The Papuan has not changed into an angel

overnight. He didn't volunteer to help chase the Jap out of his own country; and he obeyed very unwillingly or perhaps only because, by so doing, his dependants would be fed by the Army.' It added a further reminder that 'A considerable proportion of our carriers deserted.'[73]

Such emphasis, however, on the dedication to duty of the 'fuzzy wuzzies' obscured the poor conditions many labourers faced, as well as the fact that many were recruited against their will.[74] As Reed has noted, representation of Papuans as 'fuzzy wuzzy angels' was an Australian colonial construction depicting the Papuans as a homogenous 'other', reflecting a desire to 'maintain control over what had remained the preferred image of the colonised subject'. Certainly, the fact that Papuans were a colonised people – subdued, conscripted, ill-treated, with some even preaching independence – is ignored in Australian popular narratives.[75]

The deification of the 'fuzzy wuzzy angel' helped create a myth surrounding the relations and roles of Papuans in Australia's war against Japan. While the good rapport and attitudes between many Australians and carriers remains significant, the popularity of the 'fuzzy wuzzy angel' within Australian narratives overshadows the insidious face of colonialism also evident within the New Guinea campaign. Not only does it celebrate Papuan and New Guinean loyalty by overshadowing the fact that they judged the situation for themselves and chose sides accordingly but it also fails to consider the poor treatment meted out to the Papuan and New Guinean people by the Australians. A major point of difference between the AIF forces in Asia and the AIF forces in the Pacific was their attitudes toward native labour. In Malaya the AIF refused to act as strike-breakers, and many men were sympathetic toward the low wages and conditions endured by the Asians. Such anecdotes were significant in the way Australian troops defined themselves as being different from the British colonisers. However, in New Guinea the Australians did not have the British to bounce off, and this fundamentally affected their attitudes and behaviour.

In the south-west Pacific manpower was an integral component of the kinds of campaigns pursued there. The campaigns in New Guinea were some of the most difficult staged throughout the Second World War and were unique in that they relied on the brawn, skill and bushcraft of the local people for success. With few roads, the normal reliance on motor transport and the unyielding thirst for petrol to support an advance was minimal. Airdrops played a role, but it was the carrier lines that kept Australian and American – and Japanese – forces fighting in the rainforests, swamps and mountains, fed and armed the men, and carried away the wounded. The success of campaigns such as Kokoda and the following drive on Gona, Buna and Sanananda would certainly have been impossible without the carrier lines. 'Native' labour also supported the construction of airfields, the most vital commodity in the Pacific War, and performed important roles in scouting and intelligence gathering.[76] As Parer's newsreel *Assault on Salamaua* unsubtly declared: 'say a Digger: "No boongs, no battle"'.[77]

ANGAU played a central role in the New Guinea campaigns, and one of its primary responsibilities was the recruitment of labour for the military forces. Civilian field staff of military age and fitness who had served the old administrations were given rank in ANGAU, and their wartime roles contrasted sharply with their pre-war roles as detached supervisors of recruiting. It was also an about-face for villagers and kiaps (village heads), as ANGAU officers recruited aggressively, often contravening pre-war standards of recruitment.[78] Following the Japanese advance through Kokoda and their drive towards Port Moresby in 1942, an early decision to recruit volunteers only from areas affected by the war and to restrict recruiting to 25 per cent of fit adult males was hastily discarded once the military situation became critical. Indeed, historians have claimed that the army was far more unforgiving in its recruitment methods than any civilian employers who remained within the law during peacetime.[79]

In June 1942 Major General Basil Morris invoked the National Security (Emergency Control) Regulations. These terminated all existing contracts of service in Papua and New Guinea and provided the means for the conscription of native labour for the military. ANGAU, as the arm of the services responsible for the recruitment of labour, was therefore given full authority. Papuans and New Guineans could now be forced to contract their labour for up to three years. On top of this, they were required to meet military expectations of discipline and loyalty. It was forbidden to desert, be absent without leave or refuse to perform work as instructed.[80]

For the labourers, recruiters could be particularly ruthless. A report by the district officer of Purari made no apology for their methods. Of the 2598 men who were recruited in their area, fewer than 100 were volunteers.[81] A significant departure from the pre-war practice was the compelling and forcing of labourers to 'sign on'. The former ANGAU officer Peter Ryan knew of villages in which 100 per cent of all fit males over the age of 14 had been recruited (in some villages, according to Ryan, unfit males were also conscripted). Such villages suffered severely without men to cultivate, hunt, and maintain houses and canoes.[82] Likewise, although the treatment of the carriers varied, in the main conditions were harsh, particularly during the campaigns of 1942. Carriers on the Kokoda, Bulldog and Rigo trails in particular suffered during this period, as Nelson has documented: 'underfed, inadequately clothed for the altitude and overworked they sickened and died at an appalling rate'. Nevertheless, conditions gradually improved during 1943 and 1944. The rate of death among labourers was 2 per cent in 1943 – still an increase upon the pre-war average of 1.5 per cent – but it dropped to 0.88 per cent by 1944 thanks to the improved rations and health services provided by ANGAU.[83] Nevertheless, it has been argued that by late 1944 ANGAU had not only failed to prevent the undue exploitation of labourers but had also helped facilitate its allowance.[84]

Ryan noted how some 'old hands' among his colleagues thought it an 'extravagance' and 'pampering' when ration scales for labourers were increased in 1944 following medical advice, having been condemned in 1942 by the Director of Army Catering and Director General of Medical Services. For his part, Ryan felt that providing sufficient food for men doing hard work played a crucial role in sickness levels dropping by 4 per cent.[85] Other ANGAU officers also expressed concern at the issues and conditions facing the carriers. As Captain G.H. 'Doc' Vernon, the medical officer responsible for the carriers at Kokoda, wrote:

> The conditions of our carriers ... caused me more concern
> than that of the wounded ... Overwork, overloading
> (principally by soldiers who dumped their packs and even
> rifles on top of the carriers' burden), exposure, cold and
> underfeeding were the common lot. Every evening scores of
> carriers came in, slung their loads down and lay exhausted
> on the ground; the immediate prospect before them was
> grim, a meal that consisted only of rice and none too much
> of that, and a night of shivering discomfort for most as
> there were only enough blankets to issue one to every two
> men.[86]

Lieutenant Colonel Ian Hogbin, who had an anthropological background, was more understanding of Indigenous affairs than many ANGAU officers. Hogbin heavily criticised the use of labour, labour officials and camps. In a 1944 report he found that labourers were employed in tasks that should not have been prescribed as they were not conducive to the overall war effort. These included the construction of churches in American camps, officers' clubs, recreational halls, theatres, office buildings, decorative gardens and a swimming pool; working as waiters at army mess tables or as personal servants to Allied troops (a personal servant, it was reported, could be procured from an ANGAU officer for a bottle of gin); and being used to make souvenirs for officers to on-sell to servicemen. Of further concern was that labourers were employed beyond their contract terms and kept away from their home villages unnecessarily. Hogbin openly criticised and condemned a majority of Native Labour Overseers as having 'no real interest in native welfare', their primary concern being to maintain and increase figures for their own promotions. He also criticised 'old hands' for their routine brutality. Furthermore, conditions and accommodation within labour compounds were described as substandard. Strong resentment existed among conscripts who had disliked being herded in with so many strangers and who were worrying about the wellbeing of their wives and families. They had also been subjected to many broken promises, particularly in the form of repeated false assurances that when a particular job was finished they would be allowed to return home. Both American and Australian armies made use of labour far beyond their operational needs and very much to the disadvantage of Papuan and New Guinean village society.[87] The predicament of native carriers, as described by Schrijvers, was like that of pawns in a chess game, and because of their value as labourers they in essence 'became part of the rich raw materials of the region'.[88]

A number of factors may have discouraged potential recruits. A report by ANGAU officer John Blencowe on re-establishing administrative control in New Guinea detailed the problem of desertion among indentured labourers. He reported the detention of 23 deserters from the Doa plantation – the second such group he knew of from this plantation – who claimed that the manager had been 'hitting them and making them work while sick'. He also reported that the labourers were particularly susceptible to yaws and tropical ulcers, stating that these were found to be in an advanced state due to their prolonged stay in the bush.[89] Another factor is revealed within a report on the operations of the 3rd Division in the Salamaua area of New Guinea in 1943, which noted that while 12,494 labourers were required only 2293 were contracted or available for contract. Potential recruits may also have been concerned by the working conditions. For instance, it was decided that 'accommodation should not be provided for native labour as large concentrations of buildings would provide easy targets for Jap planes and bombing or strafing would lead to mass desertion'.[90]

In addition, disregarding individual labourers' contracts, virtually no labourers were released during the first two years of the war, and even by 1945 men who had seen out the duration of their contracts were prevented from returning to their homes unless replacements were available. Furthermore, labourers gained little reward or wealth. They were paid at the lower New Guinea rate until August 1943, when the army accepted the Papua rate of ten shillings a month.[91] Compounding matters, certain officers used their positions of power within the army to secure pigs, women and practically anything else that they wanted from native villages. Such officers were described by Stanton as types 'no army wants', and certainly as types that did the white man's standing disservice. One officer, Stanton reported, cunningly extracted from the inhabitants of an offshore island £220/13/10 for war bonds. Stanton noted with irony how newspapers would report this as a voluntarily contribution by the 'fuzzy wuzzies' for the war effort; they had, in fact, been demanded by the patrol officer. Stanton added, cynically: 'it's easier to pay a fine than to go to gaol'.[92]

Punishment for offences such as desertion or theft of food, tools or clothes from supplies could be particularly cruel. To coerce deserters to return, threats were made that the sons of the deserter would be conscripted. In one incident, recaptured deserters were bent over a hot 44-gallon fuel drum (in which a fire burned) and publicly whipped.[93] Although such punishments were not sanctioned by ANGAU, and in fact were strictly forbidden, Powell suspects that senior officers turned a blind eye to such practices, particularly during the desperate months of 1942.[94] Such incidents were not isolated; there are reports of village elders being flogged for concealing fit men from conscription, and of the beating of men who attempted to avoid recruitment. So severe were some of these beatings that the victim could be left unconscious.[95] Physical punishment could also be handed out for matters far more trivial. For example, Stanton wrote of an ANGAU district officer who beat a Papuan with a fence paling because he persisted in smiling while being spoken to. According to Stanton, some native labour overseers took delight in hitting those under their care.[96] Ryan states that assaults on labourers were not systematic, and that ANGAU's reputation remained credible.[97] However, as the historian Riseman has noted, rather than read the warning signs and address the root of the problem by improving food and conditions ANGAU chose instead to punish those most affected by its own inadequacies.[98]

Papuans and New Guineans accused of treason or assisting a public enemy faced severe punishment. When Papuans turned over parties of Australians fleeing Rabaul to the Japanese, tough justice was handed out by Australian soldiers once they regained control of the area. In one particular case, 22 men were hanged on purpose-built gallows at Higaturu over two days in 1943. The executions (17 of which occurred on a single day) were watched by hundreds of local villagers. Figures vary, but one estimate has it that as many as 100 Papuans were hanged by Australian troops in several locations during the war for various offences, including treason, assisting a public enemy and wilful murder.[99] ANGAU officer Clarrie James clearly felt uncomfortable about his role as official witness and assistant to the hanging of eight Papuans at Misima in February 1944 for their involvement in the murder of a party of 11 men, including an ANGAU officer, two members of the Royal Papuan Constabulary and a village policeman, as well as their seven companions. Every able-bodied male on the island had been ordered to attend (the reason for attending having been withheld), and had to watch the events unfold over more than four hours. Although James believed the sentences imposed by the court of law were just, he felt conflicted between his duty and his conscience.[100] For the people of Misima it brought the Australians – 'as a race' – into contempt.[101]

More disturbing still, military command did not inform the Australian government that these hangings had taken place. The army had, in essence, been acting on its own whim; this was 'frontier justice'. When Prime Minister John Curtin and his federal cabinet eventually found out in April 1945, the Minister for External Territories, E.J. Ward, ordered that the hangings cease. Through either deliberate fabrication or incompetence (we can only speculate), army officers had falsified the numbers in their reports to Ward, grossly underestimating the number of men who had been hanged. It is estimated that Ward's intervention saved another 50 Papuans who were on death row.[102]

There remains, however, a question over the legality of such punishments. Where the punishment was for the act of wilful murder, the cases have not raised controversy. However, where punishments were for the crime of treason the cases enter murky legal grounds. The pre-war administration of Papua had administered the law under the provision of the Queensland Criminal Code, which included the civil offence of treason. However, though residents in an Australian territory, the Papuans and New Guineans were not citizens; they did not vote in Australian elections or receive Australian pensions, nor were they allowed to settle in Australia. Furthermore, Papuans and New Guineans had seen the Australians take over from one colonial master only to be superseded by yet another. They did not understand the conflict between Australia and Japan, and did what they could to survive. Making these cases even more unusual was that a board of inquiry investigating Japanese executions of Papuans and New Guineans recognised that the Japanese were entitled to treat those who had assisted Australians as guilty of treason. The effect of this decision was to acknowledge that the Japanese were in legitimate control of areas it had conquered and, ipso facto, Papuans and New Guineans must lawfully obey their orders. When the Australians returned, however, they nevertheless claimed a right to try 'natives' who had assisted the Japanese. Put simply, as a report by the Chief Legal Officer of the army in New Guinea attests, as non-British subjects acting in areas not under British (but Japanese) control, Papuans and New Guineans could not be tried with treason under the Queensland Criminal Code. Furthermore, treason was a civil offence, yet the civil judicial process was not followed as trials took place under ad hoc military tribunals. Papuans and New Guineans could, however, be tried with assisting a public enemy under the Commonwealth *Crimes Act*. Unknown to the Minister of the Army or the Minister of External Affairs, the military had been hanging men for crimes after having arrived at sentences by a different process to that used by civil authorities. While each incident needs to be considered on a case-by-case basis, the measures taken against Papuans and New Guineans were less likely to have met Australian understandings of fairness and justice.[103]

Ryan later reflected, rather sympathetically, upon the plight of the carriers in ANGAU's hands on the Kokoda Trail. The carriers had performed 'too well for their own good, or the good of their Indigenous brothers', noted Ryan. Once an 'admiring army saw the job they could do', he wrote, its 'appetite for carriers and labourers became ravenous'.[104] Another ANGAU officer, John Bain, later recounted the friendships he had established, believing the work he did in rehabilitating and giving opportunities to the people of New Guinea would lead them to a 'new life'. Postwar, he continued to subscribe to *Pacific Islands Monthly*, and for 20 years 'dreamed' of Papua. However, his dream was sullied when he returned many years later on a visit to find that the people from the village in his former district, whose native tongue he had learnt, told him that they owed the Japanese a lot and the Australians nothing; they had been treated badly, they told him, 'and that generally, we were a pretty hopeless bunch of patronising, paternalistic bastards'.[105]

Men of the AIF, most of whom had far less contact with the Indigenous population than an ANGAU officer, viewed ANGAU's role more positively. An officer with the 8th Battalion on Bougainville, for example, described the work of ANGAU as much like that of a 'good village doctor looking after their patients'.[106] Indeed, the quality of ANGAU officers varied. Some showed genuine concern for those under their control. Keith McCarthy, for example, sent labourers home when he discovered they had been recruited against their will, or when he felt that they had dutifully served for an adequate period – while others, emboldened by the authority that they were given – sought, in the words of Captain David Fiendberg, to keep the locals 'from becoming bigheaded'. Others were concerned with making profits by selling Indigenous artefacts made under conscript labour. And, although not all ANGAU officers were disliked or feared, Fiendberg, for one, felt that the unit had a poor standing with the Indigenous community.[107] Certainly, the effects of the war on Papuans and New Guineans were profound. Even 30 years later, in the 1970s, residents of Misima used the word 'Angau' to refer to those who shouted commands; residents of Manus referred to people who took things from others as 'Angau'; and visitors could still hear a song being sung with the lyrics: 'The white man has brought his war to be fought on this land; His King and Queen have said so. We are forced against our wishes to help him.'[108]

While historians such as Powell and Nelson have discussed the issue of ANGAU and touched upon the so-called 'digger hangings', they have concluded that, despite the injustice and unfairness, ANGAU did well given the circumstances in which it worked. Powell, for example, argues that ANGAU should be judged by its influence in winning the battle for New Guinea, while Nelson has judged how much better off Papuans and New Guineans were in 1945 compared with 1941.[109] However, intriguing comparisons to what Australians considered fair and just — reflected by their attitudes in the British colonies of Southeast

Asia compared with understandings of fairness in areas of Australian imperial influence – are absent from such discussions. Overwhelmingly, darker narratives make the tale of Australian relations with 'fuzzy wuzzy angels' muddier, more complex and, ultimately, inconvenient for feel-good nationalist wartime narratives.

It is interesting to compare the separate views held toward ANGAU by Australians and Americans serving in New Guinea, especially considering that in New Guinea it was the Americans – and not the Australians, as was the case in Malaya – who were the foreign force in a colonial territory. In his history of ANGAU, Powell states: 'overall it can be said that ANGAU's special role and American appreciation of it led to one of the most harmonious of inter-Allied relationships of New Guinea'.[110] This may have been so among those who worked with the administration in order to receive quotas of labourers for the construction of airfields and bases; individual GIs, on the other hand, were more cautious in their assessments. As Schrijvers has noted, GIs believed ANGAU to be suspicious of American imperial intentions and therefore stubbornly clinging to its forces as they fought their way across New Guinea and adjacent islands with the only purpose that of re-establishing control over the Indigenous population. Furthermore, particular sights proved confronting. For example, an American sailor watching Australians overseeing a group of labourers was astonished when he observed a worker being beaten with a stick the length of a broom handle. While the foreman administering the beating exerted himself with all his might the rest of the labourers carried on as if nothing had happened. Likewise, a colonel with the US 43rd Division at Aitape wrote to his fiancée of the conditions under which the New Guineans were employed. The Australians, he wrote, kept them 'under their thumbs with a system more like slavery'. In addition, American GIs also resented ANGAU's efforts to keep villages off-limits or prevent them dealing with New Guineans for goods.[111] Such a view of ANGAU and its treatment of its charges is far removed from the 'good village doctor' view. Few Australian soldiers described the work of other Australians in New Guinea with such negative or emotive language as the GIs. However, despite such views among soldiers, historians are universal in their assessment that the Americans relied as much on native labour throughout the campaigns of the south-west Pacific as did the Australians.[112]

According to Schrijvers, some of the American behaviour was fuelled by 'overt disdain for colonial authority'. But Papuans and New Guineans viewed the Americans more positively. GIs had unwittingly increased their standing; unlike the Australian soldiers, who had little to give away, the well-supplied Americans generously fed items to people from societies in which political standing was obtained through the distribution of wealth and resources. Likewise, the sharing of food could have deep symbolic meanings of respect and trust. Furthermore, Melanesians were not dismayed by the physical segregation of African-American troops, but were impressed by the apparent equality with regard to housing, clothing, food and work. The people of Vanatinai concluded that the spirits of their own dead turned white and travelled to the United States – such was their belief in the kinship fostered through the generosity of GIs.[113] Indeed, in 1946 the community of Manus Island met with the commander of the US naval base requesting that the United States take over the island's administration because the two previous rulers – the Germans and the Australians – used them only for labour, had done little for their overall condition and had provided no schooling.[114]

Interestingly, Schrijvers has revealed how GIs – embroiled in an imperial war and seduced by the perks of colonial society – liked to think of themselves as better colonisers than others, more enlightened and more sentimental. Americans, Schrijvers noted: 'wanted to believe that the peoples of the region, like children, were responding to the benevolence of their American guardians and tutors with gratitude'.[115] Schrijvers's observations are enlightening when drawing comparisons with the attitude of Australian troops. In certain encounters diggers could be sympathetic to the colonised; in others – where there was an Australian imperial mission – there was less concern for the affairs of the subjugated and indeed an excitement about the potential for economic betterment. As official historian Gavin Long observed, Australians drove Papuans and New Guineans harder than they drove themselves. Referring to the period 1944–45, when conditions and services had improved for the then approximately 55,000 labourers, Long wrote that 'the burden of war was weighing down heavily on the New Guinea native – more heavily, man for man, than on the general run of Australian citizens'.[116] This occurred despite safeguards put in place to protect the populations and village life of New Guinea. Clearly, as historian Geoffrey Gray has highlighted, the war effort took first priority at the expense of the interests of Papuans and New Guineans. And, as has been made clear, 'native labour' benefited Australians not only by providing a crucial role in the success of Allied campaigns in the south-west Pacific but also by adorning the lives of Australian troops with personal servants and – in the words of the official historian – with 'well-drilled native waiters' at officers' clubs.[117]

Clearly, Australia's war in New Guinea presents a paradox: in seeing Australia's mission as 'civilising', were Australians viewing Asians as less 'backward' than the people of New Guinea? In a war defined by the imperialist ambitions of adversaries, is there a conscious undertone within the literature that Australians made better colonisers? In Southeast Asia the Australians were critical of the British and the conditions imposed upon the subjugated populations. However, in New Guinea there is identification with an imperial mission. Not only were individual soldiers inspired by the potential for New Guinea to become the new India or Java but the poor treatment that Papuans and New Guineans received at the hands of the Australian military also symbolises the insidious face of colonialism and the way in which the governing structure can affect how people interact across racial lines. While friendships between Australians and Papua New Guineans did arise, and while the 'fuzzy wuzzy angels' were held in particular regard, these positive aspects have been allowed to obscure the sinister nature of Australia's war in New Guinea and the nation's own colonial past. The face of colonialism in New Guinea was an Australian one, and the soldiers' attitudes toward race appear to have been influenced by this. While it remains important to acknowledge and celebrate the efforts of Papuans and New Guineans who worked for the Allied war effort, it also needs to be considered – as Riseman points out – that they were treated as subjects, in many cases obliged to work for their colonial rulers.[118]

Nevertheless, as the war progressed the interactions between Australian soldiers and the people of Asia and the Pacific saw not only the development of relations between ordinary Australians and others but also important changes in attitudes. Australian soldiers were beginning to consider some of the big questions on ideologies and international movements that were emerging with regard to how a just and lasting peace might be established in the world. As soldiers debated the causes of the war, and the objects for which the conflict was being fought, a burgeoning political awareness dawned among them, placing a particular emphasis on Asia and encouraging a newfound respect for regional affairs. By 1945 they were asking: what regional role should Australia play in postwar Asia and the Pacific?

6

REVERSAL OF FORTUNES
POW contacts in captivity

Australian soldiers made significant contacts with the peoples of Southeast Asia during the Pacific War. The conduct of the campaigns in which Australian forces were involved has been well documented; however, there are certain aspects of the experiences of Australian soldiers in Asia that have not received as much attention. They are the episodes in which we can see a genuine awareness of Asia and Asian affairs developing within a large cross-section of Australian society. During their captivity in Asia, Australian prisoners of war found themselves in a situation few white men had experienced. Now lacking power and prestige – and many enslaved by the Japanese – they interacted with Asian communities in an unprecedented way. In all the places of their internment assistance was given by Asians which in certain circumstances proved crucial to the prisoners' survival. Rather than fleeting, some personal contacts and friendships proved to be long-lasting.

Prisoners of war were acutely aware of the reversal of fortunes in which they had taken part. They had witnessed, and some had been sympathetic to, the subjugated Asian civilians in the British colonies during the days of peace. Now, following the fall of Singapore on 15 February 1942, British and Australian prisoners were on the other end of the racial hierarchy. This was evidenced by well-known survivors' accounts with titles such as *White Coolies* or *Slaves of the Samurai*.[1] Some prisoners found their circumstances, in full view of Asian civilians, 'a most humiliating experience'.[2]

The official war artist Murray Griffin, recalling the march from Singapore to Changi in full view of the locals, later wrote: 'What a change from rulers to slaves, to a position more lowly than theirs in so short a time. Some of the Malays laughed.'[3] Such sentiments were emphasised in Australian press reports at war's end which tended to accentuate that in their employment of labour the Japanese had failed to distinguish between white European prisoners and the *romusha*, the Asian labourers forced to work for the Japanese.[4]

While they were prisoners of war, Australian encounters with local populations could further enhance or reinforce attitudes toward particular groups. During the campaign and battle for Singapore some were paranoid about Malayan fifth columnists, whom they perceived as deviously waiting at the ready to sell information about troop movements to the enemy.[5] In Singapore one suspect caught carrying a mirror (which it was believed he used to signal the enemy) was executed.[6] This was not an isolated case. Such treasonous behaviour was confirmed for Braddon when marching into captivity at Pudu Gaol in Kuala Lumpur; he described streets lined with Malays 'who only a fortnight before been hysterically pro-British', but who now flung stones and spat at the line of British and Australian prisoners. It is of little surprise that, later on in their captivity on the Burma–Thailand Railway, prisoners who had their few remaining possessions stolen by the locals felt that 'as a nation we found the Thais excessively dishonest and thieving'. However, some of the Australians, Braddon added, reciprocated wholeheartedly in these endeavors by stealing from the Thais. More so, some had little sympathy for the conditions of the *romusha* they encountered in Thailand. Some 200,000 Asian labourers worked on the railway alongside the 60,000 Allied prisoners of war, and perhaps 90,000 *romusha* died in its construction. These Asian labourers did not have the military structures or organisation to which prisoners of war were accustomed, and their camps and conditions were bleak. One prisoner described a camp previously occupied by *romusha* as 'littered with excrement, seething with flies, and in condition of unspeakable filth which only Asiatics can attain'.[7]

The dominant narrative to emerge from the prisoner-of-war experience, however, was one that highlighted the qualities inherent in the Anzac legend: resilience, resourcefulness, egalitarianism, good humour and mateship. In this way prisoners of war are seen as exemplars of the national character.[8] With a particular focus on Australian mateship as a key to surviving captivity – the emphasis on Australians looking out for fellow Australians – lost are the stories of humanitarian goodwill and responses to the suffering of prisoners by Asian civilians. Accounts emerge as early as the Allied forces' retreat down the Malayan peninsula in the face of the Japanese onslaught in 1942. When Australian stragglers fell behind the lines, more than in any other circumstance these men felt like strangers in a strange land. In this environment they were isolated, marooned from the reassurances of others of their own race and nationality. However, these stragglers and survivors of the withdrawal down the peninsula received comfort and compassion from the many Chinese–Malay residents who helped alleviate their hunger and thirst and assisted them in returning to their own lines. For some, the journey was more than a hundred kilometres through jungle and swamp.

As an example, survivors of the encirclement at Parit Sulong spoke of being given food and drink by Chinese, who risked Japanese retribution if caught.[9] One soldier who spent 11 days behind enemy lines in Malaya – cold, shivering, worn out and hardly able to walk – was given refuge in a Chinese house where his energy was restored with hot food and coffee before being guided by the house owner to a river crossing and the safety of British lines.[10] Not all locals were prepared to assist the Australians, however. One airman was reportedly hidden within a Chinese community for over two months until he was 'sold to the Japs by Malayans for 10 dollars'.[11] Looking back on the 1942 campaign, Major General

Bennett proclaimed that 'the Australian soldiers in Malaya will never lose their admiration for the Chinese and will remember with gratitude their loyalty and kindness'.[12] Mant felt especially grateful as he recognised the many grievances facing the Chinese under British rule, citing the case of a Chinese manager of a large British store who was paid less than his European clerk in the name of 'British prestige'.[13]

Assistance was also given to those who had fled Singapore and made the arduous journey through the Indonesian archipelago toward Australia aboard an assortment of vessels. One soldier noted: 'Saved as usual by some Malays carrying burning torches … taken to village … given food, clothes, and a hut … The Malays behaved as if they acted as hosts to shipwrecked evacuees every night.'[14]

In almost all of the locations of Australian prisoners' suffering there were acts of generosity from the local populations. In many reminiscences there are references to such acts from unknown Chinese, undertaken at great personal risk; those caught by the Japanese faced severe punishment and the ethnic Chinese populations of Asia suffered great persecution under Japanese occupation.[15] On the long march to Changi the day following the fall of Singapore, Chinese women, 'displaying a provoking contempt for the Japanese', provided coffee to the passing column of prisoners.[16] Later, when Australian prisoners of war were on work duties at places such as the Municipal Nursery in Singapore, they too were brought coffee, food and cigarettes by Chinese from nearby *kampongs*. The prisoners were very appreciative of such kindness. As one prisoner of war wrote in his diary, the Chinese 'are marvellous, bought me bananas, pineapple and paw paw. Also given a packet of cigars'.[17]

From the very first days of imprisonment Australian prisoners witnessed the horrific treatment of the Chinese communities of Singapore by the occupying forces. Japan had been waging an imperialist war in China since 1937. As an extension of this, when conquests were made in Southeast Asia and the Pacific in 1941–42 the Japanese purged local Chinese communities in attempts to eliminate anti-Japanese elements. In Singapore, all male Chinese had to report to screening centres.[18] The repercussions were well documented in the diaries of Australian prisoners of war such as William Miggins. Just days after his arrival in Changi, Miggins volunteered for a work party to alleviate the boredom, not knowing the grisly task that awaited at Changi beach. There, 'spread along the water's edge were the bodies of 108 Chinese murdered by machine gun fire from a range of about 10 yards. They had been stripped with their hands behind their backs'. The prisoners were to serve as the burial party. These were just some of the approximately 25,000 Chinese massacred on Singapore Island in 1942 (a purge known in Singapore as *sook ching*).[19] Two months later, Miggins wrote in his diary: 'Anzac Day. Saw a Chinese being tortured today. They had him upside down and giving him the water treatment.'[20] They were scenes common to work parties across the island. At Serangoon Road Camp, prisoners wrote of the decapitated heads publicly displayed on poles lining the road.[21] When the Chinese were beaten up by the Japanese for supplying the prisoners with food or medicine, one Australian wrote that 'their spirit never wavered', and the supplies continued.[22] By 1944 the prisoners could see that the population of Singapore was worse off than they were, with Chinatown suffering many deaths due to malnutrition. Again, to the admiration of the prisoners, the generosity of the Chinese persisted and supplies continued to arrive.[23] The significance of these observations in 1944 is that they were made by prisoners just recently returned from working on the Burma–Thailand Railway. Such scenes and thoughts are well documented within diaries written in Changi, or in other camps where work parties were billeted around Singapore.

Such scenes were not isolated to Singapore. From Burma, Jack Turner, a member of the 2/2nd Reserve Motor Company, wrote of his admiration for his Chinese, Thai, Indian and Burmese friends

– as well as others who were total strangers to him – who had provided him with cigars, bananas, breadfruit, paw paw and coffee during the period of his captivity. One Burmese woman who gave him food was married to an Australian miner and had a son in the AIF.[24] On Java, Indonesians gave imprisoned nurses flour and palm oil, which were used to make fried scones.[25] Trade and black-market activities, another key source of sustenance for the more devious or entrepreneurial prisoner, relied very much on contacts within local communities.[26]

Many locals in Thailand also assisted prisoners. The most famous was Weary Dunlop's great friend, Boon Pong Sirivejjabhandu, a riverboat trader and captain in the Free Thai movement. With his riverboat, he continually risked his life smuggling food, money and medicines to prison camps along the River Khwae.[27] At Tamarkan, the goods provided by Boon Pong between June and November 1943 amounted to a staggering £3500 sterling. During this time the rate of deaths at Tamarkan fell from four per day in August to one per week in October. Boon Pong's goods provided a great lift not only in health but also in overall morale.[28] This appreciation was reciprocated postwar when ex-prisoner-of-war associations heard that Boon Pong was struggling financially and funds were raised to help out the man who had done so much to aid the prisoners. The friendship between Dunlop and Boon Pong was genuine and lasted a lifetime. A medical scholarship is named in their memory. Within his diaries, Dunlop was understandably covert in discussing his dealings with Boong Pong in order to protect his friend's identity in case the diaries came into the possession of the Japanese. Given such circumstances, while Dunlop was glowing in praise for Boon Pong and the underground movement in his preface to the published diaries, references in the text to the 'faithful Thai trader' or that the hospital obtained 'most useful drugs and money' do not do justice to the full story of their collaboration.[29]

Many memoirs describe similar generosities from Thais who

were not publicly associated with the Allied cause. Ken Barrett wrote of women selling fruit at a railway station near Bangkok who gave their goods for free to the prisoners when their train stopped at the station.[30] Another example is the extraordinary scene witnessed during a forced march in Thailand following a harrowing train ride from Singapore. In great despair the men passed through a small village where on both sides of the road stood villagers with 'rows of charcoal braziers on which pots and pans bubbled with rice and vegetables, eggs, banana fritters, fish and peanuts; fresh fruit in baskets, limes and papayas, small sweet bananas, coconuts and acidic fruit stars'. The food was offered 'not for sale, but as friendly gifts pressed on us with unlimited generosity'. When the Japanese arrived they treated the villagers with ferocity.[31] A similar situation occurred in 1945 when, after the completion of the railway, a group of Australian prisoners found themselves in the town of Lopburi in central Thailand. When the men went for their daily wash, they would find hard-boiled eggs on the banks of the river that had been left for them by the locals.[32]

In Borneo men such as Chin Chee Kong, a young boy scout, and Koram bin Anduut, a sergeant major in the constabulary, risked their lives assisting Australian prisoners of war. Initially, Chin assisted in supplying medicine and cigarettes to prisoners; later, he and Koram helped eight Australians escape from the camp near Berhala Island to the Philippines, where the prisoners then joined guerrilla forces. When a member of the underground movement betrayed his colleagues, the *kenpeitai* (Japanese secret police) arrested Chin and he was subjected to four days of torture. Despite the excruciating pain, he told his captors nothing. With the extent of his role undiscovered he was sentenced to eight years imprisonment with hard labour.[33]

Prisoners on the receiving end of such generosity were forever grateful. In the days following the war's end, Jack Kerr wrote in his diary at Changi that 'the Chinese stand very high in our regard

Reunited in Changi following its liberation in 1945, these local Chinese had worked alongside these medical officers in an AIF hospital before the surrender in 1942. Many prisoners of war later praised the efforts of local Chinese who assisted in providing food and medical supplies at great personal risk.
Australian War Memorial 019326

for they have taken great risks and have helped us all they can'.[34] Another wrote that when 'the day of freedom arrived' at Changi 'there was a great reunion between the AIF and their Chinese friends'. When the men drove through Singapore on their way to the docks and the awaiting transport ship for their long-awaited journey home, one former prisoner of war wrote of how 'the Chinese lined the streets, giving the V-sign, while the children waved and cheered for joy. Such was the bond that had grown up between the right kind of yellow man and the white man'.[35] Such scenes were moving and reiterated for the freed prisoners that the war – and all their troubles – had not been fought in vain. The great Allied victory was as much theirs as anybody else's.

Such acts of generosity were widely reported in newspapers following the prisoners' release in 1945. For example, Melbourne's *Argus* reported the praise given by civilian internees in Singapore toward the local Chinese, and the villagers of Banka Island were commended for assisting Vivian Bullwinkel, the only survivor of a massacre that took place on 16 February 1942. Additionally, Rohan Rivett, in his series of exclusives in the *Argus*, wrote glowingly of the efforts of traders in Thailand and Burma, and of the Chinese in Singapore, in aiding the prisoners' survival.[36] It was a theme continued in his memoir, published shortly after the war. In *Behind Bamboo*, Rivett declared that 'the families of Allied POWs in Siam owe a tremendous debt to all those in this brilliant organized underground society, which helped save the lives of hundreds of British, Dutch and Australian prisoners'.[37] Similarly, in a radio broadcast from Saigon following liberation, Captain David Nathan promoted the great assistance provided to the prisoners by locals in the form of money, food and medical supplies. He did not wish to identify on air one particular Chinese merchant in Bangkok whom he singled out for praise, since he felt that, even with the war over, there was danger of retribution. Without such assistance, he stated, thousands more prisoners would have died.[38]

Despite these early reports, a popular narrative of the experiences of prisoners of war emerged postwar highlighting qualities that positioned them as inheritors of the Anzac legend. Of particular note was the tale of mateship; in simple terms, a myth persists that Australian prisoners survived at better rates than others by helping fellow Australians.[39] Despite this immediate publicity,

Asian assistance toward Australian prisoners of war has been marginalised in favour of more nationalistic and inward-looking tales of Australian camaraderie and mateship. Tales of compassion, generosity, goodwill and tolerance between Australians and Asians were evidently lost among the wider audience. Nevertheless, due gratitude was not lacking among many of the ex-prisoners themselves. For those who suffered and survived internment, clear feelings of friendship and tolerance were established toward Asian communities in Southeast Asia who aided their survival, and important and lasting relations were established through ex-servicemen's associations.

For instance, a historian travelling with a group of ex-prisoners to Singapore and Thailand in the 1980s wrote of his astonishment when a toast was declared to Singapore's brave Chinese.[40] Indeed, ex-prisoners have provided practical measures to preserve the memory of their relations with Asian communities. The Australian Ex-Prisoners of War Association oversees the AIF Malayan Nursing Scholarship awarded annually to candidates from Malaysia and Singapore. With the first recipients beginning their training in 1947, the program – decided upon at war's end, before the prisoners had even left Changi, to help repay their 'debt to the Chinese' – is still in existence today as an official 'living memorial' of the 8th Australian Division.[41] Also, the Gull Force 2/21st Battalion Association has been involved in many projects on Ambon since the 1960s, including a medical aid project, books for local schools and universities and a trust fund for scholarships.[42] Former prisoners of war have also been prominent in community groups such as the Asian–Australian Association, founded in 1956, which carried out social and welfare work, provided lectures, organised host-family schemes for Asian students, administered technical advice (such as providing engineering and agricultural specialists) and provided specialist medical treatment in Asia. Two of the associations' founding members were prominent ex-prisoners Sir Albert Coates and Sir Edward 'Weary' Dunlop.

While we know little about the motivations of those who assisted Australian stragglers and prisoners of war at great personal risk, what remains important is that such acts of generosity were not forgotten by the individual Australians involved. Importantly, these transactions constituted important aspects of personal narratives. In some cases they were the beginnings of lasting relationships between individuals or between veterans' associations and local communities.

The subject matter so far has revolved around Australians and their interactions with people who shared a common foe, but discussion of prisoners of war demands that the topic of Australian encounters with Japanese also be addressed. While differences may have yet existed between the 'right kind of yellow man and the white man', the experience of captivity also broke down barriers between Australians and the Japanese. Much is known about the atrocities and bitter hatred generated during the war in the Pacific, and the plight and suffering of the prisoners are common examples. But here, too, more complex stories emerge. Reporting and portraying the racism of earlier generations is an easy case for historians to make; teasing out the intricacies of these encounters is far more revealing.

While Australian pre-war attitudes toward Japan had not been all bad, for many – then and since – the war against Japan was seen as confirmation of earlier fears of the 'yellow peril', and cemented beliefs in what some considered at the time the barbaric nature of Asiatic races.[43] The Pacific War was fought with great ferocity. Whether in combat or in propaganda created by strategists, scientists, academics and politicians far from the front lines, the dehumanisation of the enemy by both sides, as argued by historian John Dower, contributed immensely to the psychological distancing that facilitated killing.[44] Australian soldiers, as demonstrated by historians such as Mark Johnston and Karl James, had great difficulties understanding their enemy. Language and cultural differences were hard to bridge, and combat experiences therefore often reinforced stereotypes. Furthermore, the racist language of the pre-war era and that maintained by wartime propaganda served as a means of expressing frustrations derived from battle. Japanese soldiers were often described by Australian soldiers fighting in the islands in animalistic terms: as apes, rats or vermin.[45] At the extreme end of the scale was the Commander-in-Chief of the Australian Military Forces, General Sir Thomas Blamey, who during the fighting around Buna in late 1942 and early 1943 told troops that 'beneath the thin veneer of a few generations of civilization he is a sub-human beast, who has brought warfare back to the primeval'.[46] The Australian, he said, was 'infinitely superior to the race against whom you are pitted', and 'we must exterminate the enemy if we are to live ... If civilization is to go on the Japanese must be exterminated'.[47] Days later he told a *New York Times* reporter: 'We are not dealing with human beings as we know them. We are dealing with something primitive ... vermin.'[48]

However, as Johnston has noted, it cannot be assumed that Australian soldiers swallowed propaganda fed by the likes of Blamey. Most did not regard their senior commander as 'an oracle of wisdom'.[49] Such are the complexities of war that as well as being an intense source of hatred the Australian soldiers also respected the bravery and toughness of Japanese soldiers and their ability to endure appalling conditions.[50] But what of prisoners of war and their contacts with the Japanese? Postwar memory of the prisoner-of-war experience was heavily influenced by the successful and well-known published memoirs by authors such as Braddon and Rivett, who tended, as Robin Gerster has stated, to 'spread the gospel of Japanese barbarism with a passion'.[51] Such works excited readers with tales of atrocities, massacres, starvation, disease, skeletal figures and death. Yet to appreciate the complexities of the prisoner-of-war experience it is important to move beyond the standard go-to texts of Braddon, Rivett and their ilk.

Certainly, many generalisations and stereotypes exist regarding the prisoner-of-war experiences. The horrors of the Burma–

Thailand Railway and Sandakan death march have become ingrained in the imagination. Yet each prison camp was different; the conditions and the attitudes of camp commanders and guards were not uniform, which could lead to quite diverse experiences. In many ways each of the 22,000 Australians who became prisoners of the Japanese has a unique story to tell depending on their own journey through captivity. In some places – Sandakan, Burma, Thailand and Ambon, as we well know – conditions and treatment of prisoners were truly horrendous. But conditions in other camps could be better – Changi is the prime example – with relatively few deaths taking place. Most attention has been given by historians to places and events in which conditions were the worst. Nelson has ascribed this to a fascination in the extreme suffering in these locations and the demand for explanation. They make compelling narrative, but the result has been the failure by historians to demonstrate the range of prisoner-of-war experiences.[52] This is not to say that some prisoners had it easy or were treated well – far from it. But it is important to recognise that conditions and experiences varied and that there was no singular experience across all camps.

For example, the familiar narratives of the Burma–Thailand Railway have been contrasted with tales of sporting events, which the prisoners valued as a welcome distraction from their predicament. Therefore, the occasion of a soccer match between Australian prisoners and Japanese guards in Burma on 15 February 1943 to mark the anniversary of the fall of Singapore – in which the Australians won three to one – presents a paradox. Such instances of levity, which also included basketball and baseball games between guards and captors, or individual Japanese guards in Changi joining a rugby or soccer team made up of Australian prisoners, do not fit the stereotypes of captivity. Yet, as the historian Blackburn has recently reminded us, these events did happen.[53]

Pertinent to Nelson's point, whereas much has been written about the Burma–Thailand Railway, Changi and Sandakan, historians have by and large neglected the Australian prisoners of war who spent time in Japan. Their stories, if they appear at all, tend to feature as footnotes following the completion of the railway, yet these Australians, encountering ordinary Japanese citizens, form a unique and important group. By early 1945 there were approximately 3500 Australian prisoners of war in Japan. Many had survived the railway and all endured the treacherous journey by hellship from Java, Singapore or Saigon to Japan. Conditions in camps across Japan varied according to local circumstances. In total around 190 Australian prisoners died while captive in Japan. Most died of disease – many were seriously ill on arrival, following their time on the railway and the hazardous ocean voyage – but others were killed in industrial accidents, which were common, or in the Allied bombing campaign.[54]

Prisoners of war in Japan worked in factories, foundries, mines and the dockyards. Conditions varied depending on the camp and place of work. Each day camp guards would escort the prisoners to the workplace. On arrival the guards would hand them over to those who would supervise them during work hours. At the dockyards at Nagasaki this meant the Japanese navy and *kenpeitai*. The workers here were kept on a tight rein and beatings were not uncommon.[55] At the Yoshiwara Vegetable Oil Company factory in the suburbs of Kobe, supervisors were made up of factory security police. Some of these security police – usually old veterans – turned a blind eye to the prisoners' pilfering of supplies, mostly because the guards benefited directly from it by later trading with the prisoners for the stolen goods. These guards felt it better that prisoners risk being caught stealing highly sought-after goods. On occasion guards would encourage the prisoners, and would even direct and show them where the 'loot' was stored, on the condition that the prisoner understood the guards would not be able to intervene if he were caught red-handed by the *kenpeitai*. The thefts improved the lives of not only the prisoners but their security police overseers and their extended families,

Australian prisoners of war in Japan worked in mines, dockyards and factories alongside ordinary Japanese civilians. Here, Private Allan Chick, now of the British Commonwealth Occupation Force in 1948, visits former co-workers at a Nagasaki foundry where he once worked as a prisoner of war in 1945.
Australian War Memorial P00208.003

too.[56] Japan had been devastated by the US naval blockade and daily goods produced in the factory, such as cooking oil, were not widely available to Japanese citizens.[57]

At their places of work Australian prisoners of war found themselves working alongside ordinary Japanese civilians. In some workplaces a standard team of five was mixed, made up of two or three Japanese civilians and two or three prisoners. Some prisoners considered that 'the civilians who worked with us were just as bad as the guards'.[58] One prisoner felt that the Omuta Camp and work in the nearby Miike coal mine were the worst conditions he faced; even worse than on the railway. The guards were brutal, he said, and the Japanese civilians whom they worked alongside, too old or unfit for military service, 'were the boss and let us know. The kicking, the hitting, the shouting – it was a living hell inside the blasted coal mine'.[59]

In some places prisoners took note of the poor conditions in which ordinary Japanese workers toiled on a daily basis. On the docks at Nagasaki they observed children as young as five working until 5 pm before attending school late into the evening, as well as middle-aged women carrying heavy pieces of scrap all day long.[60] What many may find extraordinary is that in some workplaces, just as small groups of Australian soldiers formed special bonds, there also existed camaraderie between the Australians and Japanese assigned to the same work gang. At a Toyo Steel foundry in the suburbs of Kobe, the civilian workers made sure that the same prisoners of war were on their work gangs each day. Each morning they would wait for the arrival of the prisoners and signal to their regulars to join them. One foreman regularly brought the Australian prisoners in his team something extra to supplement their midday meal. Such a small gesture could make a big difference for a prisoner suffering vitamin deficiencies, malaria, pneumonia or pleurisy.[61] Similarly, working at the Besshi copper mine, Miggins described the old retired miner in charge of them: 'He was a kindly man and treated us very well. He often gave us small amounts of tobacco to smoke.'[62] Another Australian prisoner reflected on how three Japanese women with whom he worked at a chemical factory saved his life by bringing him food and showing him how to find good seaweed to eat and cook.[63]

Accidents on work sites were common and afflicted all workers. A collapsed mine, a fallen scaffold, even the American bombing – all were indiscriminate, maiming and killing prisoners and civilians alike. On an occasion of bad weather and rough seas at the Ohamagumi firm at Kobe dockyards, where the prisoners lumped goods from barges on the wharf to nearby warehouses, Albert Armstrong of the 2/26th Battalion dived into the maelstrom of the 'mountainous' waves and saved from drowning a fellow female worker who slipped from a barge.[64] In other circumstances, following the heavy American bombing of Kobe on 5 June 1945, the Australian prisoners reached out to do what they could to aid the 'terror stricken and shocked' civilians. By this stage bombing raids had destroyed 51 per cent of the city. In the aftermath the prisoners carried the young and old to places of safety and medical officers and orderlies did what they could for the injured, even drawing upon their own meagre medical resources.[65]

One example of humanitarianism is that of Tom Uren (later a minister in the Whitlam and Hawke governments). He was captured on Timor with the 2/40th Battalion and imprisoned in Java before being sent to work on the Burma–Thailand Railway. Put to work in a Japanese copper smelting plant, he worked alongside Korean indentured labourers and old Japanese workers. There he saw the compassion of human being to human being. Unlike the prison camp guards he had encountered on the railway, he found the Japanese workers 'comradely' and 'decent people'. This helped change his perception of and attitude towards the Japanese. The factory workers – prisoners, Japanese and Koreans alike – worked together and bathed together, and in an act of consideration for his fellow workers Uren shared the only Red Cross parcel he received during his time as a prisoner with his fellow Japanese

At war's end Australian and Allied prisoners of war retrieve drums of supplies dropped by American aircraft at Kobe, Japan, in August 1945. Some Australian prisoners of war shared the food they received from such airdrops with local Japanese civilians.
Australian War Memorial P02597.021

and Korean workers, realising that it was not the Japanese people who were the enemy, per se, but rather Japanese militarism.[66]

From the records available, Uren's actions do not seem unusual among prisoners of war working in Japan. Announcing the end of the war in a speech to the assembled prisoners at Nakama

Camp (Fukuoka No. 21), Hiraishi Hiroki, the camp commandant, made special mention that:

> several days ago at one camp the prisoners presented the camp staff and factory foreman with part of their valuable food relief stuffs *and* personal belongings, while at other camps, prisoners have asked permission to present civilian war sufferers with their personal belongings. This I know is an expression of your understanding and openheartedness gentlemanliness and we, the camp staff, are deeply moved.[67]

While the prisoners noted the about-face taking place among many guards and camp commanders following the end of hostilities, the sentiments expressed in this exchange appear to be sincere. At this camp only five prisoners had died, in sharp contrast with other camps in the Fukuoka district, where in some cases the death toll had been over 100.[68]

Prisoners who did not journey to Japan met Japanese who almost exclusively were members of the IJA or IJN. In contrast, prisoners of war who did go to Japan were in a position to distinguish between members of the Japanese military – their captors, who had caused much hardship and trauma – and the ordinary Japanese civilian. This became evident to a group of prisoners of J-Force shortly after their arrival in Japan in 1943. One morning, when the prisoners were travelling on the Kobe metro system for their daily commute from their camp to the factory in which they worked, another commuter, a Japanese woman, was over-anxious to board a train before all the passengers had alighted. For her impatience and audacity, the Japanese guard escorting the prisoners punched the Japanese woman in the face – two or three times – smashing her glasses in the process. She was not the only woman the prisoners saw punched in the face and having her glasses smashed by their IJA guards whilst travelling the metro. For a similar offence, Clarrie Lattimer observed the prison guards giving a Japanese businessman 'the biggest belting that I had seen'. One prisoner wrote in his diary that in these journeys he 'witnessed the supremacy of the [Imperial Japanese] Army, or rather the way that the Army maintained its supremacy in Japanese society'.[69] It was apparent that the ordinary Japanese citizen was as much under the thumb of the Japanese military as were the prisoners of war. They also observed the 'inculcating [of] militarism into the youth of the country'.[70] Such observations by prisoners in Japan were not uncommon, and these views are as strongly held today as in 1945. As former prisoner of war Charles Edwards, a member of the 2/19th Battalion, told an ABC reporter in 2013 following his first visit to Japan since the war: 'The Japanese people were so beautiful, and they still are', recalled Edwards. 'They're courteous, kind, they laugh a lot – so my opinion of the Japanese people has never altered. It was only the IJA – the Imperial Japanese Army – that were brutal to us.'[71]

Such feelings could be reciprocal. After the war, Japanese foreman Inoue Ichiji wrote to the Australian prisoners he had worked alongside at the Hitachi Shipbuilding Yard in Osaka (they had exchanged addresses at war's end). In a letter to Pierre Walton he reminisced:

> Often I remember your warm and cordial welcome given
> to me around August 20th of the year of the Japanese
> surrender 1945 when I went to see you at Chikubu of
> Fukui Prefecture. I express my hearty thanks once again
> for your many nice presents such as tobacco, canned
> goods, chocolate and coffee. I asked you then to write your
> addresses for me, promising to write you after your return.
>
> Now and then we talk about you; Because of very
> little rations of food we took pity on you while you were
> at the Hitachi Shipbuilding Yard. So consulting my wife
> sometimes I gave to you rice-balls and Japanese porridges,
> and I got many thanks from you. When No. 64, Mr. Merrie

[another Australian POW], had a high fever suffering bad
coughs, I ventured to allow him to take rest in a warehouse
without the knowledge of the authorities, giving to him
the next day the medicine I brought from my friend doctor,
and whether it worked wonders or not, he was restored
to health. Another thing fresh in my memory is that No.
90 was full of fun and mischief. I felt as if separated from
a lover when you started on board a tram-car from Taisho
Camp to Chikubu.[72]

Such correspondence does not fit the grain of popular understanding regarding wartime encounters between Australians and
the Japanese.

Elsewhere, at war's end, a now ex-prisoner-of-war on a work
party in Singapore sat quietly musing over the news and felt compelled to approach the Japanese guardhouse to share his billy of
tea in an effort to cheer up the guards.[73] But fraternisation was not
just an experience of prisoners. The war may have been fought in
a vicious cycle of violence but, while in some places the fighting
continued, when the surrender was signed men were by and large
curious to meet Japanese soldiers.[74] Across the region such fraternisation (still strictly forbidden under orders) between curious
groups of Australian soldiers and their former adversaries was not
unusual. Clearly, Australians were keen to learn something from
those who could speak English. They posed for photographs and
some exchanged or provided gifts of food and cigarettes. One
photograph taken by a soldier in Borneo was of a Japanese naval
officer; tears can be seen running down his cheeks. The officer
had been confronted by Australian soldiers over his First World
War service medals in the belief they had been stolen from an
Australian body. The officer then spoke in English, explaining
that he had been in the navy in the First World War, in which
his ship had provided the escort for the Australian troops who
would eventually serve on Gallipoli. He had liked the Australians,

he said, as they were friendly, and he was quite upset when their nations had gone to war.[75] So widespread were such encounters that they became of concern to the military, and instructions were issued across the region forbidding Australian troops from further fraternisation and the exchanging of gifts.[76]

Japanese prisoner of war Hirano Masuto was captured on Bougainville and later wrote to the Australian soldier who guarded him, Kenneth Cooper. From the correspondence it was obvious that the two had discussed a range of topics – and exchanged contact details – but most of all Masuto wished to thank Cooper for his compassion. 'We never forgot your many sort of kindness permanently. I think all Australians have plenty of humanity, and your treatment of us, are beyond expression. It is not flattering words, but it isn't a[n] exaggeration. We don't know a way to give presents in return.'[77] Not all Japanese prisoners were treated well by Australians, and some revelled in humiliating the defeated, but this letter demonstrates the respect that did exist between some.[78]

Despite such complex scenes, the tone of the Australian press was less subtle. The intensity, outrage and vengeful nature of the coverage of the prisoners of war following the end of the war, accompanied by images officially provided by the Department of Information of emaciated men, helped reinforce the hatred expressed in wartime racial propaganda and may well have steeled attitudes and perceptions of Asia among the wider general public into the postwar era.[79] Certainly, the complexities and diversity of the prisoner-of-war experience were not represented in such correspondence, and rarely has it done so in popular retellings. One former prisoner certainly did not agree with the reporting in the press. He wrote to his brother in September 1945, stating that he believed that the papers were 'trying to stir up enmity' against the Japanese. While he confirmed that some of the stories were true, he felt only one side was being told. Within the prison camps, he told his brother, were 'good and bad Nips'.[80] Other servicemen also strongly resented what one called 'the diet of hate' being churned out by wartime propagandists and the press.[81] Indeed, there were Australians more widely who were vehemently opposed to the so-called hate campaign run by the Department of Information aimed at drumming up support for the war. A *Sydney Morning Herald* editorial in response to the 1942 'Know Your Enemy' campaign stated that the Australian government need not emulate Dr Joseph Goebbels to get people to fight.[82] In a Gallup poll on the subject, 54 per cent of Australians surveyed opposed the campaign.[83]

If soldiers in the islands – and people at home – tended to paint the Japanese with a single brush, it appears more complex among prisoners of war, particularly those who spent time in Japan. These were men who had actually engaged with, seen and lived with, and worked alongside the Japanese people. Certainly not all ex-prisoners from Japan felt this way. One prisoner observing Japanese civilians wrote in his diary: 'they appear to be a nation of sadists'.[84] Of course, there were and are prisoners of war – or the families of prisoners – who were unable to forgive or forget.[85] The difficulties in forging an accommodation with the past were evident for Kenneth Munro. Within months of returning home, feeling rather aimless and drinking heavily, he decided to write down – warts and all – all that had happened to him from his capture on Singapore to his eventual liberation in Japan. At the beginning he expressed pity for 90 per cent of the Japanese people, despite being taught since childhood to hate the Japanese. When the war finished and he had seen the burnt-out cities, like many others he distributed among Japanese civilians the food he received from American supply drops. However, on completing his manuscript, in which he had recalled all that had happened to him over the previous four years, Munro rescinded his original feelings of pity, instead stating that these feelings were made in the exaltation of remembering the moments following liberation. He concluded that he did, after all, hate the Japanese.[86]

The prisoner unable to forgive or forget, or to articulate his immense hatred of his former adversary, is a common typecast, but it is not a reflection of all. The experiences of prisoners of war and their engagement with the people of Asia were far more dynamic, far more complex. In a large survey conducted in the 2000s among veterans and families affected by the war a majority, including half of the ex-prisoners surveyed, proclaimed to carry no anti-Japanese sentiment.[87] Some had mellowed in their views or changed attitudes over the decades since the war but, as we have seen from the evidence detailed here, some had formed their opinions much earlier. Undeniably, prisoners of war – even if representing a minority of veterans or the Australian community at large – were among the first to break down barriers. For these reasons the cordial contacts between Australian soldiers and Asian communities – including ordinary Japanese citizens – during the Second World War are significant, for they go against the grain of how people generally view the attitudes of returned prisoners toward Asia. Perhaps, as Allan Chick, an ex-prisoner who returned to Japan with the British Commonwealth Occupation Force and later married a Japanese nurse, pointed out in a letter home to his mother: 'It's a funny thing but the people back home who never actually contacted the Nips are more hostile than the chaps who fought them.'[88]

Confining the prisoner-of-war experience to the Anzac narrative in which Australian mateship was key to survival ignores the important contacts and relationships developed between the Australians and others. Likewise, dwelling on the racism of postwar Australia serves little purpose and tells audiences little they do not ordinarily know. Without ignoring the cruelties and brutality of the war, delving into the complexities of the Australian Second World War experience in Asia provides a richer narrative of the diverse outlooks that existed toward the peoples of the region.

7

AT WAR'S END
Facing the new Asia

As the war came to an end, Australian soldiers witnessed events that would shape the region and the world for decades to come. Importantly, in viewing the civil unrest and nationalist power struggles between the imperial powers and independence movements, a real, newfound understanding of Asian political affairs is evident – no matter an individual's political views. During the war the 7th and 9th divisions had taken part in campaigns on Borneo at Balikpapan, Tarakan and North Borneo. When the war ended, these Australians in the Netherlands East Indies found themselves in the unexpected position of re-establishing European colonial order in the face of a local independence movement quick to assert its position in the power vacuum created by the sudden surrender of Japan and the absence of the Dutch. Elsewhere in the region, freed prisoners of war were also witnesses to civil unrest and disorder in the wake of Japan's defeat. Firsthand observance of such events ensured that many of the troops became well informed – if not better informed than other Australians – as to the political affairs shaping the region. It also led to the formation of strong opinions regarding imperialism in Asia, independence movements, and some of the bigger questions regarding why the war had been fought. In this way, we can see awakening a burgeoning awareness and knowledge of Asian affairs among a broad section of the Australian population.

In Japan, Australian prisoners saw the birth of the atomic age. On 9 August 1945 at Nagasaki one group, including 24 Australian prisoners, was less than two kilometres from the epicentre of the blast. All were extremely lucky to survive; they just happened to be in their prison at the time of the blast rather than on a work party, and the bricks and mortar of the collapsed building protected them from exposure to the heat. Jack Johnson recalled:

> Suddenly there was a brilliant flash like a photographer's magnesium flash … Then came the blast with a deafening bang and I felt as though I had been kicked in the guts. I found myself gasping for breath, pinned under a lot of rubble and unable to see. The world was black. Very gradually the dust started to thin out.[1]

Another described it as being like 'jumping into a shimmery mirage that you see on the road sometimes'.[2] In the confusion that followed, many could not comprehend what had happened. Some thought it an earthquake, but as they made for the safety of nearby hills, and saw ships ablaze miles out to sea, they knew it was something else. A number of other Australian prisoners were also working in industrial sites and mines around Nagasaki or in the region of Hiroshima on 6 August. Many of them recalled variously the single B-29 bomber in the sky, the great flash, the mushroom cloud and the big wind.[3] In the days that followed at Nagasaki some Australian prisoners were tasked with searching for survivors or the remains of workers killed in the blast.[4] After their recovery by Allied forces the surviving prisoners in Japan boarded ships in Nagasaki for their long-awaited return journey to Australia. En route they passed through the ruined city. In some places the only things left standing where houses once stood were pipes and water taps.[5] Following his return home Private Bernard O'Keefe – one of the 24 Australians in Nagasaki at the time of the bomb – told reporters about the devastating scene. Speaking of the fatal effects of the raid he spoke of the horrific burns that appeared on the skins of the locals, of people with their hair falling out and with bleeding gums. The atomic bomb, he proclaimed, 'was worse than the most deadly poison gas'.[6]

On 15 August, days after the dropping of the atomic bombs, Hugh Clarke recounts that prisoners all over Japan went to work as usual. Working at a lumberyard in Fukuoka, everything stopped at noon as all the guards and workers began assembling around a loudspeaker. The prisoners did not know at the time but the Emperor of Japan was addressing his people in a radio broadcast for the first time in history. Announcing the surrender, the prisoners watched as the Japanese listeners 'stood stunned and tears rolled down their face'. It was a scene repeated and experienced by prisoners all across Japan.[7]

With the war now over, and with the temporary absence of European control, Australian military personnel stationed across Asia were among the first outsiders to witness conflict between groups attempting to take advantage of the power vacuum created by the war's abrupt end. Freed prisoners of war, in particular, found themselves in prime positions to observe the unfolding civil unrest that was to shape the future of Southeast Asia.[8] Unwittingly, Australian servicemen and servicewomen were witnessing, often firsthand, the creation of a 'new' polity.[9] In Singapore, for example, many ex-prisoners observed the fighting that took place among the Chinese and Malayan communities following the Japanese surrender. Incidents included looting and revenge killings.[10] In the meantime a handful of Australians in Malaya who had been cut off in 1942, including Sergeant Arthur Shepard, were kept hidden in jungle camps, training and fighting alongside Chinese communists until September 1945.[11] Known as the Malayan Peoples' Anti-Japanese Army during the Second World War, this was the precursor to the Malayan National Liberation Army. Better known to British Commonwealth forces as 'Communist Terrorists', it was due to the insurgency of this group that Australian forces would again be sent to the Malayan peninsula in the 1950s during the Malayan Emergency.

Elsewhere, freed prisoners observed the civil unrest escalating in Saigon and Bangkok. In Saigon, where there were over 265 Australian prisoners, Stan Gilchrist watched Vietnamese youths marching through the street clashing with the French. As the procession broke up into running skirmishes, the Vietnamese escorted the prisoners back to the safety of their camps. These prisoners had to be careful not to be mistaken for Frenchmen lest they be attacked by the Viet Minh.[12] One group of prisoners, free of their camp and looking for a meal and a beer, found themselves confronted by a much larger group of Vietnamese with sharpened bamboo spears. Once they had explained in poor French that they were not Frenchmen but Australians they were provided a great feast.[13] These Australians were witnessing the beginnings of the French Indochina War, an evolving conflict that would last in various guises until 1975 and include an Australian military deployment to South Vietnam. In Bangkok in 1945 an RAAF nurse assisting with the repatriation of ex-prisoners wrote of a harrowing experience when a night at a theatre was interrupted as fighting broke out on surrounding streets between 'Chinese communists and the Thailanders'. She remembered 'bullets and hand grenades going off right and left. All lights went out and we scurried into shelter in a large building until a temporary lull then a mad rush to the car, neck break speed out of such chaos'. The scene was apparently met with intrigue and curiosity rather than concern. 'Another experience to add to my list, it certainly was exciting', she wrote.[14] The fighting took its share of Australian casualties: within Bangkok, freed prisoner Staff Sergeant Edwin Jenkins was 'accidentally' killed in the turmoil.[15]

In fact, some members of the AIF actively supported – or even participated in – such movements. In the Netherlands East Indies, some prisoners who had been in close contact with the Indonesians during their internment were reconciled with the aims of the independence movement following the Japanese surrender. Because of their sympathies to the rebellion, Harry Medlin described how he and other prisoners were placed under virtual house arrest because of their political position until their eventual evacuation to Singapore. Elsewhere, in a camp on Sumatra, Betty Jeffrey recalled being the object of aggression as nurses gathered at a local railway station for evacuation at the end of the war. With their white skin they were obviously viewed no differently than the Dutch as a crowd gathered to make their feelings known. Violence broke out as some Japanese arrived, and eventually two of the male Australian prisoners kept the crowd at bay with a pair of revolvers.[16]

The political issues facing the region were complex, a point recognised through experience by some of the ex-prisoners. One of those was Private Bill Marshall of the 2/3rd Machine Gun Battalion, who had been captured and imprisoned on Java. Following his return to Western Australia he wrote to newspapers and spoke at self-organised public meetings about what he had learned about the Indonesian situation. Having received 'great hospitality from Indonesians' but also having been 'betrayed by those people to the Japanese' when he attempted to evade capture, Marshall felt it his duty to inform his fellow citizens of the complexities of the different Indonesian peoples, their cultures, and their divided loyalties.[17]

These were issues that became evident to the Australian soldiers who would occupy parts of the Netherlands East Indies until January 1946. Almost 50,000 Australian soldiers were stationed in Borneo at war's end. It had not been planned that Australian troops would be in charge of re-imposing the old Dutch administration post-surrender across vast regions of the Indonesian archipelago. Original planning had been that South East Asia Command (SEAC), under the command of Admiral Lord Louis Mountbatten, would take postwar responsibility for the whole of the Netherlands East Indies. However, due to the sudden and unexpected circumstances which led to the Japanese surrender on 15 August 1945, the Australian forces that had been campaigning in Borneo were ideally placed to be given the responsibility for restoring colonial rule in all of Borneo and eastern Indonesia.[18] Therefore, with very little planning, the Australians found themselves responsible for keeping the peace before the restoration of Dutch rule.[19] For a period of four to five months after the completion of hostilities Australian commanders, finding themselves caught between the feuding Indonesian nationalists and the Dutch, faced an extremely difficult task and had to deal with a variety of problems.

What made this such a delicate act was the unilateral declaration of independence by Indonesian nationalists immediately following the Japanese surrender. Having worked closely with the Japanese, these nationalist leaders, led by Dr Sukarno and Dr Mohammed Hatta, were encouraged and permitted by the Japanese to take over the government of Indonesia prior to the surrender. The Indonesian underground movement, on the other hand, which did not want to be seen to be given independence by the Japanese, had been organising a series of uprisings against the occupation. However, the sudden end to the war meant that the Japanese army remained in control until the formal surrender took place in Tokyo Bay on 2 September. Pre-empting this, on 17 August Indonesian leaders broadcast a declaration of independence. By the end of the month they had formed a cabinet, with Sukarno proclaimed as the President of the Republic of Indonesia.

On the ground, Australian commanders had to choose whether to use their own troops to suppress any outbreaks of violence or to extend some form of recognition to moderate nationalists who may have some influence over the armed republicans.[20] General Sir Thomas Blamey, the commander of the Australian army, was told by Mountbatten that Allied forces were to deal only with the Japanese, and that the Indonesians were to be given no grounds to think that the occupying force recognised their claim to independence.[21]

Indeed, Allied forces across the region faced quite a dilemma.

Indian soldiers arriving on Java were faced with the distasteful task of policing an anti-colonial revolutionary movement. Within Vietnam, the British forces restoring order on behalf of the French re-armed the Japanese in order to keep control away from Ho Chi Minh's revolutionary movement. Given the size of the area the Australian forces were to occupy, they too would rely on the defeated Japanese – 180,000 strong across Indonesia – to continue to administer and maintain order in areas yet to be brought under Australian or Dutch control, and also to guard valuable stockpiles of food and supplies.[22]

Given the fragility of the situation, Australian troops were issued with strict instructions that their role was to maintain law and order so as to prepare for the resumption of the Netherlands East Indies government and to prevent disease. Soldiers were not to communicate with leaders of the Free Indonesia Movement (FIM) – as the Australians called the republicans – except for the purposes of maintaining the peace, as anything else might be interpreted as recognition. It was recommended that 'displays other than recognised national flags' and the wearing of 'special emblems' should be neither authorised nor forbidden by AIF commanders, who were told to 'adopt an impartial attitude'. Additionally, processions and demonstrations were not to be allowed in areas occupied by Australian troops.[23]

Amid such an environment, it was understandable that the occupation proved a difficult job. A review of the 7th Division's unit diaries reveals the problems faced by Australian troops. On 10 October, following the implementation of the surrender by the Japanese force, the AIF was informed that the FIM intended to hold a political demonstration and raise their flag. In the interests of peace and security, Lieutenant Colonel E.M. Robson, commander of the 2/31st Battalion at Balikpapan, issued orders to the leader of the movement stating that there would be no raising of flags, no large-scale demonstrations, and no distribution of 'subversive' political pamphlets. The FIM leader agreed to these orders and, as a token gesture for his co-operation, minor processions and the wearing of rosettes in the Indonesian national colours were permitted.[24] Such cooperation was not universal. Despite similar orders issued in November by Major A.C. Robertson, commanding the 2/25th Battalion at Samarinda, and guarantees and assurances made by the FIM leaders, a rally went ahead. On news of this, AIF troops were dispatched to restore order, but the gathering dispersed before their arrival.[25]

South Sulawesi in the Celebes proved to be the major trouble spot in the Australian area of control. Brigadier Ivan Dougherty, the commander of the 21st Brigade (made up of the 2/14th, 2/16th and 2/27th battalions) and effectively the military governor of the Celebes, proved a good man for the situation.[26] His correspondence with Indonesian leaders demonstrated his care and diplomatic skill. In a speech to Indonesian youth leaders on 16 October he outlined that, while the United Nations had made the Netherlands Indies Civilian Administration (NICA) responsible for the re-establishment of the Dutch colonial government, the international community had no desire to prevent Indonesians from occupying positions of trust. 'It is not for me to differentiate between anybody, who is eligible to come into government. I am sure everything will be well if the people are patient.'[27] This echoed an earlier plea in a speech delivered to village chieftains. Dougherty acknowledged, 'I am not allowed to talk to you about politics, as I am just a soldier', and could promise only that the United Nations would establish the 'right government at the right time'. What he did make clear, however, was that the NICA was the only administration currently recognised by the occupation force.[28]

In a gesture of goodwill at Parepare in the South Sulawesi, the 2/14th Battalion organised a friendly soccer match between them and the local side. This provided an opportunity for a public display that could not be passed on by the Indonesians. The match was therefore preceded by a procession to the stadium through

An Australian soldier stands on guard in front of a
2000-strong crowd attending a speech by Brigadier
Ivan Dougherty at Makassar in September 1945. In his
speech, Dougherty made it clear to the Indonesians that
the occupying force did not recognise their claim to
independence. However, while the Australian army played an
important role in restoring Dutch rule, individual Australian
soldiers formed their own opinions regarding Indonesian
independence and European colonialism in Asia.
Australian War Memorial 119406

the city streets, headed by the local team. Flags waved and red-and-white badges were proudly worn. At the stadium the 2/14th representatives awaited. Once the procession finished the match got under way in good faith. Following a 'very good display of football' in which the teams were locked for a two-all draw, Captain Edward Clarke diplomatically addressed the crowd. While the battalion had 'thoroughly enjoyed the match', he had to point out that in line with the Australian forces' policy he disagreed with the fact that the event had been used to hold a political rally.[29]

A less-diplomatic, no-nonsense approach was adopted by Captain Jack Gerke of the 2/16th Battalion. Gerke was not political but was determined to fulfil his orders, and as the primary objective was to oversee the restoration of Dutch authority, he felt 'the quickest way was to pinch the independence thing in the bud'. No expression of nationalism by the local Raja was tolerated by Gerke, and when Indonesian flags were raised, his men immediately pulled them down. Indeed, on several occasions the flags were deliberately destroyed by Australian soldiers in front of the crowds. When the nationalist leader Dr Ratulangie – who had been designated the governor of the Celebes by the republicans in Java – attempted to address a meeting of between 500 and 1000 people, Gerke went immediately to the scene in a jeep with four or five troops and unceremoniously escorted Ratulangie out the door. Despite such an unsubtle approach, relations between the Australians and Indonesians remained genial.[30]

In other places, such as at Gorontalo in the northern Celebes, a strong local Indonesian leader refused to meet with the Australian commander. With some 600 followers being drilled outside of town, and with boycotts of Chinese and Arab communities, it was decided to remove the local leader by shipping him off to Manado. As a means of maintaining the peace this course of action proved effective, and a satisfactory agreement was soon reached with his followers.[31] In locations such as Sumbawa and

Flores the Australians did all they could to downplay potential problems in an effort to convince the Dutch that there were no impediments to their return – this was done in the hope that the diggers might be allowed to return home before Christmas.[32]

In southern Borneo and South Sulawesi the occupying forces faced a number of undesirable and difficult situations. Many examples are evident within 7th Division unit diaries from October to December 1945. These include the witnessing of bashings and killings by extremists of Dutch, Ambonese or Chinese nationality for offences such as removing political posters; intervening in Dutch and Indonesian confrontations, such as when a 45-strong gang armed with knives and spears ambushed an NICA jeep; investigating the murders of NICA officers, police and civilians; and recovering stolen weapons. In places such as Banjarmasin, the Australians resorted to protecting the Dutch flag from FIM demonstrators under armed guard (it was a practice to tear down the Dutch flag and remove the blue strip, leaving behind the red-and-white of Indonesia). A degree of tact and diplomacy was always required considering that small (though well-armed) patrols were often heavily outnumbered. In Banjarmasin, for example, a group of 500 armed Indonesians demanded that an NICA patrol hand over their weapons and leave the Indonesians to their own affairs.[33]

The most significant incidents occurred in the major centres of Makassar (which had a population of nearly 100,000), in the centre of power in the Celebes and South Sulawesi, and in Parepare, the second city of South Sulawesi. On 2 October in Makassar, undisciplined Dutch troops fired on Indonesians wearing republican colours. Reprisal killings of Ambonese and Dutch citizens followed. The presence of Ambonese, who were Christians, within the Dutch colonial forces was also a source of tension for Indonesian Muslims. On the night of 15–16 October, large gangs of young Indonesians roamed the city and, after a bloody night of violence, dozens were left dead and wounded. One member of the 2/27th Battalion recalled that on several occasions these gangs 'swept through the white quarters killing as they went'.[34] Days later, similar scenes began in Parepare.

The Australians therefore found themselves mediating to defuse tensions. Such an example occurred in the Gowa region, South Sulawesi, where the AIF acted as intermediaries between the Dutch, nationalists and local rajas in an attempt to bring under control groups armed with grenades and firearms who threatened and intimidated anybody who co-operated with the NICA.[35] Communication was a key issue when negotiating with local leaders; at times local Indigenous dialects had to be translated into Malay, then from Malay into English.[36] Misunderstandings could have consequences. The Australians acted as intermediaries not only between Indonesians and the Dutch but also between Indonesians and the Japanese, and in areas where villages remained under Japanese administration the refusal to co-operate with the NICA was well organised.[37] In other circumstances Australians had to investigate and discipline overzealous Japanese guards – enlisted to protect important supplies and stores from looting – for mistreating Indonesians. They also had to investigate reports of the Japanese hiding weapons in areas still occupied by Japanese troops. Such investigations clearly relied on tip-offs from and guidance by Indonesians.

As the Australians attempted to keep the peace, casualties occurred on both sides. In an incident in which a patrol by members of the 2/27th Battalion was attacked by a gang wielding swords and knives, more than a dozen members of a group of 'free Indonesians' were killed and one Australian soldier was wounded, the latter having been slashed on the neck and arms.[38] In such a politically strained environment, actions had repercussions. In response to the deaths incurred while fighting the 2/27th patrol, extremists within the Indonesian movement took reprisal against innocent Ambonese civilians.[39]

After nearly two months of occupation, the battalion commanders of the 21st Brigade based around Makassar convened to outline a set of guidelines to advise their troops. However, there could be 'no hard and fast rules ... for the conduct of troops in dealing with civil disturbances'. Invariably, in each and every case it was recognised that circumstances varied, and therefore it was agreed that 'the officer in command on the spot must exercise his discretion'. The unnecessary use of force could lead to provocation, the guidelines warned.[40] Significant responsibilities, therefore, particularly in an environment they were not accustomed to, fell on the shoulders of junior officers and NCOs. Following incidents such as the aforementioned attack on Dutch and Ambonese residents in Parepare, Australian commanders negotiated with nationalist leaders and local rajas to help cool tensions. However, as a meeting between Brigadier Chilton and Dr Ratulangie made clear, discussion and negotiation 'did NOT imply any recognition of Ratulangie as the leader of any political party'.[41] It was quite the balancing act. As Brigadier Dougherty later noted, 'the spirit of unrest' made for a difficult task. The situation was explosive, and could be 'likened to a powder keg filled with political dynamite'. So well did the 21st Brigade perform during its period in South Sulawesi that Dougherty believed it was through them that a tragedy was avoided.[42]

Overall, the Australians did a good job in maintaining the peace while caught between conflicting groups. While the situation was perhaps more tenuous in Java, where the British were in open conflict with republicans, the fact that such an outbreak of violence did not occur in the Australian areas of occupation is a credit to the leadership displayed by commanders on the ground. In performing their duties, the Australians' brief occupation played an important role in restoring Dutch colonial rule. Furthermore, confrontation with such a situation gave the troops an important grounding in the politics that were to shape the region, no matter whether they were impartial observers or more favourably aligned with either the Indonesians or the Dutch.

It is clear that Australian soldiers on the ground were concerned by their intervention in affairs that they believed required resolution at the highest diplomatic level, especially considering that, given the delicate circumstance, the smallest action could have dire and wider consequences.[43] In the days, weeks, and months following the Japanese defeat, no soldier wanted to become a casualty in somebody else's conflict; they simply wanted to return home safely. Therefore, it does not seem unusual that soldiers looked to somebody for blame. This role, overwhelmingly, was filled by the Dutch. Increasingly, Australians felt that Dutch actions were provoking the Indonesian situation, heightening tensions and therefore placing Australian troops at greater risk. It was the Australians, after all, who would have to intervene in a riot, or worse. Some of this blame, Dougherty believed, lay with the 'old hands' – the Dutch colonials. Having been shut off from global affairs during the occupation and only recently released from internment camps, these former colonists could not appreciate the changes that had taken place. They wanted an immediate reversion to antebellum times. 'The situation in 1945 required such an appreciation of those changes', according to Dougherty, and could have been handled with greater tact had the Netherlands sent out new administrators mindful of the change. Also, when 'old hands' who had suffered internment considered an Indonesian's behaviour during or after the occupation to be treacherous it created a poisonous atmosphere.[44]

On the other hand, Australians either could not or did not distinguish between Indonesians who had and had not worked alongside the Japanese. What is certain is that widespread antipathy toward Dutch officers clearly existed among Australian soldiers. Although the soldiers generally knew little about the Indonesians, bad experiences with Dutch officers could result in their siding with the Indonesian cause despite orders to the contrary. Reid believes that the anti-Dutch stories told by practically 'every Australian soldier' who served in Indonesia may have resulted

Members of the 2/27th Battalion trade with locals at Makassar in September 1945. For some soldiers, contact with local communities helped inform their views on Asian affairs and Australia's role and place in the region.
Australian War Memorial 120834

from battle-hardened soldiers resenting being given instruction by 'know-all' foreign civilians in brand new Allied uniforms who had been given the rank of officers in the NICA. To many Australians, the Dutch colonials appeared arrogant, hierarchic and pretentious. They further disliked proclamations from the Dutch that Indonesia was theirs and, as in Malaya and elsewhere in 1941, also resented attempts by the colonial authorities to prevent or manage relations between Australians and Asians.[45]

Additionally, a common view among Australian soldiers was that the Dutch had done little to defend the island chains, and that this had imperilled Australia itself.[46] The Australians, desperate to return home at war's end, also resented being charged with overseeing the peace until the islands' eventual return to Dutch control. In particular, Australian troops resented Dutchmen intervening when Australians and Indonesians fraternised. While orders were in place to bar Australian troops from fraternising with the locals, these were widely ignored by the Australians. In policing these orders, however, there were instances when medical supplies given to Indonesians by Australians were confiscated by NICA forces and the recipients of such aid were punished with imprisonment or hard labour.[47] Such actions did not endear Australian witnesses to the Dutch cause.

Further discrediting the Dutch, rumours spread among Australian troops in the Indies that Dutch officials were complaining about the extent of the damage following bombardments at the landing sites of Balikpapan and Tarakan, and were seeking compensation for damages.[48] Less diplomatic in his private diary than in his official history, Gavin Long wrote: 'The Dutch are most resentful about the damage that has been done, an extraordinary attitude considering that they are getting back their Indies – a vastly more productive area than Australia – practically undamaged, after having done little to defend it and less to recapture it.'[49] While the claims for compensation were only rumour, that they had currency suggests that, as seen in Malaya and New Guinea, such claims were a source of bitterness among those who had done the fighting and the dying. It raised questions about for whom and why they had fought. With such dissatisfaction directed toward the Dutch, and with the Indonesians seeking support, what effects might such rumours have had on the troops' outlooks?

A group of Indonesian district leaders in South Sulawesi appealed to the Australians – whom they acknowledged as the only force charged with maintaining peace and order – that the NICA's 'intention was to take over the Civil Administration with force'. They also alleged that Dutch troops had been identifying themselves as part of the Australian army in order to gain access to food supplies. Stating their belief that 'Dutch suppression was being carried out now in contrary to the Atlantic Charter in particular [and] to democracy in general', they called the 21st Brigade to send Australian soldiers to their region 'and not NICA soldiers'.[50]

To what degree dislike of the Dutch among Australians led to sympathy towards Indonesians is unclear. However, for the small minority of communists in the ranks of the 7th Division who were actively pro-independence it was a cause for which they could attempt to generate broader support within the division. In one example, a communist-initiated petition on behalf of Indonesians was said to have been signed by 80 diggers at Balikpapan.[51] One historian has estimated that 4000 members of the Communist Party of Australia were serving in the Australian armed forces in 1945. Of this figure, some 1400 were serving within the 7th and 9th divisions. Others were among headquarters and education services, or within the air force. Members or sympathisers within the RAAF provided a service as couriers, bringing leaflets, pamphlets and instructions from Indonesian organisations working in Australia. Once it was on the ground there were men in the AIF who would help with the distribution of such propaganda. Advice on political and military tactics was also given to the republicans by these Australian soldiers.[52]

Indeed, the 7th Division was, to use the words of the official historian, 'embarrassed' when on the morning of 14 November between 6000 and 8000 Indonesians assembled for a demonstration within the NICA compound at Balikpapan. There they raised flags and banners and displayed their emblems. What proved embarrassing for the AIF was not so much that the demonstration took place but the presence of a group of ten to 15 Australian soldiers pro-actively supporting the movement by 'inciting' the Indonesians. The demonstration was broken up by Dutch troops; however, the Australian antagonists disappeared before the AIF provosts arrived, so the identities and the motives of these men remain clouded.[53] Such scenes were not isolated incidents. In similar circumstances at Tarakan, a small group of Australian communists in the ranks of the 9th Division organised a rally and distributed pamphlets. An instigator there was later identified as Corporal Ernie Foyle of the 2/11th Field Ambulance, but having already returned home to Australia his identification came too late for him to face disciplinary action. His accomplice was an unknown airman.[54]

One soldier whose motives for his activities as a CPA member in Indonesia are known is John Cohen. Cohen helped distribute pamphlets printed by pro-independence groups back in Australia. The pamphlets claimed to be written in the official voice of Allied policy. Cohen, however, was not one of the individuals at the demonstration at Balikpapan; he had transferred to Makassar in the hope for more 'interesting action'. There he met Dr Ratulangie (who had been educated in Zurich and spoke Cohen's native German), as well as other nationalist leaders.[55]

The Dutch may well have been aggrieved by the situation surrounding their return to the Indies. First, they found themselves the junior partners to the Australians. Before the official return to Dutch control, the NICA was an agent and its actions the responsibility of the AIF. The official position of the Australians, who held legal jurisdiction as agreed upon by Blamey and Dougherty, was that arrests would 'NOT be made for political reasons, but for inciting to break law and order'.[56] Following the clash between Indonesians and the Dutch and Ambonese in Makassar in mid-

October, Dougherty exerted his authority over the Dutch by placing restrictions on the NICA, local police, and the Royal Netherlands Indies Army (RNIA) carrying arms. He also ordered that no NICA or RNIA personnel 'interfere with or remove any badge or emblem worn by any person'.[57] To the Dutch, who during their reign of the Indies had not allowed Indonesians to form political groups or unions, the Australians must have appeared overly lenient.

Furthermore, the Dutch claimed that some Australian soldiers were providing arms to the republicans. This was an allegation that was formally acknowledged at the time by the public relations department for the army. Returning soldiers in 1946 admitted that substantial quantities of light arms and ammunition from Australian stockpiles had 'fallen into the hands' of republicans. With the war over, authorities did not maintain strict inventories, and relaxed guards on munitions stocks apparently turned a blind eye.[58] The 21st Brigade command was aware of and clearly concerned by such developments, reporting in November on the number of Australian, Allied and enemy arms and equipment illegally passing into civilian hands. With the weapons received by 'barter and otherwise', the Brigade made clear that it was more than black-market activity that fuelled these transactions. Directly implicating Australian involvement, it added that members of the AIF had been detected making such trades.[59] While these likely involved a minority of troops stationed in the region, Lockwood asserts that such was the extent of Australian soldiers' sympathy toward the Indonesian movement more broadly that it influenced political decision making on whether Australian troops should be sent to Java to intervene in the conflict there between SEAC and the republican movement.[60]

Other servicemen got themselves involved in other ways. In October 1945 the ship's company of HMAS *Manoora*, repatriating from Australia to Java nearly 1000 Indonesian refugees who had first been transported by the Dutch from the Netherlands

East Indies to Australia on their retreat from the islands in 1942, refused requests by armed Dutch soldiers to hand over the passengers to Dutch jurisdiction on arrival. What made this matter delicate was the presence of political prisoners within the group. Having become friendly with the Indonesians during the voyage, *Manoora*'s company was determined to hand its passengers over to the care of the republican government. When faced with the Dutch demands *Manoora*'s captain, Alan Paterson Cousin (who was notably described by his crew as an arch-conservative), contacted a nearby Gurkha regiment that had landed at Batavia to request that the Gurkhas escort the repatriates under guard to republican territory (almost 100 kilometres away). Furthermore, the Dutch were given a stern warning that the Australian sailors were prepared to break out their weapons to ensure their orders were obeyed. These Indonesians later spoke of their gratitude, paying tribute to the actions of Cousin and his crew.[61]

Australian soldiers who were active trade unionists also supported what became known as the 'black bans' on Dutch shipping. This was an anti-Dutch and pro-Indonesian stance widely adopted by the Australian union movement.[62] In Sydney Australian soldiers and airmen joined Indian seamen in their protest march from the Lido Hotel (which had been occupied by Indian and Indonesian seamen) across the Harbour Bridge to the city offices of Dutch shipping firm KPM. Described by Lockwood as the 'first great demonstration by Asians ever seen on the streets of Sydney', the presence of Australian servicemen in the movement is clearly noticeable in the 1948 documentary film *Indonesia Calling*, which featured images of (and re-enacted) some of these events. In one scene, soldiers can be seen holding placards with inscriptions such as: 'We fought side by side [for] Freedom.'[63] Indeed, to what degree sympathy existed more widely among Australian troops is hard to define. One soldier reflected after the war that the Australians' 'sympathies lay with the Indonesian people. It seemed to us that if these people, who had endured the barbarity of the Japanese occupation, and also the violence and barbarity of our invasion, should now have no right to freedom, then we are condoning a crime'.[64]

Certainly, anecdotal evidence suggests that Indonesians themselves saw a difference between the Dutch colonials and the men who had liberated the islands from the Japanese. While it was at first 'extremely difficult to explain the relationship between NICA and the AMF', an Australian report proclaimed, the Indonesians soon 'separated the two identities'.[65] This appears, on surface, to be true. Ali Alatas, future Indonesian foreign minister, was a young teenager when the Australian soldiers arrived in his village in 1945. He would often recall that their slouch hats caught his eye, and was surprised when the diggers waved and smiled at the villagers: this was something that neither the Dutch nor the Japanese had ever done.[66] Another example is the story of a nationalist in Balikpapan who stated that his happiest memory of the Australians was when an exhibition soccer match in which the Australians were defeating a Dutch team ended in a massive brawl, with the Indonesian spectators cheering wildly for the Aussies.[67]

Furthermore, as the Indonesians lived in a society in which dissidents were denied many democratic rights, some believed that because Australian unions favoured the republic the Australian Army must naturally be on their side as well. Such attitudes lessened over time as it was realised that the AIF was actually restoring Dutch rule. However, this initial view is evident in a letter from local rajas which offered Dougherty 'cordial thanks for the sympathetic attitude of a great part of the Australian people regarding the movement for national freedom of the Indonesians'.[68] In locations such as the Celebes, where the 2/14th Battalion had come to turn a blind eye to Dutch violence and were themselves arresting republicans, and where machine-guns were set up for no other purpose but to discourage the showing of political support, retaliatory attacks were planned against the AIF by the independence movement. These would certainly have taken place if not for sympathetic Australian soldiers who were able to persuade the republicans to call off the attacks by drawing upon the goodwill created by the 'black bans' against the Dutch back in Australia.[69] In contrast to affairs in the Netherlands East Indies, in neighbouring British North Borneo the 9th Division was honoured by the inclusion of a heraldic image representing the division upon that state's coat of arms.

Wider Australian sympathies for the independence movement in South Sulawesi appeared to wane following several incidents. The first was when whole families of Ambonese were murdered by radical gangs in revenge attacks against undisciplined Dutch colonial troops.[70] Based on a letter printed in the *Sydney Morning Herald* from a soldier in South Sulawesi, it was reported that an Australian soldier was killed trying to defend Ambonese and Dutch residents from such attacks. The author of the letter stated: 'You can inform any wharfie or unionist who happens to be supporting the Indonesian movement that they have one Australian life on their conscience so far.'[71] The basis of this letter has led historians to claim that the death of this Australian soldier led to outright hostility toward the independence movement and its supporters. Reid even identified the soldier killed as belonging to the 2/14th Battalion at Parepare, and a mate of the anonymous letter-writer.[72] However, as there are no records of an Australian soldier being killed by nationalists during this period (the only member of the 2/14th Battalion killed during the occupation was in a jeep accident on 25 December), it is possible the unidentified soldiers' claims were based on rumour, perhaps following an assault.[73] Regardless, the emotion and sentiment expressed in the letter stand. A similar change in attitudes by Australian troops was noted by the Dutch military commander for Borneo and East Indonesia, who commented on how the Australian garrison had come to fully support the Dutch administration at Makassar after an Australian sentry was struck a single blow to the head.[74] These incidents should not be confused with a later incident in which three Australian war crimes investigators – Squadron Leader Frederick Birchall, Flight Lieutenant Hector McDonald and Captain Alistair Mackenzie – were murdered by Indonesian extremists on Java in April 1946. These incidents occurred after the occupation force had returned to Australia in February.

More broadly, across the straits in Java the British responses to the Indonesians were unflinching following the death on 30 October of Brigadier A.W.S. Mallaby, who was shot at point-blank range in his staff car by an Indonesian during the battle of Surabaya. Exacerbating tensions and hardening opinions, Mallaby's death was widely reported in the press as a murder, an assassination, and an atrocity. In Australia, conservative political leaders such as Arthur Fadden used the incident to discredit political opponents who may support or sympathise with the Indonesian cause and remind them of the continuing danger that faced Australian soldiers in the Indies.[75] It is unclear if any of these incidents – whether they were based on truth or rumour – were the decisive factor, but whatever the catalyst it is clear from the records that the Australian stance in South Sulawesi hardened from early November. By December there was little confidence in the FIM in South Sulawesi among the wider populace as the movement's activities were limited to extremists working from rural areas. By this time the local rajas and village leaders had signed their allegiance to the AMF and, by extension, the NICA administration.[76] From this point until the end of the Australian occupation in February 1946, events passed by peacefully.

The examples of the various issues facing the men of the AIF in restoring European colonial rule in the Netherlands East Indies are important episodes in Australian history. First, we see contradictions between Australian official positions – as demonstrated by the role the AIF was ordered to play in paving the way for a return to Dutch control – and the actual ideas and attitudes of individuals on the ground. Importantly, as Reid notes, an Australian government that professed sympathies for the Indonesian cause did little to guide soldiers in the field as to how these sympathies may have been promoted. Instead, the Australians played a pivotal role in the restoration of Dutch rule in the areas in which they were stationed, and this ultimately contributed to a gulf between the two halves of Indonesia.[77] Secondly, and most importantly, the newly released ex-prisoners and the men stationed across Indonesia were witnesses to the powerful political forces that would shape the region in the decades to come. Their experiences demonstrate – whether individuals took a neutral stance or held a political position one way or the other – the existence of a growing awareness and understanding of Asian affairs.

But outlooks remain complex. Did the different colonial structures in place affect the behaviour and outlook of soldiers entering particular regions? Where Australians had reacted in particular ways to British colonial society in Southeast Asia, and in regions of Australian colonial rule in New Guinea, were reactions in the Netherlands East Indies responses to Dutch colonialism in particular? Was there a feeling that the Australians, and to a lesser degree the British, made better colonisers? Would soldiers with Indonesian sympathies act and behave the same way toward locals if found in similar circumstances in New Guinea or Malaya?

What can be determined, as will be dealt with in the following chapter, is that there were men in the AIF who had by the end of the war – and some as early as 1942 – adopted a political position in regard to these issues. Some were clearer and more forthright in their views than official government policy at this time. Significantly, discussions of Asia were strongly linked to soldiers' debates about some of the big issues and ideas emanating from the conflict, such as why the war had been fought (as officially outlined by the Western powers within the Atlantic Charter) and the creation of the United Nations Charter in order to establish a lasting peace. If changes in attitudes to race and racism were ambiguous within the encounter between the AIF and Asia then

a newfound awareness of the region can be seen in the growing
knowledge, recognition and perceived importance of Asian affairs
to Australia's own national destiny.

'GOOD NEIGHBOURS' OR 'POLICE DOGS OF IMPERIALISM'?

Attitudes to empire

Australian troops arriving in Borneo and parts of the Nether-lands East Indies in 1945 often recalled the hearty welcome they received. The 7th Division's diary, for example, documents the memorable tribute given to the 2/31st Battalion by the local Chinese community of Banjarmasin. More than 8000 people, in spotless white suits and dresses with Chinese republic rosettes on their chests, stood in long banks behind giant banners inscribed with: 'Welcome Chinese Community'. Their leaders gave a personal message to the Australians:

> Our heartiest congratulations to your victory. We greet you heartily on your safe entry into this city to free us from the tyranny and savagery of the Japanese. They killed many of our best people. We have lived every day afraid of arrest, torture and death. Today we live. We thank you heartily.

As the battalion marched toward the heart of the city, Chinese lined the streets waving flags and holding banners inscribed with the word 'welcome'. Also along this route it was reported that a laughing and excited crowd of Indonesians waved British and American flags. The following day cheering throngs of Indonesians and Chinese also surrounded the surrender ceremony, and as the Australians marched off to the music of bagpipes and kettle drums the crowds followed with wild cheers of joy.[1]

Similar scenes were repeated elsewhere. At Kuching a double celebration was held to commemorate the Allied victory and the Chinese national day (Double Ten Day) on 10 October 1945. The Chinese community and the AIF organised a series of concerts, displays of craft, and sports meetings in celebration.[2] In Sarawak the Australians threw a party for the people after liberation. 'Fellows made swings and slippery dips and we had races,' Bill Corey recalled. 'Cooks made thousands of lollies and cakes, buns and everything. And that was the first time those kids had ever really laughed.'[3] Even in the trouble spot of South Sulawesi the Australians met similar scenes. Captain Jack Reddin of the 2/27th Battalion remembered with great fondness the 'ecstatic' crowd as his jeep nosed through the cheering throngs at Kendari. It was 'a most moving experience', recalled Reddin, 'faces beaming, many crying, they rained thousands upon thousands of flowers and flower petals over and into the car. The eyes blur a bit, even now'.[4] When the Australians left, in a number of places units were presented with banners and pennants as farewell gifts. One banner presented by the people of Beaufort in North Borneo – where the Australians had rebuilt the local school – was inscribed with the message (written in Chinese): 'During this war, our educational institutions were destroyed to nothing by the Japanese Army ... The recovery of our education system depended on the Australian military giving us the greatest sympathy and help.' Another pennant thanked 'the friendly Australian Army'.[5] Amid such goodwill, Australia's official role in the Indies of re-establishing European colonial rule led to major debates among troops as to why the war had been fought, demonstrating the development of the Australian soldiers' important new understandings of Asian affairs.

In the course of current debates about the growing movement for the commemoration and celebration of the so-called 'battle for Australia', an Australian nationalist perspective has emerged asserting that the war was fought in the Pacific so that Australia

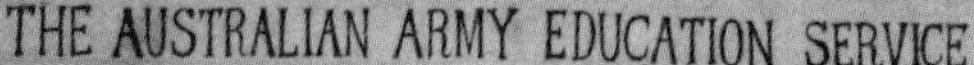

THE AUSTRALIAN ARMY EDUCATION SERVICE.

THE STAFF AND PUPILS OF THE BEAUFORT PUBLIC SCHOOL. HAVE MUCH PLEASURE IN PRESENTING THIS SMALL GIFT AS A TOKEN OF APPRECIATION FOR THE RESTORATION OF EDUCATION IN BEAUFORT.

THE BEAUFORT PUBLIC SCHOOL,
BEAUFORT, NORTH BORNEO.
28th Oct. 1945.

在這次戰爭中，我們教育的設施，悉被日本軍破壞無遺．

澳洲軍第九師二十四旅克復保佛後，蒙軍事部關懷我們的教育，設立民衆學校一所，給我們作教育之研討．

我們教育的復興，端賴澳洲軍團給我們以最大同情與幫助．我們敢不感激．

這小小的禮物，藉表我們的熱誠和感謝！

北婆羅洲保佛民衆學校敬贈

This banner was presented by the local Chinese community to Australian soldiers in North Borneo in 1945 in appreciation for the Australians' efforts in reopening a local school and restoring education in the community following the Japanese occupation.
Australian War Memorial RELAWM20254

and Australian freedoms could be saved from Japanese invasion. The view that Australians were defending the nation from a planned Japanese invasion – now officially recognised each year on the first Wednesday of September – is strongly criticised by historian Peter Stanley, who states that 'if Australians fought for anyone' it was for such Asians as those mentioned in anecdotes by soldiers; those who had endured three-and-a-half years of the Japanese occupation.[6] Critics have been quick to jump on what they call the idealism of Stanley's claims –that Australians should celebrate the contribution the nation played toward the defeat of fascism and global struggle for democracy (and for freedom of speech, freedom of worship and freedom from fear) – by citing the role the AIF played in returning much of Asia to colonial rule. If Stanley 'thinks the war was about fighting Japanese tyranny and liberating Southeast Asia, someone should tell the Malays, Vietnamese, Timorese and Indonesians', said a letter-writer to *The Age*. 'If anything, we were fighting to reimpose the colonial tyranny they laboured under before the Japanese invasion.'[7] However, despite criticisms, there is no doubt that some troops were fighting for exactly the reasons Stanley gives. The difference in opinion between officials – as demonstrated by the Australian government and the role played by the army – and individual soldiers is more dynamic and complex.

Furthermore, within Australian popular memory there has been a tendency to lay the blame for anti-Asian sentiment at the feet of returning soldiers after the Second World War. In their discovery of Asia and the Pacific – and as a possible result of their interactions with the people, cultures, colonial institutions and power structures of the region – a burgeoning political awareness of Asia was clearly beginning to form among Australian soldiers by the end of the war. No matter their political stance on a particular issue, in their diaries, letters and correspondence to forums such as *Salt* magazine Australian soldiers can be seen engaging in and responding to debates about Asian independence movements,

colonialism and a range of opinions regarding Australia's position
and role in the future of the region. How wide these opinions
really were remains difficult to determine, although they were certainly not uncommon. The development of some of these views
can be seen to be germinating among troops in Asia as early as
1942. However, with the announcements of the Atlantic Charter
(1941), the Declaration by United Nations (1942) and the United
Nations Charter (1945), as well as an increase in Australian troop
activity in the south-west Pacific and Netherlands East Indies by
the completion of hostilities in 1945, these issues became increasingly important to soldiers who had developed a personal interest in regional affairs. In essence, the soldiers were debating why
they believed the war had been fought, and these were debates in
which the issue of colonialism in Asia was at the forefront.

Just as politicians were directing Australia away from its reliance on Britain by forming a more independent outlook on world
affairs, the soldiers who had served or were currently serving in
the region quite naturally debated the merits of such government
posturing and policy, and their musings crowded the pages of *Salt*,
the monthly publication produced by the Army Education Unit.
This publication has been underutilised by historians. By 1944
it had a circulation of 185,000 copies, with which, if multiplied
by the estimated number of three readers per copy – as *Salt* was
intended to be shared among the troops – it may have reached a
significant audience of over half a million servicemen and servicewomen. It was never made available to the general public; therefore, soldiers who read the journal were probably better informed
on war and postwar issues than Australian civilians back home
who, at the time, had access to only limited reports in local newspapers and brief radio broadcasts. One important area in which
Salt differed from other AIF newspapers was the inclusion of editorial content. Although the journal was supposedly neutral in
its party politics, it was accused by both sides of parliament for
its content and alleged bias.[8] Significantly, the debates in *Salt*

demonstrated that some soldiers were knowledgeable and opinionated on the issues of decolonisation and Asian affairs, issues that were unlikely to have been on the political agenda for these men before the war.

Within the pages of *Salt*, from as early as 1942 soldiers began debating a series of issues regarding Australia's future role in the region, Australia's relations with Asia, and the future of the Asian nations. Australian racism, for example, was one hotly debated topic. Some Australian soldiers abhorred the habitual racism of their compatriots toward the people of the region. One letter took issue with a verse previously published in the magazine which had included the line 'no Yellow force on victory shall elate'. The author felt that if such an assertion were true then Australia must surely face defeat:

> This gratuitous insult to our great Chinese ally is typical
> of many irresponsible references made from day to day
> about the 'Yellow Peril' or those 'little Yellow –'. We are
> fighting the Japanese not because their skin is yellow, but
> because their armies are brutal aggressors, because their
> Fascist rulers are trying to extend their oppressive rule to
> our people, and to other peoples, white, black, brown and
> yellow – just as their 'white' Nazi allies are trying. In the
> Pacific arena of the world war we are fighting shoulder to
> shoulder with the courageous Chinese … Another oriental
> race, the Filipino, is fighting alongside our American allies
> … To make distinctions of race and colour is to surrender
> to the Nazi creed. We, British, American, Russians – who
> happened to be White – together with the Chinese, who
> happen to be yellow, and with Indians and Negroes will
> defeat the Fascist Axis – which includes white Nazis as
> well as Japs. But we will postpone the day of victory if
> we continue to split the unity of our alliance by ourselves
> raising fascist racial barriers.[9]

Salt's editors fully agreed with the anonymous author. In a following edition, Gunner D.E. Moffit further supported the role played by Chinese soldiers in the war against Japan. He suggested that Chinese soldiers were superior to Japanese soldiers, and implored readers not to undervalue their contribution.[10]

The White Australia policy was another hotly debated issue among soldiers. Corresponding with Evatt's defence of the White Australia policy at the United Nations conference in San Francisco (25 April to 26 June 1945), debate on the future of the contentious policy raged within the pages of *Salt*. Suggestions that Australian postwar immigration should be open only to people from European nations was strongly opposed by some Australian soldiers, some of whom served in Asia and the Pacific. Gunner M.D. McGrath, for example, was moved to respond to a letter by A.B.E. Harris which suggested 'Asiatics' be excluded from post-war immigration. McGrath felt that 'this closed door policy to particular races … fans the embers of war. It fosters mistrust and widens the gap between countries'. Believing that restrictions on immigration should apply, but not on the basis of race, McGrath felt that 'man's relationship to man is in the form of a brotherhood, disregarding pigmentation of his own skin, when he can call the world his country, we will be able to enjoy perpetual peace'.[11] Harris replied: 'Gnr McGrath advocates an influx of Asiatics. I oppose this policy.' Harris further cited the Pegging Act introduced in South Africa 'to prevent Asiatics from acquiring more property, and the expense to which South Africa is prepared to go to ship them back to India'. He believed that as a result of this situation in South Africa both races held half-castes in contempt. He also cited 'racial riots in America' to further his point of view. Furthermore, Harris recalled 'the fight our forefathers had to keep Australia white, starting against the low-living Chinese on the goldfields', and asked: 'is any man prepared to accept a coloured man as his son-in-law or boss?' If Australia was open to Asian immigration, Harris continued, 'Australians, as we know them today, would cease to exist'.[12] Captain B.H. Evans agreed with such sentiments, arguing that 'Australia would be saddling itself for a minority problem'.[13]

Concerned by such xenophobic feelings among many of his compatriots, Sergeant G.S. Brett felt that in light of the terms within the Atlantic Charter demanding a 'more equitable treatment of coloured races' Australia must heed the increasing criticism of the White Australia policy. Brett believed that, 'in some quarters, our enthusiasm borders on the sphere of racial superiority', adding:

> We are a small, young nation, unskilled in diplomacy, but it will richly repay us if we endeavour to substitute our oft-stated hopes for a better 'good neighbour' policy in the Southwest Pacific. It is distressing to find, among both civil and service populations, a carry-over from pre-war days of the distrust and scorn from foreigners despite the opportunities afforded servicemen of mingling with them on terms of equality, often sharing their troubles. We have [a] valuable contribution to make in world affairs, and it is hoped that there are among us some with sufficiently matured and broadened vision to mould public opinion in immigration matters.[14]

Private A.J. Taylor agreed: 'Wasn't war in Europe over the master-race theory? Well in the eyes of the world, the White Australia policy must sound like "master race".' A veteran of the island campaigns in the south-west Pacific, Taylor asked:

> Could we, who have seen the sacrifice made and the help given by the coloured people of the Pacific say to those people who have helped us in the war at the cost of their own homes and families, to preserve our homes and families from the Japs, 'we have a White Policy; you can't come and

live with us'? Already there is talk of German children being emigrated to Australia and so, to me, the White Australia policy is terribly fascist like.[15]

In similar vein, a second letter in the same edition reiterated the belief that the White Australia policy was offensive to Australia's neighbours and allies in India, China and the Netherlands East Indies.[16] There was certainly a truth to these fears, as they existed among policy makers in Canberra and had, in fact, been expressed to Australian diplomats in Delhi.[17]

Significantly, soldiers stationed throughout Asia during the war observed the growing political movements and, on occasion, the civil unrest that would grip the region following the cessation of hostilities with Japan. Even within the early years of the war, the cities of Bombay, Calcutta, Rangoon and Colombo could be dangerous places at night-time for British soldiers who, particularly from 1942 onward, could be systematically targeted by political activists from the Indian National Congress and Quit India movements. In 1942 the Indian National Congress was split on the question of whether full support should be given to the Allied war effort while a time frame for Indian self-governance remained unclear. Following the failure of the Cripps Mission – the British government delegation led by Stafford Cripps to India in 1942 – to address such a time frame, as well as the unacceptable offer of limited dominion status, the congress launched the Quit India Movement. This movement aimed to force Britain to the negotiating table by attempting to hold the Allied war effort hostage through non-violent, disobedient actions. However, as well as mass strikes, there were acts of sabotage, arson and violence against the military and government installations, and it was in this way that British soldiers would be targeted by political activists.[18]

When Australian servicemen went on leave in these ports of call they were not allowed to carry arms, and at times found themselves particularly vulnerable. Having heard reports of rickshaw pullers taking British soldiers to darkened alleys where congress 'gangs' would set upon them, one group of diggers in the darkness of Calcutta's blackout instigated a violent confrontation with a rickshaw puller out of fear that they were being led to an ambush. One soldier kicked the rickshaw puller in the head before fleeing for his life.[19] In another incident in Bombay in 1942, amid stories of British soldiers being 'strangled or stabbed nightly in lonely parts' of the city, a group of lost soldiers trying to find their way home from a theatre were suddenly confronted and showered with stones. Grabbing chairs from a neighbouring teahouse to defend themselves against the assault – as previously noted, men on leave were not permitted to carry weapons – they were lucky to be rescued by 'the providence of a Tommy patrol van'.[20] Similarly, a soldier stationed on Ceylon in 1942 wrote in his diary of the fear of going off the 'beaten tracks of Colombo' as he would fall victim to stones hurled from the darkness.[21] Such scenarios greatly differed from the languid and luxurious vision of life in the region that had been envisaged on their arrival. While the Australians were more than likely to be viewed no differently to the British by those who led such assaults, the former quite naturally felt it was unjust that anger caused by Britain's treatment of colonial subjects should be taken out on them, and it furthered their desire to differentiate themselves from the British. Furthermore, these anecdotes demonstrate how soldiers who may have been encountering the region for only a short period could be subject to eye-opening experiences when it came to colonial issues.

For those who were in the region for a much longer period, these issues became ingrained in the facets of daily life. In Singapore's major prisoner-of-war camp at Changi a number of the guards were Indians, previously from the British regiments, who had changed sides following the surrender by joining Subhas Chandra Bose's Indian National Army. Australian and British prisoners considered these men traitors. Some of these Indian guards took out years of British-borne humiliation on their prisoners by punishing them for misdemeanours such as failing to salute with military precision or sloppy dress. Any Australian on the receiving end of such punishments – usually a slap or an order to stand to attention for a prolonged period in front of the guardhouse – resented treatment for what they considered British sins. The Indian soldier, however, failed to identify the distinction. There was an even stronger sense of injustice felt by Australians when they believed that the offences of Dutchmen and Frenchmen were being taken out on them.[22]

Amid the political turmoil unfolding in front of Australian soldiers throughout the region at the end of the war, it was not surprising that Australian military personnel serving in Asia and the Pacific were forming strong opinions – canvassing both sides of politics – regarding the concept of self-determination, independence from colonial rule, and the future role Australia and Australians could play in the region. Indeed, Australian soldiers showed particular concern for Australian government policy in the region, with a clear interest in justifying for themselves what they had been fighting for and what the war in the Pacific was about. A member of the 2/5th Independent Company, for example, was hostile to the idea of what he believed were plans by the government for an 'Austrasia' – a proposed Australian Empire that incorporated New Guinea, Timor, the Solomons, New Caledonia, Fiji and British Borneo.[23]

The course of the conflict, or possibly their experiences abroad in the services, may have led Australian soldiers to debate the futures of India, the Netherlands East Indies and New Guinea.[24] The implementation of the Atlantic Charter by Churchill and Roosevelt following the Placentia Bay conference of 1941 determined eight points of agreement between Britain and the United States. The charter acknowledged that neither party sought aggrandisement, nor did they desire territorial changes without the freely expressed agreement of the peoples concerned. It respected the right of all peoples to choose their governments and it was desired that self-government be returned to all who had been forcibly deprived of it. Other points were concerned with access to wealth and resources and the establishment of lasting peace. The USSR later adhered to the charter and it subsequently became the basis of the Declaration by United Nations (1 January 1942), to which Australia was a signatory. Understandably, the charter compromised British relations with and policies towards its colonies. This was especially the case with India, to which Britain refused to apply the Atlantic Charter, much to the criticism of the United States. This refusal had the strong support of Winston Churchill, who, fiercely proud of India's imperial role, was profoundly hostile to India's national aspirations.

Publications such as *Salt* provided soldiers with a forum in which to express their views on a wide range of social and political issues, such as the terms outlined within the Atlantic Charter, the events unfolding in India regarding the Cripps Mission, and the Quit India Movement in 1942. One letter-writer to *Salt*, Warrant Officer R. Saunders, felt that protests by the India Office against self-rule on the grounds of internal disunity were 'most insincere'. It was vital that India be mobilised 'behind us in this war', he noted. This, however, could not occur unless the Indians were given 'freedom to fight for'. He added:

> If insincere reasons are given for not granting freedom, it would appear that the real reason is the old one of vested interests pulling strings to retain their privileged position in India. We cannot afford to let this go on when our very lives and outcome of this war may depend upon us giving this great nation some of the freedom for which we fight. If we give India self-government in time, then we shall have won the biggest political and strategic victory of the Pacific War zone.[25]

Debate continued in a following edition, with Corporal P.F. Mortimer writing: 'It's not too late to win India.' Tellingly, Mortimer cited critics of the American struggle for independence, pointing out that the same criticisms were now being applied toward India. Just as 'America had proved these prophets wrong', he wrote, 'it would be wise carefully to analyse the dire predictions about modern India'. Citing the political and religious differences within India that critics claimed made Indian independence impractical, Mortimer believed that Indians were quite capable of dealing with the challenges that would face them, especially considering these groups lived side by side. 'If we are to gain the active support of India we must face that. Immediate independence for India is, admittedly, not a practical step', he wrote, 'but, immediate steps to prove to the Indian people our sincerity in the ideals expressed in the Atlantic Charter, would be of immense importance in the Pacific arena'. He added: 'A united India can be won for our war effort. Our Burmese experiences show us how necessary this is.'[26] The very next edition of *Salt* contained letters from soldiers in response to Mortimer's article. One letter-writer supported Mortimer's view while another, a Colonel, strongly opposed it, arguing that the success of the American nation was because 'America was predominantly British', implying that the Indian nation could not succeed on racial assumptions.[27]

As the war drew to a conclusion the issue of India would again become prominent. In June 1945 Gunner B. Harwood made a well-informed argument outlining his concerns that conditions such as those faced by many citizens in nations such as India could be detrimental to winning the peace:

> The problems of occupied countries of Europe have
> been widely publicised in Australia. Of much more vital
> concern to Australia is the problem of India, our backdoor
> neighbour, which has been occupied for the past 200
> years. India is fertile, well watered and endowed with rich
> mineral resources – mostly undeveloped. Yet in that land of
> potential plenty, over 400 million people (1931 census) live

in poverty and starvation. Education has been shamefully
neglected and medical facilities are also so hopelessly
inadequate that every year hundreds of thousands die
of curable diseases. According to Prof. Shah of Bombay
University, the average income is just sufficient to feed
two out of every three people with the minimum ration of
the cheapest food ... The importance attached to religious
differences has been greatly exaggerated ... In the interest
of justice we owe it to the Indian people, and to ourselves,
to offer every assistance in their struggle. No lasting peace
can be established so long as one subject people remains in
the world.[28]

Some of these views among the ordinary rank-and-file men of
the AIF may have been influenced by service alongside Indian
soldiers in North Africa and Southeast Asia, and by experiences
of leave in Bombay. In his survey of AIF veterans, Barrett has
noted that the Gurkhas in particular were held in highest esteem
by AIF troops when compared with other British and dominion
troops.[29] Indian divisions fought with distinction alongside AIF
divisions in North Africa and the Middle East. In Burma, much of
the victory was owed to the Indian Army, such was their heavy
involvement in that campaign. However, Indian formations did
not perform as well in Malaya, and members of the 8th Division
were certainly critical. Indeed, members of the 2/15th Field Regiment attached to the 45th Indian Brigade at the battle of Maur
dubbed the soldiers 'the galloping Gwahlis' for their actions in
the face of the enemy.[30] Certainly, Major General Bennett and
Australian official historian Wigmore were both more diplomatic
and practical in their reasoning for the poor Indian performance,
citing the young, raw recruits of the Indian divisions and lack of
training and equipment suitable to jungle warfare.[31] In review of
the Malayan campaign, historians such as Warren point out that
while Indian troops have been heavily criticised for the defeat

they were as well represented as British and Gurkha troops, and at any rate the defeat was a team effort (in which Australians played their part).[32]

However, while many members of the 8th Division were critical of the performance of Indian soldiers in the Malayan campaign, the plight of Indian prisoners of war who chose not to join – or resisted joining – the Japanese or Indian National Army (INA), and who were starved and tortured due to their loyalty to the Allied cause, won much respect. In particular, the poor conditions faced by Indian prisoners of war who had remained 'loyal' to the empire and were interned in Singapore, those who endured starvation and torture by the Japanese attempting to force them into the INA, and those encountered by Australians in New Guinea moved some soldiers to write of the encounters in their diaries.[33] From December 1944 onwards, Australian soldiers in New Guinea had been encountering and helping escaped Indian prisoners of war. An officer of the 6th Division witnessing a group of Sikhs and Punjabis arriving at the Australian lines in May 1945 proclaimed them 'a great race – Sikhs and Punjabis – great in adversity. It is most inspiring to see them come in'. He went on to note that despite their ordeals there remained pride in their appearance, concluding that their ennobling 'spirit of service' and sacrifice was something that was 'sadly lacking in so much of our country at present'.[34] The respect was mutual, as when the Indians finally departed New Guinea in 1946 there was an emotional farewell and much praise for the compassion, 'sympathy, care and affection' shown toward them by the 6th Division. They had, according to one of the Sikh officers, Jemadar Chint Singh, 'worked as Angels for us'.[35]

Just as the future of India remained a growing concern for a number of Australian soldiers toward the end of the war, Australian military involvement in the Netherlands East Indies provided provocation for some to question the continuing role of the Dutch in Indonesia. An article in *Salt* stressed that, far from being of 'no concern to Australia', 'the future of Indonesia, Malaya, Indo-China, and other Southeast Asian lands urgently concern this Commonwealth and its 7,000,000 people'. It was not just a question of the Atlantic Charter and democratic ideals generally, it was argued, but a 'question of Australia's safety'; unlike the European powers and the United States, the author believed Australia's 'destiny is linked eternally with those near neighbour Asiatic countries'. The article argued that Southeast Asia's millions could either work with Australia to the benefit, protection and progress of all or they could be a 'menace' and 'depress living standards'. Pre-war conditions could not return, it was argued, as in Malaya people on a low wage and with no vote saw no reason to fight. The days of white residents being free from income tax and paying for duty-free goods while Asians lived around them in poverty had to end. Unions, it was argued, should not be repressed, especially since it was jailed Chinese union leaders who had organised resistance to the Japanese occupation and assisted prisoners of war. Likewise, the fact that 70 million Indonesians lived on a 'coolie wage' was a 'menace' to the Australian nation both economically and for security reasons. High incomes and better education could open trade to the benefit of both Australians and Indonesians, it was argued, and the Dutch reluctance to arm Indonesians directly threatened Australian defence. The author concluded that in these ways the future of the region was crucial to Australia, and there should be recognition for the Indonesian cause.[36]

It appears that many agreed with these sentiments, recognising the hypocrisy of liberating the island from one unwanted foreign power in order to pave the way for return of the islands to another. Sergeant W.B. Buchanan demanded answers to his growing concerns about Australian military involvement in the liberation of the Netherlands East Indies:

Australian troops are now fighting for the liberation of
the Dutch East Indies. What future is proposed for these

Members of the Indian army who had been prisoners of war since the fall of Singapore mingle over a cup of tea with Australian soldiers in New Guinea, 1945. The Australians were impressed by the loyalty shown by these soldiers, who rather than enduring the hardship of imprisonment might otherwise have joined the Indian National Army. One AIF officer was moved to describe the Sikhs and Punjabis as 'a great race'. Following their experiences of the Pacific War, many Australian soldiers formed strong views regarding the question of India's independence and colonialism in Asia.
Australian War Memorial 098714

islands? Have any proposals been made for increasing the independence and improving the conditions of the native people? Presumably Holland took part in the San Francisco Conference, one of the proposals of which was to enable dependent countries to take the path to independence and political democracy as soon as possible; yet it appears that all political parties are still illegal under Dutch administration – and even trade unions are illegal … We must liberate the islands because they could never achieve democracy and independence under Japanese rule. However, some blame for the ease with which the Japanese conquered the islands and threatened Australia must be laid on the pre-war treatment of the natives. Hence Dutch policy in the Indies vitally affects our security as well as our Pacific trade. Australia is playing its part in liberating these islands. What assurances has it sought [for] their treatment when liberated?[37]

Driver R. Lewis took umbrage at Buchanan's assertions, stating that the schemes drawn up for the Netherlands East Indies were similar to Minister for External Affairs E.J. Ward's 'New Deal' for New Guinea and were 'so much eyewash' because 'native labour in any of these islands must be exploited to cut labour costs and keep alive the spirit of inferiority in the native mind'. These islands, according to Lewis, were liberated because they belonged to Australia's ally, the Netherlands, and because they produced a major proportion of the world's rubber and oil supplies. Furthermore, Lewis argued, it was not pre-war treatment of 'natives' but poor defence that resulted in the loss of these islands, and anyway, it was 'none of Australia's business what treatment the natives get after the war'; according to Lewis, 'it was Holland's concern'.[38] Lewis drew strong criticism from Private P.L. Smith, who suggested there were 'shades of *Mein Kampf!*' in the former's statement. Ignoring the Atlantic Charter, by which 'the basic principles around which world peace and postwar rehabilitation must be built', was perilous as it 'contained no reference whatsoever that could be construed, by any stretch of the imagination, as excluding coloured people of any nationality, whether they may be Indian, Chinese, Indonesian, Papuan or other colour, colonial or subject people'.[39] Essentially, these men were debating the real reason they were (or had been) fighting. Of further importance was the fact that knowledge of Asian and regional affairs and the reflection of prospective legacies of the war in Asia and the Pacific were central to discussions.

This was reflected by the deep concern held among a group of soldiers that the articles of the Atlantic Charter and United Nations Charter were not being implemented by the Allies in Southeast Asia at war's end. These discussions corresponded with debates at the United Nations regarding the return of European control and independence movements in Asia, which undermined the sincerity of the terms outlined within the charter and brought into question the very notion of why the war had been fought. Indonesia was of particular concern for Sapper C.G. Mathews. 'With the ink hardly dry on the surrender documents, we see reactionary forces in the United Nations striving to bring to nought the aims for which the peoples of the United Nations have fought, worked and suffered for the last five years,' he wrote, referring to the practice by which the SEAC re-armed Japanese soldiers in order to restore colonial order in Netherlands East Indies and French Indochina:

> Look at Indonesia. Living on the verge of starvation, under
> the most violent repression by Japanese Imperialism, the
> Indonesian people yet organised their own underground
> resistance movement, adding their bit to the mounting
> offensive against the Jap. Now the Resistance Movement
> has declared Indonesia a republic. They are determined to
> be done with Imperialism forever, be it Japanese or Dutch.
> Yet we read of British commanders ordering Jap troops to

the Netherlands East Indies to 'maintain order', pending
the arrival of Allied interventionary forces. Is this the way
we are going to put the principles of the Atlantic Charter
into action? Is this 'self-determination for all peoples'? Did
we work and fight for democracy, or was our aim the use
of the same Jap Army that killed so many of our men, the
same Gestapo that held the people of Asia in slavery, as the
police dogs of imperialism in these areas?[40]

Supporting this viewpoint, Corporal F.G. Lynch argued that:
'Demands by the Annamites from the French, by the Indians and
Egyptians from the British and the Indonesians from the Dutch,
should greatly disillusion Australians who have fought a war to
stop Germans, Italians and Japanese from dominating other peoples.' Lynch argued similarly that the people who inhabited some
of the richest islands in the world within Indonesia were of importance to Australia because of their geographic proximity and their
potential trade value. 'We should give the national aspirations of
its people our sympathy and gain their friendship.'[41] Sergeant J.L.
Brown was similarly concerned that the leaders of the resistance
and voices for democracy in Indonesia were being forgotten.[42]

Likewise, Warrant Officer G. Steele was also concerned that
the intervention in Indonesia violated the principles of the Atlantic Charter, arguing that a strong and independent Indonesia was
necessary for Australia's future safety.[43] Such views were shared
by Private N.L. Rosser, who lamented: 'Dutch interests appear to
believe that democracy can only be restored in the Indies when
the Indonesians are held down with guns and their leaders thrown
back into concentration camps. That would be a remarkably queer
type of democracy.' Rosser added succinctly that 'smashing' Japanese fascism was the priority in the Pacific, 'not the smashing of
independence movements which are a barrier for future conflict'.[44]
These views were not shared by all. Among the dissenters was
Private E.E. Taylor:

As a remnant of a frontline unit, I would like to claim
that units are wholeheartedly behind the White Australia
Policy: I was fighting for that in particular. Australian
whiteness and high standards are realities. To what extent
is the Atlantic Charter a reality? Christianity is fighting
a losing battle if it fights for the minority of colours and
races. Give the best people, even by science. People
are definitely failing the spiritual force behind them;
therefore the people must be improved. Upward White
Australia.[45]

Yet even Taylor's view could be considered reactionary, as it reinforces the point that in one way or another the political views of
Australian servicemen were being tested by their encounter with
the region.

It was not only in the pages of *Salt* that these kinds of debates
took place. Stanley has similarly noted the interest soldiers on
Tarakan took in the affairs unfolding around them. One of the
informal polls conducted by troops asked for respondents' views
on 'the Indonesian question'.[46] Even within the confines of Changi
prisoner-of-war camp, political groups were formed and a 'mock
parliament' regularly assembled to debate social issues and topics
such as Australia's future and immigration policy. 'The prevailing
opinion in the ranks', it was noted, 'was leftist, but seldom violently so'. A key figure in the creation of the mock parliament was
the conservative MP, Alexander Downer (senior). Writing about
politics in Changi, he stated his belief that prisoners of war would
return to Australia 'more enlightened, more tolerant, more sympathetic, and better citizens'.[47]

It was not only Asian political concerns that were on the
minds of the troops. Reflecting on the war in New Guinea, an
area in which Australians had shared interests for some time, a
number of diggers called for independence, believing that it was
time Australia honoured the ruling of the mandate granted by the

League of Nations. An article by a *Salt* staff writer entitled 'Salute to Boong' reflected such a view:

> The debt we owe them cannot be discharged with less than
> a resolve that they, and all native peoples under charge,
> shall share fully in the fruits of victory. They must have
> their due place in a world where humanity and justice are
> reinstated. It is not enough that we wipe out the stain of
> the black birding era. All exploitation must cease. To do
> less would be to mock Australian soldiers, who in their
> thousands honour and respect the black stalwarts who
> shared their perils and whose great souls counted no
> sacrifice too high for their tabauda brothers.[48]

Another soldier shared this viewpoint, stating that nearby villagers 'love the Australian soldiers, who behave as paternal friends toward the natives working around them'. The story of the heroism of the Papuans on the road to Buna had 'no parallel in unselfishness co-operation between white man and coloured'. Those working with the casualty clearing station had 'their shoulders rubbed raw with the rough, home-made stretchers', and 'the stretcher bearers look after their wounded almost entirely by themselves now'.[49] More forthright in his views was Sergeant J.V. White:

> It is with feeling of disgust that I, and cobbers of mine, read
> that 'a campaign to the Fuzzy Wuzzies for their services to
> the troops in NG' is to be launched by a Diggers' group.
> Imitation jewellery for services rendered, plus blood, death
> and misery … The mere thought of such an idea would rile
> all Australian and Allied servicemen. The associations of
> returned soldiers of the last war did not strive for 'imitation
> jewellery' for its members during the depression years of
> 1929–34 and afterwards. No, Sir! They strived, or should
> have striven, for work, food and decent housing conditions,

which all wanted but very few received. This war is being
fought for equality of relationships between peoples of
all colours, creeds and nationalities. And this includes the
Fuzzy Wuzzies, who have endeared themselves in the eyes
of Australian soldiers, not only for their energy but their
devotion and wonderful ability to learn quickly. We soldiers
want to see the Fuzzy Wuzzies receive, during and after
the war, democratic education, scientific facilities to solve
unhygienic and unsanitary conditions, and freedom from so-
called 'white' plantation and mine-owners.[50]

Evidently, there was support for the views expressed by White.
Others also wrote of their dislike for the continued usage of the
term 'boong'.[51]

Another sergeant, E.J. Johnston, also expressed strong views
regarding Australia's role in New Guinea. Responding to the
announcement within the early months of 1944 that civilians
were to return to New Guinea, Johnston raised the question of
Australian policy for the Papuan people, whom he felt had 'earned
the right to all the help we can give them'. It was hoped such
policies would be 'devoid of racial superiority' and would 'help
them achieve better health and education, higher standards of
living, [and] democratic independence'. The best students could
be trained in Australia as teachers, a wider system of hospitals
should be developed, and large-scale schemes to combat malaria
– such as the one carried out by the military authorities – should
all be key policies. Importantly, all agricultural land should be
native-held, with up-to-date agricultural methods and machinery
employed, and 'native administration should be trained as the first
step toward self-government'. Most important were the issues of
wages and conditions:

Wages and conditions of labour are key points of our whole
policy. The system of indentured labour should go and

with it the disgraceful rates of pay. (10/– per month for
most natives). The natives' present restricted scale of needs
only reflects his past low standard of living and, even if the
individual native cannot make good use of Australian wages,
this is no reason for giving employers cheap labour – part
of the wage could be paid into a fund for the benefit of the
native population. To permit old wage standards to continue
is to exploit native backwardness, to create a commercial
and financial group with vested interest in the perpetuation
of these wages and the natives' backward status.[52]

Furthermore, Johnston believed that to 'build up a pool of cheap
labour deliberately is a threat to our own Australian standards'.[53]
Others agreed with Johnston. 'Many New Guinea natives have
been away from their families longer than our blokes, and are out
of touch with their villages,' wrote Sergeant H.W. Forster. 'During
the war they have seen machinery turning earth, carpenters tools,
mosquito nets, RAPs [Regimental Aid Posts], and know their
farms can be tilled better, that fevers can be prevented and cured,
that meat can be a staple part of the diet.' Government initiatives,
according to Forster, made it possible that 'with the introduction
of machinery, medical, agricultural and general education by sympathetic administrators, the New Guinea native can step from the
Stone Age to a fuller life'.[54] Signaller W.M. Nicholls argued for
democracy for the people of New Guinea, noting that Australian
manpower problems would have increased and many more Australians would have been called up for military service had it not
been for their loyalty. 'They have proved themselves our equals
on numerous occasions', he wrote, and they therefore deserved
democratic freedoms.[55] Anthropologist Donald Thompson added
further spice to the debate when he commented:

thousands of Australians who had fought in the jungles
of New Guinea had come to know and understand the

Papuans, and to these men, their friends and relatives at home, the boong is more than a potential coolie. He is a fellow human being with a sense of humour and a destiny of his own.

A *Salt* article insisted that such changes in attitudes should not become just another piece of political window dressing.[56]

Others, however, criticised the concept of a 'free' New Guinea. One author, identified only by his service number, argued in an article entitled 'Fuzzy wuzzy fetish' that 'progress of the idea of equality to its logical conclusion in native self-government is ludicrous at this present stage of development and would be like a suggestion to place the government of Australia in the hands of 16-year-old school boys'. The author was an ANGAU officer. Stating that provision of education, medicine and 'general betterment' had been provided for only 50 years in Papua and 20 years in New Guinea, he criticised those who proclaimed themselves as advocates of New Guinea affairs as having 'only just discovered them to be in need', and their interest nothing but a 'hobby horse'. The author then defended the labour system against charges of exploitation, proclaiming that the facts quoted within his summary were 'vouched for by actual experiences and should be an effective rejoinder to all those who have so misguidedly and misinformedly "discovered" particular exploitation of the native in the labour system of New Guinea'.[57] Strongly reflective of Social Darwinist principles, these views were also supported by other contributors to *Salt*. Major F.G.T. Place, for example, argued that New Guinea should be thrown open to 'Asiatic' immigrants after the war. Its many natural resources would provide living for them and this action would, according to the Major, 'placate Asiatic members of our Empire' (a reference to Asian opposition to and resentment of the White Australia policy). Australia would remain in administrative charge and would share in the benefits from the island's increased trading capacity, according to Place,

Members of the 2/17th Battalion chat with a local Malayan man in Brunei following the liberation of his village from Japanese occupation in 1945.
Australian War Memorial 109297

and from such a population a fair standing army could be maintained in order to provide 'a trusty shield between Australia and the Pacific'.[58]

These discussions provide a unique glimpse into the attitudes of some Australian military personnel between 1942 and 1945. Most interesting is that within the debates emerging in *Salt* we can see a pattern regarding the demographics of the contributors. Those who supported the independence movements of Asia and advocated a democratic postwar New Guinea free of white exploitation – or even an independent New Guinea – were overwhelmingly made up of NCOs and Other Ranks (a total of 22). There were two officers (both captains) who supported one of these positions. The men with what may be termed more traditionalist viewpoints, declaring their support for the European colonial presence in the region, featured three Other Ranks and four officers ranging from the rank of lieutenant to colonel. While this sample is limited, we can see a pattern in the letters written within the 148 issues of *Salt* whereby officers feature heavily among those with more traditional viewpoints; meanwhile, Other Ranks feature overwhelmingly among those who took positions that could be generally described as supporting the terms of the Atlantic Charter and United Nations Charter.

Overall, whatever their rank, we can see that Australian soldiers who may have possessed little knowledge or understanding of Asian affairs before the war were by 1945 demonstrating a maturing political awareness of the region regardless of their political positions. These men were essentially pondering the question: 'Why did we fight?', and were engaging in a national debate on the subject. Crucially, the issue of Asia and the region's future was central to discussion. That soldiers were possibly ahead of the wider general public on these issues can be partly demonstrated by the results of the 1944 referendum on postwar reconstruction and democratic rights, which included the safeguarding of rights to freedom of speech and freedom of religion. Where only 44.49 per cent of the electorate voted yes, 52.38 per cent of the 417,082 members of the armed forces voted yes, a larger percentage than any individual state or the Commonwealth as a whole.[59] It is worth noting that some of the correspondence cited demonstrates that soldiers were beginning to draw conclusions on the region as early as 1942. Here was a group much more forthright in its views than the Australian Labor government of the period under prime ministers John Curtin (October 1941 to July 1945) and Ben Chifley (July 1945 to December 1949). In 1945 Labor did not fully support the idea of a 'free' Asia. It was not until the late 1940s that Australia took a firm stand on this issue, backing the transfer of India in 1947 and in 1948 taking the issue of Indonesian independence to the UN Security Council against the wishes of both Britain and the United States.[60] While Lee has noted how the policy stance of the Chifley government reflected 'a clear sense of the coming ascendency of Asian nationalism', it is clear that soldiers on the ground had been increasingly aware of this phenomenon since 1942.[61]

Of further importance, these debates show how soldiers, peripherally thrown onto a nation's frontiers where they engage with and meet people from different backgrounds and cultures, can develop a more open and tolerant viewpoint. While the sample discussed here may represent a minority of troops, the views it represents appear not uncommon. Furthermore, returning veterans may have continued to discuss these issues within their homes, among family members, at the workplace, or in clubs and pubs; possibly having further influence throughout the Australian community. While a number of historians have demonstrated how politicians, diplomats, academics, businessmen, journalists and writers – who could be all termed 'social elites' – have influenced the changing attitudes toward Asia across the 20th century, an important outcome of the Second World War was that a large group of ordinary Australian citizens who had served in Asia and the Pacific were better equipped to understand, more knowledgeable about, and even more open toward the importance of the more thorough engagement Australia was to have with the 'new' nations of Asia over the second half of the century.

CONCLUSION

The extraordinary experiences of Australian troops across Asia and the Pacific during the Second World War and their diverse encounters with the people and cultures of the region have not received due attention within the social, cultural and military history of conflict. Dominating narratives of the Second World War are tales of heroism and survival at Kokoda, at Changi and on the Burma–Thailand Railway. Such narratives, however, are devoid of the complexity, diversity and even the uniqueness of Australia's wartime experience in Asia and the Pacific. However, these first-time encounters between large numbers of ordinary Australians and the peoples and cultures of Asia remain some of the most distinctive and colourful Second World War accounts.

Central to addressing popular misunderstandings regarding Australia's Second World War, Australia's Pacific War encounters offer insights into attitudes toward Asia, empire and nation. The views of soldiers, as documented herein, demonstrate that defending Australia – either from invasion or in the event of a 'battle for Australia' – was not of immediate concern within soldier debates. On the other hand, it is clear that Australian soldiers were not only conscious but proud of the part they were playing in a wider global struggle for democracy and the right to personal freedoms. They were proud of the role they played in the downfall of Nazism and Japanese militarism. In a global struggle,

Australian soldiers were not only aware of the wider international issues but also motivated by them.

The arrival of Australian forces in Asia in 1941 demonstrated how ingrained concepts of empire, race and nation were entwined in tales of travel. Entering the region believing they were partners in the British Empire, ostracism from white colonial society challenged Australian soldiers' sense of dual loyalty. Such experience raised difficult questions for some soldiers about their sense of racial belonging and Australia's role in imperial affairs.

The Australian soldiers' first encounters with Asian peoples, cultures, languages and religions were eye-opening. Members of the armed forces proved a curious group, eager to learn something of the world around them. Some found themselves sympathetic toward the plight of the oppressed and subjugated peoples of the region, but many were not. Regardless, their exclusion from British colonial society meant that Australian soldiers promoted themselves as more egalitarian in their attitudes and relationships with Asians. Deeper examination showed that the Australians often asserted their stance within the racial hierarchy and crudely imitated the colonial style. Nevertheless, descriptions of the Australians' initial contact with Asians, however manufactured or contrived, helped provide a mechanism against which the perceived traits of the Australian character could be benchmarked in opposition to the stuffy British colonials they encountered. This wartime engagement with Asia, therefore, provided Australian soldiers with an opportunity to proclaim a different world outlook.

With the absence of the British as a counterpoint, Australian interactions in New Guinea offer an important insight into the workings of imperial and colonial encounters. These interactions demonstrate the sinister way in which particular colonial structures in place in Asia and the Pacific could influence the perceptions and affect the behaviours of outsiders entering the region for the very first time. Where contact with Asians played an important role by which Australians could differentiate themselves from the

British and even question the equality of empire, such misgivings and grievances were certainly not shared toward the Indigenous populations of Papua and New Guinea, who toiled under the governance of Australian military authorities. The idealistic and comfortable image of the loyal Papuan overshadows the darker and more insidious narratives of Australia's war in New Guinea. Importantly, such narratives – while barely registering among a wider audience – are hardly hidden histories, given their placement in popular and well-read contemporary publications. If Australians were beginning to question the sincerity and equality of their partnership in empire during the Second World War then the extension of such feelings toward subjugated peoples within territories under Australian political control was not so forthcoming.

By war's end, the Asia-Pacific region was in the grip of political turmoil and upheaval; the Japanese surrender created a power vacuum not immediately filled by the returning pre-war colonial powers. Newly freed former prisoners of war witnessed the civil unrest, and Australian troops across Indonesia found themselves policing and intervening in political affairs that would shape the region for decades to come. Amid such scenes, Australia's loyalties between the old world of European empires and the new world of free and independent Asian countries were tested. The Allied powers had proclaimed that the Second World War was fought for freedom: freedom of choice, freedom of religion, freedom from fear and freedom to democratically choose one's government – ideals enshrined in the 1942 Declaration by United Nations. Many Australian soldiers bought into these ideals only to witness them being denied Australia's Asian neighbours. This little-told tale of Australians witnessing one of the greatest political upheavals in modern history – and the compromises it required – reveals the unique perspective those soldiers had on the process of decolonisation in Asia. No matter the political persuasion of or the stance taken by individual soldiers on such issues, knowledge of Asia and the importance of Asian affairs drove discussion and debate on why the war had been fought. Significantly, Australia's Pacific encounters would challenge, shape and even orientate individual soldiers' outlooks on Asia, empire and their sense of Australia's place in the wider world. Far from being ignorant or ill-informed about Asia or Asian affairs, as a cross-section of Australian society the men of the AIF were possibly better informed and more knowledgeable than most, and some – including those who were prisoners of war in Japan – were even more understanding and accepting of Australia's Asian future.

Overall, Australia's Pacific War encounters reveal complex and fascinating accounts of personal engagement with the old world of European colonialism and the new world of a free Asia. Not only did the Second World War mark great change in the world but many Australian veterans – however small their role – were immensely proud to have been a part of it. In a speech at Port Moresby on Anzac Day in 1992, former Australian Prime Minister Paul Keating said: 'The Australians who served here in Papua New Guinea fought and died, not in the defence of the old world, but the new world. Their world.'[1] Soldiers at the time – no matter which side of the political spectrum they supported – were deeply invested in the importance of the campaigns in which they fought, not only for the future of Australia but also for the future of Asia, the future of empires, Australia's future relations with Asia, and its future role in regional and global affairs.

BIBLIOGRAPHY

Australian War Memorial

Official records
AWM52, 1/5/14, 7th Australian Division War Diary.
AWM52, 1/5/18, 8th Australian Division War Diary.
AWM52, 1/5/19, 8th Australian Division, No. 1 Prisoner of War Camp Changi War Diary.
AWM52, 1/5/62, Kuching Force War Diary.
AWM52, 1/10/1, Australian New Guinea Administration Unit War Diary.
AWM52, 8/2/17, 17th Brigade War Diary.
AWM52, 8/2/21, 21st Brigade War Diary.
AWM52, 8/3/13, 2/13th Battalion War Diary.
AWM52, 8/3/14, 2/14th Battalion War Diary.
AWM52, 8/3/16, 2/16th Battalion War Diary.
AWM52, 8/3/22, 2/22nd Battalion War Diary.
AWM52, 8/3/27, 2/27th Battalion War Diary.
AWM54, 80/2/1, History of ANGAU from the viewpoint of the employment and treatment of the native population in Australian New Guinea 1942–45.
AWM54, 506/1/4, A file dealing with trials held for various offences committed by natives, 1943–44 (March–February 1944).
AWM67, 2/88, Gavin Long, diary, August 1945.
AWM67, 3/109, Ivan N. Dougherty correspondence with Gavin Long, 1945.
AWM 3/173–3/680, 749/69/21 box 27, postcards and souvenirs.
AWM 3DRL 0369 50/7/14, 8th Australian Division (Australian Army).
AWM 363 Item 1/27, photo no. 14028.
AWM RC02398, Entertainment for Troops Collection.

Unpublished records
Arneil, Stan, diary, PR88/076.
Arneil, Stan, 'Aerodrome at Changi Point', 1945, 3DRL 0369 50/7/14.
Barrett, Ken, papers, MSS0764.
Barker, Howard, letters, PR90/048.
Beros, Bert, 'The fuzzy wuzzy angels', EXECDOC134 album 3.
Bills, Walter, letters, PR03205.
Blencowe, John, diary/papers, PR00282.
Burrey, Edward, diary, PR90/048.
Dale, F., letters, PR 90/121.

Dandie, Alex, papers, PR01193.
Chick, Allan, letters, PR85/189.
Cottier, James, diary, PR00989.
Downer, Alexander, 'POW politics', 1945, 3DRL 0369 50/7/14.
Faulkner, Thomas, leaflet, PR03205.
Filkins, Colin Joseph, papers, PR01604.
Geisler, Victor, interview, S00505.
Griffin, C. David, 'The Changi backdrop', 1945, 3DRL 0369 50/7/14.
Hirano, Matuso, letter, PR00736.
Ingrim, Robert, letters, PR03447.
Inoue, Ichiji, letter, PR04859.
Jacob, Helen, diary, PR02064.
Kelly, Charles, diary, PR02043.
Kerr, Jack, papers, PR86/191.
Lennon, John, diary, PR00875.
Little, Alec, interview, S00927.
Marien, William, diary, PR03595.
McGrath-Kerr, Peter, interview, S028989.
Miggins, William, diary, PR00373.
Mitchell, Thomas, papers, 1940–80, PR87/134.
Moore, James, papers, PR91/043.
Munro, Kenneth, manuscript, PR01687.
Nathan, David, radio broadcast, S04844.
Nevell, John, diary, PR00252.
Reddin, Jack, memoir, PR00902.
Shepard, Arthur, diary, PR91049.
Skinner, Bob, diary, PR00908.
Tracy, C.P., 'Singapore work party', 3DRL 0369 50/7/14.
Tuckey, Stirling, diary, PR00440.
Turner, Jack, papers, PR00651.
Tye, Allen, diary, PR00746.
Unknown author, 'Peace comes to X Party', 3DRL 0369 50/7/14.
Wall, Don, film, *Malayan Moments*, 1941, F03436.
Walton, Pierre, papers, PR04859.
Weir, Clarence, manuscript, PR01968.
Woodgate, W.H.L., diary/papers, PR00606.

Photographs, artworks and heraldry items
005982
009249/15
011303/30
014028
015155
015157
025722
030137/01
030135/01
101095
115157
P00102,035
P02491.099
RELAWM20304

RELAWM32543

SEA0146

ART22772, Roy Hodgkinson, *Souvenir hunters*, 1945.

ART22775, Roy Hodgkinson, *RAN in Colombo*, 1945.

ART22777, Roy Hodgkinson, *HMAS Napier entering Colombo graving dock*, 1945.

ART24308, Roy Hodgkinson, *Two RAAF groundstaff in Old Delhi street*, 1945.

ART26653, William Dargie, *Stretcher bearers in the Owen Stanleys*, 1947.

ARTV09053, *A united 'fighting mad' Australia can never be enslaved*, 1943.

ART25915, William Dargie, *Patrol in Arcadia*, 1943.

State Library of Victoria

Manuscripts

Barrett, K.T., 'My experiences as a prisoner of the Imperial Japanese Army', MS11567.

Bethune, Norman, papers, MS10346.

Bryant, James, diary, MS9540.

Conroy, Thomas, papers, MS9595.

Hawkins, John, diary, MS9615.

Holt, Fred S., memoir, MS11154.

Lambert, Eric, papers, MS10049.

Lyndon, Donald, diary, MS14445.

McIllree, Bob, letters, MS11301.

Murray-Smith, Stephen, letters and journal, MS8272Y.

Plante, Isabelle, papers, MS9215.

Rodwell, Joan, letters, MS12357.

Ross, Walter, letters, MS11469.

Sawford, Bertie, letters, MS11709.

Thomson, Max, memoir, MS10959.

Unknown Author, diary, MS14800.

Wallin, Arthur, diary, MS10172.

Wannan, W.F., papers, MS7777.

Williams, J.F., letters, MS12719.

Published memoirs and diaries

Arneil, Stan, *One Man's War*, Sydney: Macmillan, 2003 [1980].

Barber, Jack, *The War, the Whores and the Afrika Korps*, Sydney: Kangaroo Press, 1997.

Bennett, Gordon, *Why Singapore Fell*, Sydney: Angus & Robertson, 1944.

Braddon, Russell, *The Naked Island*, Melbourne: Penguin Books, 1993 [1952].

Darling (nee Gunter), Pat, *Portrait of a Nurse: Prisoner of War of the Japanese, 1942–1945, Sumatra*, Mona Vale: Don Wall, 2001.

Dawes, Allan, *'Soldier Superb': The Australian Fights in New Guinea*, Sydney: F.H. Johnston Publishing Company, 1943.

Duffy, James, *Australians in Malaya: and other tales of the Malayan Campaign*, Sydney: F.H. Johnston Publishing Company, 1943.

Dunlop, E.E., *The War Diaries of Weary Dunlop: Java and the Burma–Thailand Railway 1942–1945*, Melbourne: Nelson Publishers, 1986.

Griffin, Murray, *Changi*, Sydney: Edmund and Alexander, 1992.

Hamilton, Thomas, *Soldier Surgeon in Malaya*, Sydney: Angus & Robertson, 1958.

James, Clarrie, *ANGAU: One Man Law*, Sydney: AHMP, 2005 [1999].

Jeffrey, Betty, *White Coolies*, Sydney: Angus & Robertson, 1954.

Johnston, George, *New Guinea Diary*, Sydney: Angus & Robertson, 1943.
Johnston, George, *War Diary 1942*, Hong Kong: William Collins, 1984.
Kent-Hughes, Wilfrid, *Slaves of the Samurai*, Melbourne: Oxford, 1946.
Lambert, Eric, *The Twenty Thousand Thieves*, Melbourne: Newpont, 1951.
MacDonald, Roderick, *Dawn Like Thunder*, London: Hodder & Stoughton, 1944.
Mant, Gilbert, *You'll Be Sorry*, Sydney: Frank Johnson, 1944.
Mant, Gilbert, *Grim Glory*, Sydney: Currawong Publishing, 1955.
Nelson, Hank (ed.), and Stanton, Eddie Allan, *The War Diaries of Eddie Allan Stanton: Papua 1942–45, New Guinea 1945–1945 – Edited by Hank Nelson*, St Leonards: Allen & Unwin, 1996.
Noonan, William, *The Surprising Battalion: Australian Commandoes in China*, Sydney: Halstead Press, 1945.
Parkin, Ray, *Out of the Smoke*, London: Hogarth, 1960.
Parkin, Ray, *Into the Smother*, London: Hogarth, 1963.
Parkin, Ray, *The Sword and the Blossom*, London: Hogarth, 1968.
Parkin, Ray, *Wartime Trilogy: Out of the Smoke; Into the Smother; The Sword and the Blossom*, Melbourne: Melbourne University Press, 1999.
Peek, Ian Denys, *One Fourteenth of an Elephant*, Sydney: Macmillan, 2003.
Rivett, Rohan, *Behind Bamboo*, Melbourne: Penguin, 2003 [1946].
Ryan, Peter, *Fear Drive My Feet*, Sydney: Duffy & Snellgrove, 2001.
Shelton-Smith, Adele, *The Boys Write Home*, Sydney: Published for the Australian Women's Weekly by Consolidated Press, 1944.
Sublet, Frank *Whatever Man Dares*, Sydney: Kokoda Press, 2013.
Uren, Tom, *Straight Left*, Sydney: Random House, 1994.
White, Osmar, *Green Armour*, Melbourne: Penguin Books, 2003 [1945].

Official histories

Condon-Rall, Mary Ellen, and Cowdrey, Albert E., *The Medical Department: Medical Services in the War against Japan*, Washington DC: Centre for Military History, United States Army, 1998.
Dexter, David, *The New Guinea Offensives*, Canberra: Australian War Memorial, 1961.
Long, Gavin, *To Benghazi*, Canberra: Australian War Memorial, 1952.
Long, Gavin, *The Final Campaigns*, Canberra: Australian War Memorial, 1966.
McCarthy, Dudley, *South-West Pacific Area – First Year: Kokoda to Wau*, Canberra: Australian War Memorial, 1959.
Rexford-Welch, S.C. (ed.), *The Royal Air Force Medical Services, Volume II: Commands*, London: Her Majesty's Stationery Office, 1955.
Walker, Allan S., *Clinical Problems of War*, Canberra: Australian War Memorial, 1952.
Walker, Allan S., *The Island Campaigns*, Canberra: Australian War Memorial, 1957.
Walker, Allan S., *Middle East and Far East*, Canberra: Australian War Memorial, 1961.
Wigmore, Lionel, *The Japanese Thrust*, Canberra: Australian War Memorial, 1957.

Other official publications

A Pocket Guide to New Guinea and the Solomons, Washington DC: War and Navy Departments, 1943.
The Bombay Hospitality Committee Welcome you to Bombay: Gateway to India, Bombay: Bombay Hospitality Committee, c. 1941–42.
The Borneo Book for Servicemen, Australian Military Forces, 1945.
Colombo – Information for Visiting Troops, issued by the Troops Entertainment Committee, Colombo, 28 April 1941.
Guinea Gold.

HMAS Mk III: Written and Prepared By Serving Personnel of the RAN, Canberra: Australian War Memorial, 1944.

HMAS Mk IV: Written and Prepared By Serving Personnel of the RAN, Canberra: Australian War Memorial, 1945.

Java: Handbook for Servicemen, Allied Geographic Section, Southwest Pacific Area, 1945.

Jungle Warfare: With the Australian Army in the South West Pacific, Canberra: Australian War Memorial, 1944.

Khaki and Green: With the Australian Army at Home and Overseas, Canberra: Australian War Memorial, 1943.

Malay Course for Beginners, Australian Army Far Eastern Liaison Office, 1939.

The Native Carrier: Employment and Treatment of Native Carriers in New Guinea, Allied Geographic Section, South West Pacific Area, 9 February 1943.

News Bulletin: The Official Organ of the Ex Prisoners of War and Relatives' Association of Victoria.

The Nineteenth: The magazine of the 2/19th Battalion AIF Malaya.

On Target: With the American and Australian Anti-Aircraft Brigade in New Guinea, Written and Illustrated by Men of the Front Line Forces, Sydney: Angus & Robertson, 1943.

Pigeon Post.

Salt: Authorized Education Journal of the Australian Army and Air Force.

The Seventeenth Australian Infantry Brigade Magazine: A Record of Four Years Campaigning, Australian Military Forces, 1944.

Soldiering in the Tropics, Australian Army, General Staff, 1942.

Soldiering On: The Australian Army at Home and Overseas, Canberra: Australian War Memorial, 1942.

Table Tops.

Through: The Official Journal of the Signals 8th Australian Division.

Tropicana.

Venereal Disease in Singapore: And How to Avoid It, Singapore: Printed at the Government Printing Office by W.T. Cherry, Government Printer, 1941.

Welcome to Bombay, Bombay: B.R. Gobhad & Co., c. 1941–42.

'Wild Woodbine': Some Useful Hints for Soldiers Arriving in India, Bristol and London: W.D. & H.O. Wills, c. 1942.

You and the Native: Notes for the Guidance of Members of the Forces in Their Relations with New Guinea Natives, Allied Geographical Section, South West Pacific Area, 12 February 1943.

Newspapers and magazines

The Age
The Argus
Army News
Australian Gallup Polls
The Australian Women's Weekly
Boys' Own Annual
The Cairns Post
Chums
The Courier-Mail (Brisbane)
The Herald (Melbourne)
The Launceston Examiner
Life
The New York Times
Pacific Island Monthly
The Rabaul Times
The Straits Times

The Sydney Morning Herald
The Times (London)
The West Australian

Contemporary films and newsreels

Assault on Salamaua, (dir.) Damian Parer, Cinesound Productions, 1943.
Indonesia Calling, (dir.) Joris Ivens, Waterside Workers Federation of Australia, 1948.
Kokoda Frontline!, (dir.) Damian Parer, Cinesound Productions, 1942.
The Road to Kokoda, (dir.) Damian Parer, 20th Century Fox–Movietone, 1942.
Singapore Stands to Arms: Aussies Honour Anzac Day, Cinesound News 498, 1941.

Books and articles

Adachi, Ryoko, and McKay, Andrew, *Echoes of War: Australians Voice Their Feelings about Japan*, Melbourne: Mirai, 2009.
Barrett, John, *We Were There: Australian Soldiers of World War II Tell Their Stories*, Melbourne: Penguin, 1987.
Battersby, Paul, *To the Islands: White Australians and the Malay Archipelago Since 1788*, Plymouth: Lexington, 2007.
Bayly, Christopher, and Harper, Tim, *Forgotten Armies: The Fall of British Asia, 1941–1945*, London: Allen Lane, 2004.
Bayly, Christopher, and Harper, Tim, *Forgotten Wars: The End of Britain's Asian Empire*, London: Allen Lane, 2007.
Beaumont, Joan, *Gull Force: Survival and Leadership in Captivity 1941–1945*, Sydney: Allen & Unwin, 1988.
Beaumont, Joan (ed.), *Australia's War 1939–45*, Sydney: Allen & Unwin, 1996.
Bennett, Judith A., *Natives and Exotics: World War II and Environment in the Southern Pacific*, Honolulu: University of Hawai'i Press, 2009.
Bergerud, Eric, *Touched with Fire: The Land War in the South Pacific*, New York: Viking, 1996.
Bird, Kate, 'Confined to the mainland? Australian women war correspondents reporting from overseas during WW2', *Lilith*, no. 11, 2002, pp. 73–85.
Blackburn, Kevin, *The Sportsmen of Changi*, Sydney: NewSouth, 2012.
Blackburn, Kevin, and Hack, Karl (eds), *Forgotten Captives in Japanese Occupied Asia*, London: RoutledgeCurzon, 2008.
Blackburn, Kevin, and Hack, Karl, *War Memory and the Making of Modern Malaysia and Singapore*, Singapore: National University of Singapore Press, 2012.
Brawley, Sean, and Dixon, Chris, *Hollywood's South Seas and the Pacific War: Searching for Dorothy Lamour*, New York: PalgraveMacmillan, 2012.
Broinowski, Alison, *The Yellow Lady: Australian Impressions of Asia*, Melbourne: Oxford University Press, 1996.
Brown, Nicholas, 'Australian intellectuals and the image of Asia: 1920–1960', *Australian Cultural History*, no. 9, 1990, pp. 80–92.
Bryant, R. *Pictorial History of the British Empire, Social, Descriptive, and Biographical*, London: James Sangster and Co. [1890s?].
Buckley, K., and Klugmen, K., *'The Australian Presence in the Pacific': Burns Philip 1914–1946*, Sydney: Allen & Unwin, 1983.
Bullard, Steven, *Blankets on the Wire: The Cowra Breakout and its Aftermath*, Canberra: Australian War Memorial, 2006.
Burns, John, *The Brown and Blue Diamond at War: The Story of the 2/27th Battalion*, Adelaide: 2/27 Battalion Association, 1960.
Butcher, John G., *The British in Malaya, 1880–1941: The Social History of a European*

Community in Colonial South-East Asia, New York: Oxford University Press, 1979.
Chandler, David P., and Ricklefs, M.C. (eds), *Nineteenth and Twentieth Century Indonesia: Essays in Honour of Professor J.D. Legge*, Clayton: Monash University Centre of South East Asian Studies, 1986.
Churchill, Winston S., *The Second World War*, London: Bloomsbury, 2013.
Clarke, Hugh V., *Last Stop Nagasaki*, Sydney: Allen & Unwin, 1985.
Clarke, Hugh V., *Twilight to Liberation*, Sydney: Allen & Unwin, 1985.
Copland, Ian, *India, 1885–1947: The Unmaking of an Empire*, New York: Longman, 2001.
Curthoys, Ann, and Markus, Andrew (eds), *Who Are Our Enemies? Racism and the Australian Working Class*, Neutral Bay: Hale and Ironmonger, 1978.
Dandie, Alex (ed.), *The Story of J Force*, Sydney: self-published, 1985.
Davies, Peter, *The Man Behind the Bridge: Colonel Toosey and the River Kwai*, Exeter: Athlone Press, 2000.
Davis, Joan, 'Salt: The journal of the Australian Army Education Service in the Second World War', *Journal of the Australian War Memorial*, no. 17, October 1999, pp. 20–29.
Daws, Gavan, *Prisoners of the Japanese: POWs of World War II in the Pacific*, New York: William Morrow and Company, 1994.
Day, David, *The Great Betrayal: Britain, Australia & the Onset of the Pacific War 1939–45*, Sydney: Angus & Robertson, 1988.
Dean, Peter (ed.), *Australia 1942: In the Shadow of War*, Melbourne: Cambridge University Press, 2012.
Dean, Peter (ed.), *Australia 1943: The Liberation of New Guinea*, Melbourne: Cambridge University Press, 2013.
Dear, I.C.B., and Foot, M.R.D. (eds), *The Oxford Companion to World War II*, Oxford: Oxford University Press, 2005.
Dennis, Peter; Grey, Jeffrey; Morris, Ewan; Prior, Robin; with Bou, Jean (eds), *The Oxford Companion to Australian Military History*, Melbourne: Oxford University Press, 2nd Edition, 2008.
Dixon, Robert, *Writing the Colonial Adventure: Race, Gender and Nation in Anglo–Australian Popular Fiction, 1875–1914*, Melbourne: Cambridge University Press, 1995.
Dixon, Robert, *Prosthetic Gods: Travel, Representation and Colonial Governance*, St Lucia: University of Queensland Press, 2001.
Dower, John, *War without Mercy: Race and Power in the Pacific War*, New York: Pantheon Books, 1986.
FitzSimons, Peter, *Kokoda*, Sydney: HodderHeadline, 2004.
Frank, Richard B., *Downfall: The End of the Imperial Japanese Empire*, New York: Penguin, 1999.
Gerster, Robin, *Big-Noting: The Heroic Theme in Australian War Writing*, Melbourne: Melbourne University Press, 1987.
Gerster, Robin, *Hotel Asia: An Anthology of Australian Literary Travelling to 'The East'*, Melbourne: Penguin Books, 1995.
Gerster, Robin, *Travels in Atomic Sunshine: Australia and the Occupation of Japan*, Melbourne: Scribe, 2008.
Gerster, Robin, and Pierce, Peter, *On the Warpath: An Anthology of Australian War Writing*, Melbourne: Melbourne University Press, 2004.
Glassop, Lawson, *We Were the Rats*, Sydney: Angus & Robertson, 1944.
Goldsworthy, David (ed.), *Facing North: A Century of Australian Engagement with Asia*, Melbourne: Melbourne University Press, 2001.
Goodall, Heather, 'Port politics: Indian seamen, Australian unions and Indonesian independence 1945–47', *Labour History*, no. 94, May 2008, pp. 43–68.
Grant, Lachlan, 'Mateship, memory and the Australian ex-prisoners of war memorial:

Incorporating the prisoner of war experience within Anzac', MA (Thesis): Monash University, 2005.

Grant, Lachlan, 'The AIF and the end of empires: soldiers' attitudes toward a "Free Asia"', *Australian Journal of Politics and History*, vol. 57, no. 4, December 2011, pp. 479–94.

Gray, Geoffrey, 'The coming of war to the territories: forced labour and broken promises', *Remembering the War in New Guinea Symposium 19–21 October 2000*, online at: <http://ajrp.awm.gov.au>, accessed 12 July 2009.

Hack, Karl, and Blackburn, Kevin, *Did Singapore Have to Fall? Churchill and the Impregnable Fortress*, London: Routledge, 2003.

Hay, David, *Nothing Over Us: The Story of the 2/6th Australian Infantry Battalion*, Canberra: Australian War Memorial, 1984.

Horne, Gerald, *Race War! White Supremacy and the Attack on the British Empire*, New York: New York University Press, 2004.

Horner, David, *High Command: Australia and Allied Strategy 1939–1945*, Sydney: Allen & Unwin, 1982.

Hyam, Ronald, *Empire and Sexuality: The British Experience*, Manchester: Manchester University Press, 1990.

Hyam, Ronald, *Understanding the British Empire*, Cambridge: Cambridge University Press, 2010.

Iddries, Ion, *Gold-dust and Ashes: The Romantic Story of the New Guinea Goldfields*, Sydney: Angus & Robertson, 1933.

Inglis, Ken, 'War, race and loyalty in New Guinea, 1939–1945', *The History of Melanesia (papers delivered at the Second Waigani Seminar)*, Port Moresby: University of Papua New Guinea and the Australian National University, 1969, pp. 503–29.

Iriye, Akira, *The Origins of the Second World War in Asia and the Pacific*, London: Longman, 1985.

James, Karl, 'White, black, and brown: Attitudes to race as reflected during the Bougainville Campaign, 1944–1945', *Alpheus*, vol. 1, June 2004, pp. 1–12.

James, Karl, *The Hard Slog: Australians in the Bougainville Campaign, 1944–45*, Melbourne: Cambridge University Press, 2012.

Johnson, Carl, *Little Hell: The Story of the 2/22 Battalion and Lark Force*, Melbourne: History House, 2004.

Johnston, Mark, *At the Front Line: Experiences of Australian Soldiers in World War II*, Melbourne: Cambridge University Press, 1996.

Johnston, Mark, *Fighting the Enemy: Australian Soldiers and their Adversaries*, Melbourne: Cambridge University Press, 2000.

Johnston, Mark, *The Silent 7th: An Illustrated History of the 7th Australian Division 1940–46*, Sydney: Allen & Unwin, 2005.

Johnston, Mark, 'The civilians who joined up', *Journal of the Australian War Memorial*, Issue 29, November 1996, online at <http://www.awm.gov.au>, accessed 3 March 2006.

Johnston, Mark, *The Proud 6th: An Illustrated History of the 6th Australian Division 1939–1946*, Melbourne: Cambridge University Press, 2008.

Kratoska, Paul H. (ed.), *Malaya and Singapore During the Japanese Occupation*, Singapore: Singapore University Press, 1995.

Lack, John, *No Lost Battalion: An Oral History of the 2/29th Battalion*, Melbourne: Slouch Hat Publications, 2005.

Legge, John, 'Asian studies: from reconstruction to deconstruction', *Australian Cultural History*, no. 9, 1990, pp. 93–102.

Levine, Phillipa, *Prostitution, Race and Politics: Policing Venereal Disease in the British Empire*, New York: Routledge, 2003.

Lockwood, Robert, *Black Armada: Australia and the Struggle for Indonesian Independence 1942–1949*, Sydney: Hale & Ironmonger, 1982.

Lowe, David (ed.), *Australia and the End of Empires: The Impact of Decolonisation in Australia's Near North, 1945–65*, Geelong: Deakin University Press, 1996.

MacArthur, Brian, *Surviving the Sword: Prisoners of the Japanese 1942–45*, London: Time Warner, 2005.

MacKenzie, John M., *Propaganda and Empire: The Manipulation of British Public Opinion, 1880–1960*, Manchester: Manchester University Press, 1984.

MacKenzie, John M., *The Empire of Nature: Hunting, Conservatism and British Imperialism*, Manchester: Manchester University Press, 1988.

McCormack, Gavin, and Nelson, Hank (eds). *The Burma–Thailand Railway: Memory and History*, St Leonards: Allen & Unwin, 1993.

McQueen, Humphrey, *Social Sketches of Australia 1888–2001*, St Lucia: University of Queensland Press, 2004.

Meaney, Neville, 'Britishness and Australian identity: The problem of nationalism in Australian history and historiography', *Australian Historical Studies*, no. 116, 2001, pp. 76–90.

Moore, Bob, and Hately-Broad, Barbara (eds), *Prisoners of War, Prisoners of Peace: Captivity, Homecoming and Memory in World War II*, Oxford: Berg, 2005.

Nelson, Hank, 'The swinging index: capital punishments and British and Australian administrations in Papua and New Guinea, 1888–1945', *The Journal of Pacific History*, vol. 13, no. 3, 1978, pp. 130–52.

Nelson, Hank, 'Travelling in memories', *Journal of the Australian War Memorial*, no. 3, October 1983.

Nelson, Hank, *POW: Australians Under Nippon*, Sydney: ABC Enterprises, 1985.

Nelson, Hank, '"The Nips are going for the parker": The prisoners face freedom', *War & Society*, vol. 3, no. 2, 1985, pp. 127–43.

Nelson, Hank, 'Turning north: Australians in Southeast Asia in World War 2', *Overland*, no. 119, winter, 1990, pp. 31–39.

Newton, J., 'Angels, heroes and traitors: Images of some Papuans in the Second World War', *Research in Melanesia*, vol. 20, 1996, pp. 141–56.

Newton R.W., and McGuiness, Peter E.M., *Grim Glory: The Official History of the 2/19 Battalion AIF*, Sydney: 1/19 Royal New South Wales Regiment Association, 2006.

Noonan, William, *The Lost Legion: Mission 204 and the Reluctant Dragon*, Sydney: Allen & Unwin, 1987.

O'Hare, Martin, and Reid, Anthony, *Australia Dan Perjuangan Kemerdekaan Indonesia – Australia & Indonesia's Struggle for Independence*, Jakarta: Gramedia Pustaka Utama, 1995.

O'Lincoln, Tom, 'Battles over the war', *Overland*, no. 193, 2008, p. 83.

O'Lincoln, Tom, 'Whose liberty? Australian imperialism and the Pacific War', *Marxists Interventions*, vol. 1, 2009, pp. 83–105.

Oliver, Pam, *Raids on Australia: 1942 and Japan's plans for Australia*, Melbourne: ASP, 2010.

Powell, Allan, *The Third Force: ANGAU's New Guinea War, 1942–46*, Melbourne: Oxford University Press, 2003.

Read, K.E., 'Effects of the Pacific War in the Markhem Valley, New Guinea', *Oceania*, vol. 18, no. 2, 1947, pp. 95–102.

Reed, Liz, '"Part of our own story": Representations of Indigenous Australians and Papua New Guineans with "Australia remembers 1945–1995" – the Continuing Desire for a Homogenous National Identity', *Oceania*, vol. 69, no. 3, 1999, pp. 157–72.

Reed, Liz, *Bigger Than Gallipoli: War, History and Memory in Australia*, Crawley: University of Western Australia Press, 2004.

Reid, Anthony, 'The Australian discovery of Indonesia, 1945', *Journal of the Australian War Memorial*, no. 17, October 1990, pp. 30–40.

Reynolds, E. Bruce, *Thailand's Secret War: The Free Thai, OSS and SOE During World War II*, New York: Cambridge University Press, 2005.

Robinson, Neville, *Villagers at War: Some Papua New Guinean experiences in World War II*, Canberra: Australian National University, 1979.

Ross, Jane, *The Myth of the Digger: The Australian Soldier in Two World Wars*, Sydney: Hale & Iremonger, 1985.

Ross, Sheila, *And Tomorrow Freedom: Australian Guerrillas in the Philippines*, Sydney: Allen & Unwin, 1989.

Russell, W.B., *2/14 Battalion: A History of an Australian Infantry Battalion in the Second World War*, Sydney: Angus & Robertson, 1948.

Ryan, Peter, 'The Australian New Guinea Administrative Unit (ANGAU)', *The History of Melanesia (papers delivered at the Second Waigani Seminar)*, Port Moresby: University of Papua New Guinea and the Australian National University, 1969, pp. 531–48.

Said, Edward, *Culture and Imperialism*, London: Vintage, 1994.

Said, Edward, *Orientalism*, London: Penguin Books, 1995 [1978].

Savage, Victor, *Western Impressions of Nature and Landscape in Southeast Asia*, Singapore: Singapore University Press, 1984.

Scheps, Leo, 'Chimbu Participation in the Pacific War', *The Journal of Pacific History*, vol. 30, no. 1, 1995, pp. 76–86.

Schreuder, Deryck M., and Ward, Stuart (eds.), *Australia's Empire*, Oxford: Oxford University Press, 2008.

Schrijvers, Peter, *The Crash of Ruin: American Combat Soldiers in Europe During World War II*, New York: New York University Press, 1998.

Schrijvers, Peter, *The GI War Against Japan: American Soldiers in Asia and the Pacific During World War II*, New York: New York University Press, 2005.

Smith, Neil C., *Tid-Apa: The History of the 4th Anti-Tank Regiment 1940–1945*, Melbourne: Mostly Unsung Military History Research and Publications, 1992.

Sobocinska, Agnieskza, '"The Language of Scars": Australian prisoners of war and the colonial order', *History Australia*, vol. 7, no. 3, December 2010.

Stanley, Peter, *Tarakan: An Australian Tragedy*, Sydney: Allen & Unwin, 1997.

Stanley, Peter, '"Great in Adversity": Indian Prisoners of War in New Guinea', *Journal of the Australian War Memorial*, no. 37, 2002.

Stanley, Peter, *Invading Australia: Japan and the Battle for Australia, 1942*, Melbourne: Viking Penguin, 2008.

Sturma, Michael, *South Sea Maidens: Western Fantasy and Sexual Politics in the South Pacific*, Westport: Greenwood Press, 2002.

Sublet, Frank, *Kokoda to the Sea: A History of the 1942 Campaign in Papua*, Melbourne: Slouch Hat Publications, 2000.

Tavan, Gwenda, *The Long Slow Death of White Australia*, Melbourne: Scribe, 2005.

Thorne, Christopher, *Allies of a Kind: The United States, Britain, and the War Against Japan, 1941–1945*, Oxford: Oxford University Press, 1978.

Thorne, Christopher, *Racial Aspects of the Far Eastern War of 1941–1945*, London: Oxford University Press, 1985.

Torney-Parlicki, Prue, *Somewhere in Asia: War, Journalism, and Australia's Neighbours 1941–75*, Sydney: University of New South Wales Press, 2000.

Toyoda, Yukio, and Nelson, Hank (eds), *Pacific War in Papua New Guinea: Memories and Realities*, Tokyo: Rikkyo University, Centre for Asian Area Studies, 2006.

Turner, Louis, and Ash, John, *The Golden Hordes: International Tourism and the Pleasure of Periphery*, London: Constable, 1975.

Twomey, Christina, *Australia's Forgotten Prisoners: Civilians Interned by the Japanese in World War Two*, Melbourne: Cambridge University Press, 2007.

Twomey, Christina, 'Emaciation of emasculation: photographic images, white masculinity and captivity by the Japanese in World War Two', *The Journal of Men's Studies*, vol. 15, no. 3, 2007, pp. 295–310.

Uren, Malcom, *A Thousand Men at War: The Story of the 2/16th Battalion, AIF*, Melbourne: Heinemann, 1959.

Vickers, Adrian, 'Kipling goes south: Australian novels and South East Asia 1895–1945, *Australian Cultural Studies*, no. 9, 1990, pp. 65–79.

Wahlert, Glenn, *The Other Enemy? Australian Soldiers and the Military Police*, Melbourne: Oxford University Press, 1999.

Walker, David, *Anxious Nation: Australia and the Rise of Asia 1850–1939*, St Lucia: University of Queensland Press, 1999.

Walker, David, 'Survivalist anxieties: Australian responses to Asia, 1890s to the present', *Australian Historical Studies*, vol. 33, no. 120, 2002, pp. 19–30.

Wall, Don, *Singapore and Beyond: The Story of the Men of the 2/20 Battalion Association*, Sydney: 2/20 Battalion Association, 1985.

Warren, Allan, *Singapore 1942: Britain's Greatest Defeat*, Melbourne: Hardie Grant, 2002.

Warren, James, *Rickshaw Coolie: A People's History of Singapore (1880–1940)*, Singapore: Oxford University Press, 1986.

Warren, James, *Pirates, Prostitutes & Pullers: Explorations in the Ethno- and Social History of Southeast Asia*, Crawley: University of Western Australia Press, 2008.

White, Geoffrey, and Lindstrom, Lamont (eds), *The Pacific Theatre: Island Representations of World War II*, Honolulu: University of Hawaii Press, 1989.

White, Geoffrey, and Lindstrom, Lamont (eds), *Black and White Memories of the Pacific War*, Washington: Smithsonian Institution Press, 1990.

White, Richard, 'Bluebells and Fogtown: Australians' first impressions of England, 1860–1940', *Australian Cultural History*, no. 5, 1986, pp. 44–59.

White, Richard, 'The soldier as tourist. The Australian experience of the Great War', *War & Society*, vol. 5, no. 9, May 1987, pp. 63–78.

White, Richard, 'Sun, sand and syphilis: Australian soldiers and the Orient, Egypt 1914', *Australian Cultural Studies*, no. 9, 1990, pp. 49–64.

Whitelocke, Cliff, and George O'Brien, *Gunners in the Jungle: A Story of the 2/15 Field Regiment, Royal Australian Artillery, 8 Div, AIF*, Sydney: 2/15 Field Regiment Association, 1983.

Wieland, James, 'There and back with the Anzacs: more than touring', *Journal of the Australian War Memorial*, no. 18, April 1991, pp. 49–56.

Woolf, Leonard, *Growing: An Autobiography of the Years 1904–1911*, London: Hogarth, 1961.

Woollacott, Angela, *Gender and Empire*, New York: Palgrave Macmillan, 2006.

Ziino, Bart, 'A kind of round trip: Australian soldiers and the tourist analogy, 1914–1918', *War & Society*, vol. 25, no. 2, October 2006, pp. 39–75.

NOTES

Introduction

1   Cinesound 498, 'Singapore stands to arms: Aussies honour Anzac Day', 1941, AWM F00527.

2   Hank Nelson, *POW – Australians under Nippon*, Sydney: ABC, 1985; Mark Johnston, *Anzacs in the Middle East: Australian Soldiers, their Allies and the Local People in World War II*, Melbourne: Cambridge University Press, 2012.

3   David Walker, *Anxious Nation: Australia and the Rise of Asia 1850–1939*, St Lucia: University of Queensland Press, 1999; David Walker, 'Survivalist anxieties: Australian responses to Asia, 1890s to the present', *Australian Historical Studies*, vol. 33, no. 120, 2002, pp. 19–30; Paul Battersby, *To the Islands: White Australians and the Malay Archipelago Since 1788*, Plymouth: Lexington, 2007; Broinowski, Alison, *The Yellow Lady: Australian Impressions of Asia*, Melbourne: Oxford University Press, 1999; Nicholas Brown, 'Australian intellectuals and the image of Asia: 1920–1960', *Australian Cultural History*, no. 9, 1990, pp. 80–92; Legge, John, 'Asian studies: From reconstruction to deconstruction', *Australian Cultural History*, no. 9, 1990, pp. 93–102.

1   Australia, the war, and the world

1   Cited in David Day, *The Great Betrayal: Britain, Australia & the Onset of the Pacific War, 1939–45*, Sydney: Angus & Robertson, p. 2.

2   Joan Beaumont, 'Australia's war: Europe and the Middle East', in Beaumont (ed.), *Australia's War 1939–45*, Sydney: Allen & Unwin, 1996, p. 9.

3   Day, *The Great Betrayal*, pp. 5–7.

4   Neville Meaney, 'Britishness and Australian identity: The problem of nationalism in Australian history and historiography', *Australian Historical Studies*, no. 116, 2001, pp. 80–82.

5   John Barrett, *We Were There: Australian Soldiers of World War II Tell Their Stories*, Melbourne: Penguin, 1987, pp. 125–35.

6   Chris Waters, 'War, decolonisation and postwar security', in David Goldsworthy, (ed.), *Facing North: A Century of Australian Engagement with Asia*, Melbourne: Melbourne University Press, 2001, pp. 128–30.

7   *Australian Gallup Polls*, April 1943; Gwenda Tavan, *The Long Slow Death of White Australia*, Melbourne: Scribe, 2005, pp. 40–41.

8   *The Herald*, 18 January 1944.

9   Broinowski, *The Yellow Lady*, 13–14.

10   Adrian Vickers, 'Kipling goes south: Australian novels and South-East Asia

1894–1945', *Australian Cultural History*, no. 9, 1990, p. 66.
11 Victor Savage, *Western Impressions of Nature and Landscape in Southeast Asia*, Singapore: Singapore University Press, 1984, pp. 16–17.
12 Broinowski, *The Yellow Lady*; Vickers, 'Kipling goes south'; David Walker, *Anxious Nation*; Robert Dixon, *Writing the Colonial Adventure: Race, Gender and Nation in Anglo-Australian Popular Fiction, 1875–1914*, Melbourne: Cambridge University Press, 1995.
13 Broinowski, *The Yellow Lady*, p. 39; Robert Dixon, *Prosthetic Gods: Travel, Representation and Colonial Governance*, St Lucia: University of Queensland Press, 2001.
14 Broinowski, *The Yellow Lady*, p. 24.
15 John M. MacKenzie, *Propaganda and Empire: The Manipulation of British Public Opinion, 1880–1960*, Manchester: Manchester University Press, 1984, pp. 147–227.
16 Richard White and Hsu-Ming Teo, 'Popular culture', in Deryk M. Schreuder and Stuart Ward (eds), *Australia's Empire*, Oxford: Oxford University Press, 2009, pp. 340 and 345–47.
17 R. Bryant, *Pictorial History of the British Empire, Social, Descriptive, and Biographical*, London: James Sangster and Co. [c. 1890s].
18 For example, see the *Victorian Readers* series published by the Education Department of Victoria.
19 White and Teo, 'Popular culture', pp. 336–61.
20 *The Age*, 27 April 1939.
21 *The Herald*, 27 December 1941.
22 Beaumont, 'Australia's war: Asia and the Pacific', pp. 30–33; Winston S. Churchill, *The Second World War*, London: Bloomsbury, 2013, pp. 523–24.
23 David Horner, *High Command: Australia and Allied Strategy 1939–1945*, Sydney: Allen & Unwin, 1982, pp. 157–58.
24 Scott MacWilliam, 'Papua New Guinea in the 1940s: Empire and legend', in David Lowe (ed.), *Australia and the End of Empire: The Impact of Decolonisation in Australia's Near North, 1945–65*, Geelong: Deakin University Press, 1996, pp. 26–27.
25 David Lowe, 'Australia in the world', in Beaumont (ed.), *Australia's War: 1939–45*, pp. 175–76.
26 Waters, 'War, decolonisation and postwar security', pp. 108–10.

2   The new world: Arriving in British Asia

1 *The Argus*, 20 February 1941.
2 Richard White, 'The soldier as tourist: the Australian experience of the Great War', *War & Society*, vol. 5, no. 1, May 1987, pp. 63–77; Robin Gerster and Peter Pierce (eds), *On the Warpath: An Anthology of Australian Military Travel*, Melbourne: Melbourne University Press, 2004; Bart Ziino, 'A kind of round trip: Australian soldiers and the tourist analogy, 1914–1918', *War & Society*, vol. 25, no. 2, October 2006, pp. 39–75; Robin Gerster, *Hotel Asia: An Anthology of Australian Literary Travelling to 'the East'*, Melbourne: Penguin, 1995; Richard White, 'Sun, sand and syphilis: Australian soldiers and the Orient, Egypt 1914', *Australian Cultural Studies*, no. 9, 1990, pp. 49–64; James Wieland, 'There and back with the Anzacs: more than touring', *Journal of the Australian War Memorial*, no. 18, April 1991, pp. 49–65.
3 Robert Ingrim, letter, 15 January 1942, AWM PR03447.
4 *Through*, December 1941; Bob McIlree, letter, 10 April 1941, SLV MSB402 / MS 11301.

5   *The Times*, 16 May 1936.

6   Ingrim, letter, 15 January, 1942. Collections of postcards featuring these ocean liners were the pride of the Royal Navy and have been deposited by soldiers within the Australian War Memorial's collection: AWM 3/173–3/680, 749/69/21, box 27. Soldiers also collected menus from aboard the liners as mementoes.

7   Bob McIlree, letter, 10 May 1941, SLV MSB404 / MS11301.

8   Walter Bills, letter, 5 February 1941, AWM PR03205

9   See, for example, an article in *The Times*, 9 August 1938; Hank Nelson, 'Turning north: Australians in Southeast Asia in World War 2', *Overland*, no. 119, winter, 1990, pp. 31–39, p. 31. Writing in the 1980s, one soldier wrote of the *Queen Mary*'s manoeuvre out of convoy as a 'sight never to be forgotten': Clarence Weir, 'Return from Singapore', p. 4, AWM PR01968.

10   Cited in *Soldiering On: The Australian Army at Home and Overseas*, Canberra: Australian War Memorial, 1942, p. 53.

11   Vickers, 'Kipling goes south', p. 67.

12   William Noonan, *The Surprising Battalion: Australian Commandos in China*, Sydney: Halstead Press, 1945, pp. ix–x, 36.

13   For just one example, see: K. Barrett, AWM, MSS0764.

14   Rohan Rivett, for example, atop his prison block at first light in Moulmein in Burma, wrote: 'true to Kipling's promise, the dawn came up like thunder; and there behind us, its bells tinkling faintly in the gentle morning breeze, was a golden-topped pagoda'. While he thought that this was the pagoda from Kipling's verse, being the biggest and highest in Moulmein, Rivett felt that although 'it does lookout towards the sea', Kipling's geography was definitely astray as China was definitely not 'across the bay'. Rohan Rivett, *Behind Bamboo*, Melbourne: Penguin, 2003, pp. 174–75.

15   E.A. Nichols cited in *Through*, December 1941.

16   Noonan, *The Surprising Battalion*, p. 25.

17   Bills, letter, 19 February 1941.

18   Russell Braddon, *The Naked Island*, Melbourne: Penguin, 1993, p. 28.

19   J.F. Williams, letter, 25 April 1941, SLV Box 3515

20   Edward Burrey, diary, 2 May 1943, AWM PR90/048.

21   Arthur Wallin, diary, 15 April 1942, SLV MS 10172 MSB 597.

22   *'Wild Woodbine': Some Useful Hints for Soldiers Arriving in India*, Bristol and London, W.D. & H.O. Wills, c. 1942, AWM RC02398, 4/4/1, 419/84/39.

23   Noonan, *The Surprising Battalion*, p. 9; Similarly, in a letter to a friend Bob McIllree wrote: 'this is a very pretty country and very fertile, it rains every other day and all the growth is immense', McIllree, letter, 10 May 1941, SLV, MSB402 / MS11301.

24   Howard Barker, letter, 1 April 1941; AWM PR90/048.

25   *Australian Women's Weekly*, 5 April 1941.

26   *Australian Women's Weekly*, 12 April 1941.

27   Charles A. Kelly, diary, 14 May and 20 May 1942; AWM PR02043.

28   William Noonan, *The Lost Legion: Mission 204 and the Reluctant Dragon*, Sydney: Allen & Unwin, 1987, p. 17.

29   John MacKenzie, *The Empire of Nature: Hunting, Conservatism and British Imperialism*, Manchester: Manchester University Press, 1988, p. ix; Louis Turner and John Ash, *The Golden Hordes: International Tourism and the Pleasure of Periphery*, London: Constable, 1975, p. 174.

30   Lionel Wigmore, *The Japanese Thrust*, Canberra: Australian War Memorial, 1957, p. 71.

31 Cliff Whitelocke and George O'Brien, *Gunners in the Jungle: A Story of the 2/15 Field Regiment, Royal Australian Artillery, 8 Div, AIF*, Sydney: 2/15 Field Regiment Association, 1983. Others also wrote of tiger sightings, shootings, and the perceived threat of tigers: Wallin, diary, 25 April 1943; Kelly, diary, 24 March, 14 May and 20 May 1942; Barker, letter, 24 September 1941; *Soldiering On*, p. 61.

32 Kelly, diary, 24 March 1942.

33 For Change Alley, see: Bills, letter, 26 February 1941; for Ceylon, see: Kelly, diary, 31 March 1942.

34 James Bryant, diary, 4 February 1942, SLV, MS9540 MSB51.

35 David C. Griffin, 'The Changi backdrop', 1945, AWM 3DRL/369 50/7/14.

36 *Australian Women's Weekly*, 12 April 1941.

37 Williams, letter, 12 May 1941.

38 Joan Rodwell, letters, 18 and 30 May 1945; SLV MS12357.

39 Whitelocke, *Gunners in the Jungle*, pp. 73–74; See also photograph AWM 011303/30.

40 James Edward Cottier, diary, 1942–43, AWM PR00989.

41 *HMAS Mk III: Written and Prepared By Serving Personnel of the RAN*, p. 123.

42 Noonan, *The Surprising Battalion*, p. 142.

43 Gerald Horne, *Race War! White Supremacy and the Japanese Attack on the British Empire*, New York: New York University Press, 2004, p. 40.

44 Barker, letter, 1 April 1941.

45 Cited in Peter Dennis, Jeffrey Grey, Ewan Morris, Robin Prior with Jean Bou (eds), *The Oxford Companion to Australian Military History*, Melbourne: Oxford University Press, 2008 [Second Edition], p. 39.

46 Robin Gerster, *Big-Noting: The Heroic Theme in Australian War Writing*, Melbourne: Melbourne University Press, 1987, p. 2.

47 Whitelocke, *Gunners in the Jungle*, p. 61.

48 *The Straits Times*, 19 February 1941.

49 *The Straits Times*, 20 February 1941.

50 *Australian Women's Weekly*, 8 March 1941.

51 James Duffy, *Australians in Malaya: And Other Tales of the Malayan Campaign*, Sydney: F.H. Johnston Publishing Company, 1943, p. 3.

52 Eric Andrews, *The Anzac Illusion: Anglo-Australian Relations During World War I*, Melbourne: Cambridge University Press, 1993, pp. 179–85.

53 Whitelocke, *Gunners in the Jungle*, p. 44.

54 Allan Warren, *Singapore 1942: Britain's Greatest Defeat*, Melbourne: Hardie Grant, 2002, pp. 30–31; Christopher Bayly and Tim Harper, *Forgotten Armies: The Fall of British Asia, 1941–1945*, pp. 64–65.

55 AWM52, 1/5/19, 8th Division, No. 1 Prisoner of War Camp Changi War Diary, August–October 1941, part 1.

56 Braddon, *The Naked Island*, p. 32.

57 Glenn Wahlert, *The Other Enemy? Australian Soldiers and the Military Police*, Melbourne: Oxford University Press, 1999, pp. 141–45.

58 Braddon, *The Naked Island*, pp. 33–34.

59 Bayly and Harper, *Forgotten Armies*, p. 64.

60 Gilbert Mant, *Grim Glory*, Sydney: Currawong Publishing, 1955, pp. 30–31.

61 Bayly and Harper, *Forgotten Armies*, p. 64.

62 Mant, *Grim Glory*, pp. 31–33.

63 Karl Hack and Kevin Blackburn, *Did Singapore Have to Fall? Churchill and the Impregnable Fortress*, London: Routledge, 2003, p. 27.

64 *Through*, December 1941.

65   Kelly, diary, 7 May 1942.

66   Noonan, *The Surprising Battalion*, pp. 49 and 60.

67   *Welcome to Bombay*, Bombay: B.R. Gobhad & Co, c. 1941–42; and *The Bombay Hospitality Committee Welcome You to Bombay: Gateway to India*, AWM RC02398, 4/4/1, 419/4/68.

68   Noonan, *The Surprising Battalion*, p. 194.

69   Frank Holt, 'A banker at sea', 1942, SLV MSB454.

70   Blackburn and Hack, *Did Singapore Have to Fall?*, p. 27.

71   Whitelocke, *Gunners in the Jungle*, p. 55.

72   Gilbert Mant, *You'll Be Sorry*, Sydney: Frank Johnson, 1944, p. 81.

73   Wigmore, *The Japanese Thrust*, p. 63.

74   Whitelocke, *Gunners in the Jungle*, p. 127.

75   Bryant, diary, 2 and 3 February 1942. The Lone Pine photograph: AWM A02025.

76   8th Division, No. 1 Prisoner of War Camp Changi War Diary, February–July 1941, part 2, appendices.

77   8th Division, No. 1 Prisoner of War Camp Changi War Diary, August–October 1941, part 1.

78   Braddon, *The Naked Island*, p. 37.

79   Bennett, *Why Singapore Fell*, Sydney: Angus & Robertson, 1944, p. 28.

80   Mant, *Grim Glory*, pp. 29 and 33.

81   Wigmore, *The Japanese Thrust*, p. 72.

82   Mant, *Grim Glory*, p. 20.

83   *Australian Women's Weekly*, 12 April 1941, p. 9.

84   AWM, SEA0146. This photograph of an RAAF serviceman pulling a mate in a rickshaw is accompanied by the following caption: '"Burra Sahibs" frown on such antics by RAAF servicemen but 418274 Warrant Officer (WO) W.G. (Hap) Hazard of Lower Ferntree Gully, Vic, between the shafts of a rickshaw, knows it's only a gag for the camera.'

85   Mant, *Grim Glory*, pp. 30–31. Before the 1950s the term 'British Commonwealth of Nations' referred only to the white dominions. The word 'British' was dropped in 1949 on account of the inclusion of newly independent nations recently granted self-government.

86   Bayly and Harper, *Forgotten Armies*, pp. 50–52; for a description of a visit to the New World and Great World, see: Noonan, *The Surprising Battalion*, pp. 17–18.

87   Braddon, *The Naked Island*, pp. 38–39.

88   Nelson, *POW*, pp. 11–12.

89   Kevin Blackburn, *The Sportsmen of Changi*, Sydney: NewSouth, 2012, pp. 50–51.

90   *Welcome to Bombay*.

91   Noonan, *The Surprising Battalion*, p. 21; Kelly, diary, 30 March 1942.

92   Wigmore, *The Japanese Thrust*, p. 68.

93   Wigmore, *The Japanese Thrust*, p. 557.

94   Nelson, *POW*, p. 11; Nelson, 'Turning north', p. 34.

3   Making friends: First encounters with Asia

1   Prue Torney-Parlicki, *Somewhere in Asia: War, Journalism, and Australia's Neighbours 1941–75*, Sydney: UNSW Press, 2000, pp. 78–79.

2   Gavin Long, *To Benghazi*, Canberra: Australian War Memorial, 1952, p. 71.

3   Nelson, *POW*, p. 11; Nelson, 'Turning north', p. 33.

4   *Australian Women's Weekly*, 8 March 1941 and 12 April 1941.

5   *Australian Women's Weekly*, 12 April 1941.

6   *Australian Women's Weekly*, 22 March 1941.

7   Wigmore, *The Japanese Thrust*, pp. 62–63.

8   Neil C. Smith, *Tid-Apa: The History of the 4th Anti-Tank Regiment*, Melbourne: Mostly Unsung Military History Research and Publications, 1992, p. 27.

9   'President & Members of the Chinese Chamber of Commerce, Batu Pahat, request the pleasure of the company of Corporal R.R.J. Ambrose of the 2/30th Battalion, Australian Imperial Force, at a Tea Party on Sunday 26th October 1941 at 4.30 pm at the Chambers Premises', AWM RC02398, 4:2/1/1, Pub01035.

10   Rodwell, letter, 22 September 1945.

11   Bills, letter, 10 March 1941.

12   Williams, letter, 24 May 1941.

13   Bills, letter, 29 March 1941.

14   Blackburn, *The Sportsmen of Changi*, p. 49.

15   *Australian Women's Weekly*, 22 November 1941.

16   Peter Schrijvers, *The Crash of Ruin: American Combat Soldiers in Europe During World War II*, New York: New York University Press, 1998, p. 174.

17   *Australian Women's Weekly*, 5 and 12 April 1941.

18   Williams, letters, 4 May and 18 June 1941.

19   Nelson, *POW*, p. 12.

20   Cited in *Soldiering On*, p. 54.

21   Bills, letter, 7 March 1941.

22   Bills, letter, 10 March, 13 March and 15 March 1941.

23   AIF greeting cards from Malaya, featuring unit colour patches, also depicted rickshaws, AWM PR01064; see also postcard of Battery Road, Singapore (c. 1933); AWM 3/663 Box 27

24   Bills, letter, 15 March 1941.

25   The author continued: 'Hard to believe that those same beasts of burden are the descendants of the proud and glorious Tang dynasty, which under Emperor Kao Chung, completely routed the Japanese at Chemulpo some hundreds of years ago.' Cited in *Soldiering On*, p. 53.

26   Roy Hodgkinson, AWM ART22775, *RAN in Colombo*, 1945; AWM ART22777, *HMAS Napier entering Colombo graving dock*, 1945; AWM ART22772, *Souvenir hunters*, 1945; See also: AWM ART24308 *Two RAAF groundstaff in Old Delhi street*, 1945.

27   Walter Ross, letters, 4 January 1942 and 3 February 1942, SLV MS11469 Box 1769/7.

28   Wigmore, *The Japanese Thrust*, p. 73.

29   Nelson, 'Turning north', p. 34.

30   Kelly, diary, 14 March, 1 April, 7 April, 6 April, and 6 June 1942.

31   Bills, letter, 7 and 15 March 1941.

32   Noonan, *The Surprising Battalion*, pp. 27–28, 32, 40, 66, 70.

33   Noonan, *The Lost Legion*, pp. 119.

34   Donald Lyndon, diary, 1940, SLV PA01/18 box 1/3 R45.

35   AWM 3/668–3/670, 749/69/21 box 27; Bills, letter, 29 March 1941.

36   Kelly, diary, 29, 30 March 1942; 1, 2, 4, 7, 8, 11, 17, 21 April 1942; 8, 23 May, 1942.

37   Leonard Woolf, *Growing: An Autobiography of the Years 1904–1911*, London: Hogarth, 1961, p. 46.

38   Jane Ross, *The Myth of the Digger: The Australian Soldier in Two World Wars*, Sydney: Hale & Iremonger, 1985, p. 165.

39   Noonan, *The Surprising Battalion*, p. 3; A similar scene was also captured in photograph AWM 009249/15.

40   *The Straits Times*, 19 February 1941.

41   Duffy, *Australians in Malaya*, p. 1.

42   Nelson, 'Turning north', p. 33.

43   Lyndon, diary, 1940; Long, *To Benghazi*, p. 71.

44   8th Division, No. 1 Prisoner of War Camp Changi War Diary, February–July 1941, part 1.

45   Barker, letters, 1 April 1941.

46   Nelson, 'Turning north', p. 35.

47   Malcolm Uren, *A Thousand Men at War: The Story of the 2/16th Battalion*, AIF, Melbourne: Heinemann, 1959, pp. 24–26.

48   Uren, *A Thousand Men at War*, pp. 24–26.

49   Bills, letter, 28 February 1941.

50   This phenomenon is common among Australian travel writing of the early 20th century. See Broinowski, *The Yellow Lady*, p. 12.

51   Turner and Ash, *The Golden Hordes*, p. 145.

52   Bills, letter, 28 February 1941.

53   Isabelle Plante, letter, February–March 1941, SLV MS9215 MSB23.

54   Rodwell, letter, 27 September 1945.

55   Plante, letter, February–March 1941.

56   A photograph of impoverished Ceylonese in a Colombo park is a reflection of this: AWM, 030135/01.

57   A soldier sightseeing in Singapore who was confounded by this 'funny city' exemplifies this in a letter home to his family in Katoomba: 'Real modern in some places and in others very filthy and a lot worse than any slums in Sydney.' Barker, letter, 24 September 1941. See also: Barker, letter, 1 April 1941; T.A. Jones cited in *Through*, December 1941.

58   Broinowski, *The Yellow Lady*, p. 12.

59   Turner and Ash, *The Golden Hordes*, p. 139.

60   *Australian Women's Weekly*, 29 March and 10 April 1941; Bills, letter, 5 March 1941.

61   *Australian Women's Weekly*, 8 March 1941.

62   Bertie George Sawford, letter, 17 August 1941, SLV, box 1872/10 & 11.

63   Skinner, diary, 4 June 1944, AWM PR00908.

64   Johnston, *Anzacs in the Middle East*, p. 8.

65   Noonan, *The Surprising Battalion*, pp. 1–2. Similar descriptions are found in Darling, *Portrait of a Nurse*, p. 11, and Whitelock, *Gunners in the Jungle*, p. 32.

66   Rodwell, letter, 9 October 1945.

67   Most letter-writers and diarists in documenting their arrival in Asian destinations made note of the strong smells that permeated the atmosphere. See, for example: Bills, letters, 26 February 1941; Barker, letter, 1 May, 1941. Another wrote: 'I'll lay 10 to 1, on some of these streets for smells, "whew"', McIlree, letter, 10 May 1941. Noonan was seemingly obsessed with describing the unique odours infusing the air on his arrival at destinations across the region; in Malaya, Burma, China and India, from Port Dickson to Penange, Mandalay to Paoshan. Noonan reasoned that many Malayans slept or sat on the roadside at night because their homes were 'on the nose', Noonan, *The Surprising Battalion*, pp. 5, 8, 24, 33–34, 38, 60, 68 and 84.

68   *Through*, December 1941.

69   Johnston, *Anzacs in the Middle East*, p. 11.

70   See, for example: Barker, letter, 27 March 1941.

71   Bryant, diary, 29 January 1942.

72   Noonan, *The Surprising Battalion*, p. 13–14.

73 Skinner, diary, 6 June 1944.
74 Skinner, diary, 6 December 1944.
75 Cited in *Soldiering On*, p. 56; Bills, letter, 26 February 1941; Sawford, letter, 17 August 1941.
76 See, for example: Plante, letter, March 1941.
77 Braddon, *The Naked Island*, p. 29.
78 Noonan, *The Surprising Battalion*, p. 9.
79 Rivett, *Behind Bamboo*, p. 242.
80 *Through*, December 1941.
81 *Colombo – Information for Visiting Troops*, issued by the Troops Entertainment Committee, Colombo, 28 April 1941, AWM PR03105; Kelly, diary, 8 May 1942. Another problem was that 'one could never be so sure of getting the real thing'.
82 *Welcome to Bombay*.
83 Noonan, *The Surprising Battalion*, p. 32.
84 Bills, letters, 26 February 1941 and 9 March 1941.
85 McIllree, letter, 10 May 1941.
86 Ingrim, letter, 5 February 1942.
87 Kelly, diary, 28 and 30 March 1942.
88 F. Dale, letter, 17 December 1941, AWM PR 90/121.
89 Wallin, diary, 3 May 1940.
90 *Australian Women's Weekly*, 8 March 1941.
91 Uren, *A Thousand Men at War*, pp. 24–26.
92 AWM, P02491.099. Similar scenes document the arrival of soldiers elsewhere: Noonan, *The Surprising Battalion*, p. 36.
93 *'Wild Woodbine'*. Despite a total absence of 'please' or 'thank you', the list included 'That's enough,' 'Make it clean,' 'Take this away,' 'Where are you going?', 'Give the letter to me,' 'What are these?', 'Make the tea,' 'Bring the water,' 'What do you say?', 'What do you want?', 'Get out of the way,' and 'Shut up.'
94 Some officers had Indian servants aboard a troop ship en voyage from Australia to the Middle East in 1940: Lyndon, papers, 1940.
95 Rodwell, letter, 19 September 1945.
96 *Australian Women's Weekly*, 29 November 1941; See also: Barker, letters, 16 October 1941.
97 Whitelocke, *Gunners in the Jungle*, p. 41.
98 Kelly, diary, 30 May 1942.
99 8th Division War Diary, routine order no. 51, 19 September 1941.
100 Uren, *A Thousand Men at War*, pp. 24–26.
101 Hack and Blackburn, *Did Singapore Have to Fall?*, p. 27.
102 See, for example, the photographs: AWM, 030137/01; AWM, 025722.
103 Stanley, *Invading Australia*, pp. 1–2. Such an arrangement was turned on its head in an Australian poster of 1942 urging the construction of Beaufort bombers with the slogan: 'A united "fighting mad" Australia – can never be enslaved', juxtaposed against the then familiar image of a stereotypical Japanese businessman riding a rickshaw being pulled by an Australian worker in front of Flinders Street Station: AWM, ARTV09053, *A united 'fighting mad' Australia can never be enslaved*, 1943.
104 Rodwell, letter, 13 September 1945.
105 Sawford, letter, 22 August 1941.
106 Barker, letter, 1 April 1941. Noonan also describes a rickshaw race: Noonan, *The Surprising Battalion*, p. 33.

107 *Colombo – Information for Visiting Troops.*
108 Noonan, *The Surprising Battalion*, pp. 8, 17 and 21; Braddon, *The Naked Island*, pp. 34–35.
109 Plante, letter, February–March 1941.
110 *Welcome to Bombay*, and *The Bombay Hospitality Committee Welcome You to Bombay*.
111 Ray Parkin, *Wartime Trilogy: Out of the Smoke; Into the Smother; The Sword and the Blossom*, Melbourne: Melbourne University Press, 1999, pp. 382–83.
112 Horne, *Race War!*, pp. 60–61.
113 *The Australian Women's Weekly*, 12 April 1941; Torney-Parlicki, *Somewhere in Asia*, p. 34; Kate Bird, 'Confined to the mainland? Australian women war correspondents reporting from overseas during WW2', *Lilith*, no. 11, 2002, pp. 73–85.
114 Darling, *Portrait of a Nurse*, p. 12.
115 Nelson, 'Turning north', p. 33.
116 Williams, letter, 4 July 1941.
117 *Australian Women's Weekly*, 12 April 1941.
118 Wigmore, *The Japanese Thrust*, p. 71–72.
119 Duffy, *Australians in Malaya*, p. 27.
120 Noonan, *The Surprising Battalion*, p. 29. Criticisms of Shelton-Smith also appear in Williams, letter, 18 August 1941.
121 *Through*, December 1941.
122 Bayly and Harper, *Forgotten Armies*, p. 65.
123 R.W. Newton and Peter E.M. McGuiness, *Grim Glory: The Official History of the 2/19 Battalion AIF*, Sydney: 1/19 Royal New South Wales Regiment Association, 2006. Cartoons first published in *The Nineteenth: The Magazine of the 2/19th Battalion AIF Malaya*, 1941, vol. 1, p. 13, and vol. 3, p. 31.

4 'Nothing like Dorothy Lamour': Perceptions of Asian women

1 Noonan, *The Surprising Battalion*, p. 24.
2 Cited in Whitelocke, *Gunners in the Jungle*, p. 53.
3 Sean Brawley and Chris Dixon, *Hollywood's South Seas and the Pacific War: Searching for Dorothy Lamour*, New York: PalgraveMacmillan, 2012, p. 27.
4 Bayly and Harper, *Forgotten Armies*, p. 35.
5 Barker, letter, 27 March 1941.
6 Bills, letter, 22 February 1941; *Australian Women's Weekly*, 10 May 1941.
7 Said, Edward, *Orientalism*, London: Penguin, 1995 [1975], p. 190.
8 For further scholarship on these issues see: Ronald Hyam, *Empire and Sexuality: The British Experience*, Manchester: Manchester University Press, 1990; Ronald Hyam, *Understanding the British Empire*, Cambridge: Cambridge University Press, 2010; Phillipa Levine, *Prostitution, Race and Politics: Policing Venereal Disease in the British Empire*, New York: Routledge, 2003; Angela Wollacott, *Gender and Empire*, New York: PalgraveMacmillan, 2006.
9 Robin Gerster, *Hotel Asia*, 1995, pp. 8–10; Broinowski, *The Yellow Lady*, p. 33.
10 Broinowski, *The Yellow Lady*, pp. 65–66.
11 Peter Schrijvers, *The GI War Against Japan: American Soldiers in Asia and the Pacific During World War II*, New York: New York University Press, 2005, p. 151.
12 Noonan, *The Surprising Battalion*, pp. 18, 44.
13 Noonan, *The Surprising Battalion*, p. 64.
14 Ray Parkin, *Wartime Trilogy*, pp. 697–98.
15 'A soldier's life in Malaya', *Salt*, vol. 1, no. 11, 8 December 1941, pp. 14–15.
16 *The Borneo Book for Servicemen*, Australian Military Forces, p. 28.

17   *Java: Handbook for Servicemen*, Allied Geographic Section, South West Pacific
     Area, 1943, p. 19.
18   *The Borneo Book for Servicemen*, p. 28.
19   *You and the Native: Notes for the Guidance of Members of the Forces in Their Relations with
     New Guinea Natives*, Allied Geographical Section, South West Pacific Area,
     12 February 1943, p. 8.
20   Brawley and Dixon, *Hollywood's South Seas and the Pacific War*, p. 68.
21   Allan S. Walker, *Clinical Problems of War*, Canberra: Australian War Memorial,
     1952, p. 266.
22   *Venereal Disease in Singapore: And How to Avoid It*, Singapore: printed at the
     Government Printing Office by W.T. Cherry, Government Printer, 1941.
23   Walker, *Anxious Nation*, pp. 127–40.
24   AWM52, 8/3/20, 2/20th Battalion War Diary, February–March 1941.
25   The first of a series of articles on VD appeared in *Salt*, vol. 2, no. 5, 2 February
     1942.
26   AWM52, 1/5/62, Kuching Force War Diary, September–December 1945.
27   AWM52, 2/2/21, 21st Infantry Brigade War Diary, Routine Order,
     17 November 1945.
28   AWM52 8/3/14, 2/14th Battalion War Diary, 31 October 1945.
29   Schrivers, *The GI War Against Japan*, p. 154.
30   Kuching Force War Diary, September–December 1945.
31   Barrett, *We Were There*, p. 351.
32   Noonan, p. 33.
33   Cited in Barrett, *We Were There*, pp. 252–53; AWM52, 1/5/14, 7th Division War
     Diary, November–December 1945.
34   *Java*, p. 12.
35   *Java*, p. 24; Very similar are the descriptions within *A Pocket Guide to New Guinea
     and the Solomons*, p. 49.
36   *Salt*, vol. 1, no. 7, 10 November 1941, p. 4.
37   *Salt*, vol. 2, no. 4, 26 January 1942.
38   Williams, letter, 25 April 1941.
39   Mant, *Grim Glory*, p. 22.
40   Wigmore, *The Japanese Thrust*, pp. 62–63.
41   Kelly, diary, 25 April, 8 May and 22 May 1942.
42   *The Seventeenth Infantry Brigade Magazine: A Record of Four Years Campaigning*,
     Australian Military Forces, 1944, p. 92.
43   Noonan, *The Surprising Battalion*, pp. 8–9 and 29.
44   Letter published in *Australian Women's Weekly*, 24 May 1941.
45   Braddon, *The Naked Island*, pp. 34–35.
46   Unknown author, diary, 8 February 1942, SLV PA box 64.
47   Noonan, *The Surprising Battalion*, pp. 16 and 39.
48   Noonan, *The Surprising Battalion*, p. 193.
49   Lawson Glassop, *We Were the Rats*, Sydney: Angus & Robertson, 1944, reprinted
     in *The Australian War Classics Collection*, Melbourne: Penguin, 2001, pp. 96–104.
50   Jack Barber, *The War, the Whores and the Afrika Korps*, Sydney: Kangaroo Press,
     1997, p. 31.
51   Allan S. Walker, *Middle East and Far East*, Canberra: Australian War Memorial,
     1961, pp. 345, 466.
52   Walker, *Clinical Problems of War*, pp. 264–68; S.C. Rexford-Welch, *The Royal
     Air Force Medical Services, Volume II: Commands*, London: Her Majesty's Stationery
     Office, 1955, p. 73.
53   Walker, *Clinical Problems of War*, pp. 264–68; Allan S. Walker, *Medical Services of the*

R.A.N. and R.A.A.F., Canberra: Australian War Memorial, pp. 244 and 261.

54   Walker, *Clinical Problems of War*, p. 269. It is quite evident that this was a particular concern within the divisional unit diaries. See, for example: 7th Division War Diary, November–December 1945; Kuching Force War Diary, September–December 1945.

55   Australian Bureau of Statistics, <www.abs.gov.au/AUSSTATS/abs@.nsf/Lookup/4102.0Main+Features10Jun+2012#Sexually>, accessed 8 November 2013.

56   Walker, *Clinical Problems of War*, p. 269.

57   Mary Ellen Condon-Rall and Albert E. Cowdrey, *The Medical Department: Medical Services in the War against Japan*, Washington DC: Centre for Military History, United States Army, 1998, pp. 58 and 140.

58   Brawley and Dixon, *Hollywood's South Seas and the Pacific War*, pp. 79–80.

59   Barrett, *We Were the Rats*, pp. 345–46.

60   Schrijvers, *The GI War Against Japan*, pp. 40–43.

61   AWM52, 8/3/13, 2/13th Battalion War Diary, routine orders, 26 October 1945.

62   'Walking wounded', *Compass*, ABC TV, broadcast 13 August 2006.

63   Holt, 'A banker at sea'.

64   Allen Tye, diary, February 1946, AWM PR00746.

65   Hank Nelson (ed.) and Eddie Stanton, *The War Diaries of Eddie Allan Stanton: Papua 1942–45, New Guinea 1945–1945*, St Leonards: Allen & Unwin, 1996, pp. 121, 152, 196, 207, 226, 249, 283. While Stanton himself wrote that after nearly two-and-a-half years he had not had anything to do of a 'sexual nature with the native women', there were certainly others who used their positions to acquire women. Also, in New Guinea, photos of naked Indigenous women taken by GIs were popular trade items.

66   Barrett, *We Were There*, p. 352.

67   Cited in *HMAS MK IV: Written and Prepared By Serving Personnel of the RAN*, Canberra: Australian War Memorial, 1945, pp. 161–62.

68   Noonan, p. 47.

69   Nelson (ed.) and Stanton, *The War Diaries of Eddie Allan Stanton*, pp. 16, 81 and 291. Stanton used descriptions of the racial mix of American troops to defend the White Australia policy, and his contempt for half-castes is evident in his vindictive and callous description of the death of 70 half-castes drowned when a Japanese submarine sank the *Mamutu*. His diary reads: 'So long, half castes!'

70   Schrijvers, *The GI War Against Japan*, p. 156.

71   Gerster, *Travels in Atomic Sunshine: Australia and the Occupation of Japan*, Melbourne: Scribe, 2008, pp. 224–26.

72   Cited in Whitelocke, *Gunners in the Jungle*, pp. 44–45.

73   Barrett, *We Were There*, p. 352.

74   Barker, letter, 27 March 1942.

75   Edward William Burrey, diary, 18 August 1942, AWM PR00662.

76   Noonan, *The Surprising Battalion*, pp. 11, 44, 79 and 84.

77   Rivett, *Behind Bamboo*, p. 224.

78   For comment on the practice of chewing betel nut, see: Parkin, *Wartime Trilogy*, 694–95; Unknown author, diary, 8 February 1942; Stephen Murray-Smith, *Journal*, SLV MS8272Y box 262; Rivett, *Behind Bamboo*, pp. 365–67; Wigmore, *The Japanese Thrust*, p. 395; and Noonan, *The Surprising Battalion*, p. 8.

79   Schrijvers, *The GI War Against Japan*, pp. 151–56; Judith A. Bennett, *Natives and Exotics: World War II and Environment in the Southern Pacific*, Honolulu: University of Hawai'i Press, 2009, pp. 38–39.

80   *On Target: With the American and Australian Anti-Aircraft Brigade in New Guinea, Written*

and Illustrated by Men of the Front Line Forces, Sydney: Angus & Robertson, 1943, p. 86.

5 Myth and memory: Australia's war in New Guinea

1   'History of ANGAU from the viewpoint of the employment and treatment of the native population in Australian New Guinea 1942–1945', AWM54, 80/2/1; Hank Nelson, 'Report on historical sources on Australia and Japan at war in Papua and New Guinea, 1942–45', at <rspas.anu.edu/papers/sources.html>, accessed 9 March 2006.

2   Hank Nelson, 'Looking black', Yukio Toyoda and Hank Nelson (eds), *The Pacific War in Papua New Guinea: Memories and Realties*, Tokyo: Rikkyo University, 2006, pp. 155–56.

3   J. Newton, 'Angels, heroes and traitors: Images of some Papuans in the Second World War', *Research in Melanesia*, vol. 20, 1996, pp. 141–56; Noah Riseman, *Defending Whose Country: Indigenous Soldiers in the Pacific War*, Lincoln: University of Nebraska Press, 2012, p. 102.

4   This occurred in Iatmul village in the Sepik; Lamont Lindstrom and Geoffrey M. White, 'War stories', Geoffrey White and Lamont Lindstrom (eds.), *The Pacific Theatre: Island Representations of World War II*, Honolulu: University of Hawaii Press, 1989, p. 23.

5   Leo Scheps, 'Chimbu participation in the Pacific War', *The Journal of Pacific History*, vol. 30, no. 1, 1995, pp. 76–86.

6   Liz Reed, 'Part of our own story', *Oceania*, vol. 69, no. 3, 1999, p. 157; Liz Reed, *Bigger Than Gallipoli*, pp. 138–43.

7   Peter FitzSimons, *Kokoda*, Sydney: HodderHeadline, 2004, pp. 331–32.

8   *On Target*, p. 87; Murray-Smith, letter, 28 May 42.

9   Schrijvers, *The GI War Against Japan*, pp. 26–33.

10   *A Pocket Guide To New Guinea and the Solomons*, p. 3.

11   Allan Dawes, *'Soldier Superb': The Australian Fights in New Guinea*, Sydney: F.H. Johnston Publishing Company, 1943, p. 57.

12   Eric Lambert, *The Twenty Thousand Thieves*, papers 1945–66. As an example, Eric Lambert's New Guinea diary contains several sketches of romantic tropical beach settings, SLV, MSB 132–137.

13   Cited in David Dexter, *The New Guinea Offensives*, Canberra: Australian War Memorial, 1961, p. 500.

14   Murray-Smith, journal. Similar assertions about the fertility and abundance of food in New Guinea are made in Peter Ryan, *Fear Drive My Feet*, Sydney: Duffy and Snellgrove, 2001 pp. 61 and 70.

15   William Dargie, *Patrol in Arcadia*, 1943, AWM ART25915.

16   Lachlan Grant, 'Operations in the Markham and Ramu valleys', Peter Dean (ed.), *Australian 1943: The Liberation of New Guinea*, Melbourne: Cambridge University Press, 2013, p. 233.

17   Osmar White, *Green Armour*, Melbourne: Penguin, 2003, p. 16; George Johnston, *War Diary 1942*, Hong Kong: William Collins, 1984, pp. 95, 108 and 120.

18   *A Pocket Guide to New Guinea and the Solomons*, p. 3.

19   This was a point contemporary reviewers had also made in discussion of Ion Idriess's *Gold-dust and Ashes: The Romantic Story of the New Guinea Goldfields*, Sydney: Angus & Robertson, 1933.

20   John Percival Blencowe, diary, 1942, AWM, PR0282.

21   Murray-Smith, letter, 28 May 1942.

22   Wallin, diary, 26 February 1943.

23   *Salt*, vol. 2, no. 2, 12 January 1942, p. 12

24   W. Brian Molly in *On Target*, pp. 22–24.

25   Cyril E. Fyfe in *On Target*, pp. 25–27.

26   'Willo' in *On Target*, p. 36.

27   Lyndon, letters, 1943.

28   *A Pocket Guide to New Guinea and the Solomons*, pp. 2, 18, 21.

29   AWM 015155, AWM 015157. Schrijvers also notes the 'gold fever' that swept through the ranks of GIs who believed in rumours that Australian deserters were working abandoned gold mines in the mountains: Schrijvers, *The GI War Against Japan*, pp. 23–24.

30   Allusions to prospectors are made in Frank Sublet, *Whatever Man Dares*, Sydney: Kokoda Press, 2013, p. 89.

31   *Cairns Post*, 29 December 1942.

32   *Rabaul Times*, 7 March 1941 and 30 May 1941, cited in Nelson, 'Looking black', in Toyoda and Nelson (eds), *The Pacific War in Papua New Guinea*, p. 145. The incident of the cricket match is cited in Carl Johnson, *Little Hell: The Story of the 2/22 Battalion and Lark Force*, Melbourne: History House, 2004, p. 40. Incidents involving manual labour are cited in Ken Inglis, 'War, race and loyalty in New Guinea, 1939–1945', in *The History of Melanesia (Papers Delivered at the Second Waigani Seminar)*, Port Moresby: University of Papua New Guinea and the Australian National University, 1969, p. 510.

33   AWM52, 8/3/22, 2/22nd Battalion War Diary, routine orders, 22 July 1941.

34   *You and the Native*, p. 17.

35   *You and the Native*, pp. 2, 15.

36   *You and the Native*, pp. 1–2.

37   Nelson (ed.) and Stanton, *The War Diaries of Eddie Allan Stanton*, pp. 161, 203 and 206–207.

38   Maria Lepowski, 'Soldiers and spirits: the impact of World War II on a Coral Sea island', White and Lindstrom, *The Pacific Theatre*, pp. 220–21.

39   White wrote of one of his troublesome servants who infuriated him 'because he was impervious to any expression of anger we could assume. He took the whole business of serving white men as a rich joke, and when threatened with physical violence would giggle shrilly and imitate Joe Louis shaping up': White, *Green Armour*, pp. 57–59, 112–13, 123, 136–39 and 57–59. The AIF newspaper, *Guinea Gold*, also drew upon the responsibilities of white men in the tropics when it published information to highlight Australia's role in maintaining white prestige in New Guinea: *Guinea Gold*, no. 5, 11 April 1943.

40   Johnston, *War Diary 1942*, p. 14.

41   White, *Green Armour*, p. 61.

42   Hawkins, diary, 1943, SLV MS9615 box 2007–08.

43   K. Buckley & K. Klugmen, *'The Australian Presence in the Pacific': Burns Philp 1914–1946*, Sydney: Allen & Unwin, 1983, pp. 362–63.

44   *You and the Native*, p. 1; *The Native Carrier*, p. 20.

45   Johnston, *War Diary 1942*, pp. 39, 109.

46   Wallin, diary, 7 January 1945.

47   Nelson (ed.) and Stanton, *The War Diaries of Eddie Allan Stanton*, p. 213.

48   Wallin, diary, 3 January 1945.

49   Hawkins, diary, December 1943.

50   Powell, *The Third Force: ANGAU's New Guinea War, 1942–46*, Melbourne: Oxford University Press, 2003, p. 200.

51   Powell, *The Third Force*, p. 200.

52   Australian Military Forces, *Khaki and Green: With the Australian Army at Home and*

Overseas, Canberra: Australian War Memorial, 1943, pp. 200–202; Nelson (ed.) and Stanton, *The War Diaries of Eddie Allan Stanton*, p. 164.

53   K.E. Read, 'Effects of the Pacific War in the Markhem Valley, New Guinea', *Oceania*, vol. 18, no. 2, 1947, p. 98.

54   Bert Beros, 'The fuzzy wuzzy angels', AWM EXDOC 134, album 3; Hank Nelson, 'From Kanaka to fuzzy wuzzy angel', Ann Curthoys and Andrew Markus (eds), *Who Are Our Enemies? Racism and the Australian Working Class*, Neutral Bay: Hale and Ironmonger, 1978, p. 186.

55   George Silk, AWM014028; See also work by artists such as William Dargie: AWM ART26653.

56   *Kokoda Frontline!*, (dir.) Damian Parer, Cinesound Productions, 1942. *Kokoda Frontline!* won the Academy Award for Best Documentary in 1943.

57   *The Road to Kokoda*, (dir.) Damian Parer, 20th Century Fox–Movietone, 1942.

58   Karl James, 'Resources on the war in the Pacific at the Australian War Memorial', talk delivered at Australian National University, 9 February 2012; AWM 363 item 1/27, photo no. 14028.

59   Cited in *The Seventeenth Brigade Magazine*, p. 64.

60   Australian Military Forces, *Khaki and Green: With the Australian Army at Home and Overseas*, Canberra: Australian War Memorial, 1943. Their skills were also acknowledged by the official historians: Allan S. Walker, *The Island Campaigns*, Canberra: Australian War Memorial, 1957, p. 33; Dudley McCarthy, *South-West Pacific Area – First Year*, Canberra: Australian War Memorial, 1959, pp. 115–16.

61   R. Edmonds, 'Letter to daughter' published in Adele Shelton-Smith, *The Boys Write Home*, Sydney: published for the *Australian Women's Weekly* by Consolidated Press, 1944, p. 117.

62   D. Woolford, 'Letter to aunt' in Shelton-Smith, *The Boys Write Home*, p. 128.

63   F. Harly, 'Letter' in Shelton-Smith, *The Boys Write Home*, p. 147. Further examples of such admiration are littered throughout the individual histories of Australian battalions that served in New Guinea. For one such example, see David Hay, *Nothing Over Us: The Story of the 2/6th Australian Infantry Battalion*, Canberra: Australian War Memorial, 1984, p. 250.

64   *HMAS Mk. III*, p. 171.

65   White, *Green Armour*, p. 76.

66   *The Borneo Book for Servicemen*, p 42.

67   *You and the Native*, p. 13.

68   *Java*, p. 27; *The Borneo Book for Servicemen*, p. 21.

69   Eric Bergerud, *Touched with Fire: The Land War in the South Pacific*, New York: Viking, 1996, p. 118.

70   Inglis, 'War, race and loyalty in New Guinea, 1939–1945', p. 515.

71   Nelson (ed.) and Stanton, *The War Diaries of Eddie Allan Stanton*, pp. 269–77, 302.

72   Dawes, 'Soldier Superb', p. 51; See also Osmar White, *Parliament of a Thousand Tribes*, London: Heinemann, 1965, pp. 129–30.

73   *Pacific Island Monthly*, January 1943, p. 18.

74   *Pacific Island Monthly*, January 1943, p. 77.

75   Reed, 'Part of our own story', p. 161.

76   Powell, *The Third Force*, pp. vii, 42; Bergerud, *Touched with Fire*, pp. 109–10.

77   *Assault on Salamaua*, (dir.) Damian Parer, Cinesound Productions, 1943.

78   Peter Ryan, 'The Australian New Guinea Administrative Unit (ANGAU)', *The History of Melanesia (Papers Delivered at the Second Waigani Seminar)*, Port Moresby: University of Papua New Guinea and the Australian National University, 1969, p. 540; Nelson, 'From Kanaka to fuzzy wuzzy angel', pp. 180–83.

79   Nelson, 'From Kanaka to fuzzy wuzzy angel', pp. 182–83.

80   Powell, *The Third Force*, p. 36.
81   Powell, *The Third Force*, p. 112.
82   Ryan, 'ANGAU', p. 540.
83   Nelson, 'From Kanaka to fuzzy wuzzy angel', p. 184; For a detailed discussion on the health of native carriers on the Kokoda Trail see: Alison Pilger, 'Courage, endurance and initiative: medical evacuation from the Kokoda Track, August–October 1942', *War & Society*, vol. 11, no. 1, 1993, pp. 52–72.
84   Geoffrey Gray, 'The coming of the war to the territories: forced labour and broken promises', accessed online at <ajrp.awm.gov.au/ajrp/remember.nsf/Web-Frames/SympFrame?>, 27 July 2009.
85   Ryan, 'ANGAU', p. 542.
86   Cited in McCarthy, *South-West Pacific Area – First Year*, p. 132.
87   Powell, *The Third Force*, pp. 193–95.
88   Schrijvers, *The GI War Against Japan*, p. 89.
89   John Blencowe, '1942 report on re-establishing control', AWM PR00282.
90   'Report on operations of 3 Australian Division in Salamaua area from 22 April 43 to 25 August 43', SLV, MS 9595 box 2007–09.
91   Nelson, 'From Kanaka to fuzzy wuzzy angel', p. 183.
92   Nelson (ed.) and Stanton, *The War Diaries of Eddie Allan Stanton*, pp. 85, 235.
93   Neville Robinson, *Villagers at War: Some Papua New Guinean Experiences in World War II*, Canberra: Australian National University, 1979, p. 78.
94   Powell, *The Third Force*, p. 222; AWM52 1/10/1 Australian New Guinea Administrative Unit War Diary, January 1945, Legal section.
95   Hank Nelson, 'More than a change of uniform: Australian military rule in Papua New Guinea, 1942–1946', in Toyoda and Nelson (eds), *The Pacific War in Papua New Guinea*, p. 242.
96   Nelson (ed.) and Stanton, *The War Diaries of Eddie Allan Stanton*, pp. 57, 206–207.
97   Ryan, 'ANGAU', p. 543.
98   Riseman, *Defending Whose Country?*, p. 128.
99   'The digger hangings of World War II', *Foreign Correspondent*, ABC TV, broadcast 25 September 2007.
100 Clarrie James, *ANGAU – One Man Law*, Sydney: AHMP, 2005, pp. 144–46.
101 The quote is from a missionary who witnessed the events, cited in Malama Meleisea, Stewart Firth, Jocelyn Linnekin, and Karen Nero (eds), *The Cambridge History of the Pacific Islanders*, Cambridge: Cambridge University Press, 1997, p. 317.
102 'The digger hangings of World War II', *Foreign Correspondent*.
103 AWM54 506/1/4, 'A file dealing with trials, held by various civil offences, committed by natives, 1943–1944' (March–February 1944); Hank Nelson, 'The swinging index: capital punishments and British and Australian administrations in Papua and New Guinea, 1888–1945', *The Journal of Pacific History*, vol. 13, no. 3, 1978, p. 150; Powell, *The Third Force*, pp. 206–11.
104 Ryan, 'ANGAU', p. 540.
105 John Bain, cited in Powell, *The Third Force*, pp. 156–57.
106 Stirling Tuckey, diary, 1945, AWM PR00440.
107 David Fiendberg, cited in Powell, *The Third Force*, p. 166.
108 Maria Lepowsky, 'Soldiers and spirits', pp. 220–21; song cited in Humphrey McQueen, *Social Sketches of Australia 1888–2001*, St. Lucia: University of Queensland Press, 2004, p. 176.
109 Powell, *The Third Force*, p. 256; Nelson, 'Kokoda: and two national histories', pp. 184–88.
110 Powell, *The Third Force*, p. 177.

111 Schrijvers, *The GI War Against Japan*, pp. 73–78.
112 See for example: Bergerud, *Touched with Fire*, pp. 104–19; Schrijvers, *The GI War Against Japan*, pp. 88–89.
113 Lepowski, 'Soldiers and spirits' p. 218; Schrijvers, *The GI War Against Japan*, p. 97.
114 Powell, *The Third Force*, p. 246.
115 Schrijvers, *The GI War Against Japan*, p. 95.
116 Gavin Long, *The Final Campaigns*, Canberra: Australian War Memorial, 1966. p. 83.
117 Gray, 'The coming of the war to the territories'; Long, *The Final Campaigns*, p. 90.
118 Riseman, *Defending Whose Country?*, p. 105.

6 Reversal of fortunes: POW contacts in captivity

1 Betty Jeffrey, *White Coolies*, Sydney: Angus & Robertson, 1954; William Kent-Hughes, *Slaves of the Samurai*, Melbourne: Oxford University Press, 1946. For more on this point see: Christina Twomey, *Australia's Forgotten Prisoners: Civilians Interned by the Japanese in World War Two*, Melbourne: Cambridge University Press, 2007, pp. 41–58; Agnieskza Sobocinska, '"The language of scars": Australian prisoners of war and the colonial order', *History Australia*, vol. 7, no. 3, December 2010.
2 Stanley Arneil, diary, 24 April 1943, AWM PR 88/076.
3 Murray Griffin, *Changi*, Sydney: Edmund and Alexander, 1992, p. 47.
4 Torney-Parlicki, *Somewhere in Asia*, p. 74.
5 Mark Johnston, *Fighting the Enemy: Australian Soldiers and Their Adversaries*, Melbourne: Cambridge University Press, 2000, pp. 141–42.
6 John Lennon, diary, 13 February 1942, AWM PR00875.
7 Braddon, *The Naked Island*, pp. 98, 172–73.
8 Joan Beaumont, 'Prisoners of war in Australian national memory', in Bob Moore and Barbara Hately-Broad (eds), *Prisoners of War, Prisoners of Peace: Captivity, Homecoming and Memory in World War II*, Oxford: Berg, 2005, pp. 189–91; Lachlan Grant, 'Monument and ceremony: the Australian ex-prisoner of war memorial and the Anzac legend', in Karl Hack and Kevin Blackburn (eds), *Forgotten Captives in Japanese Occupied Asia*, London: RoutledgeCurzon, 2008, pp. 41–54.
9 Whitelocke, *Gunners in the Jungle*, p. 94.
10 C.H. Orne, 'Letter to wife' published in Shelton-Smith, *The Boys Write Home*, p. 104. A similar tale is told within Sawford, letter, 26 January 1942.
11 Bryant, diary, 4 April 1942. Examples are also found in Wigmore, including the assistance given to those who escaped Singapore and made their way through the Indonesian archipelago back to Australia: Wigmore, *The Japanese Thrust*, pp. 216, 248, 387, 505.
12 Bennett, *Why Singapore Fell*, p. 34.
13 Mant, *Grim Glory*, p. 30.
14 Cited in Wigmore, *The Japanese Thrust*, p. 387.
15 Wigmore, *The Japanese Thrust*, pp. 154–55.
16 C. David Griffin, 'The Changi backdrop' 1945, AWM 3DRL/369 50/7/14.
17 Burrey, diary, 18 August 1942.
18 Kevin Blackburn and Karl Hack, *War Memory and the Making of Modern Malaysia and Singapore*, Singapore: National University of Singapore Press, 2012, p. 136–37.
19 Blackburn and Hack, *War Memory*, p. 292.
20 William Miggins, diary, 23 February and 25 April 1942, AWM PR00373.
21 John Nevell, diary, July 1942, AWM PR00257.

22   *Salt*, vol. 11. no. 5, 5 November 1945.

23   Jack Wilfred Turner, papers, AWM, PR00651; Miggins, diary, 27 June 1944. A point is also made of this in the official history of the Malayan campaign in Wigmore, *The Japanese Thrust*, p. 519. On the conditions facing the Chinese community in Malaya during the Japanese occupation, see: Paul Kratoska, *The Japanese Occupation of Malaya 1941–1945*, Sydney: Allen & Unwin, 1998, pp. 93–109; Bayly and Harper, *Forgotten Armies*, pp. 208–30.

24   Turner, papers, 1944–1945.

25   Darling, *Portrait of a Nurse*, p. 34.

26   C. David Griffin, 'The Changi backdrop' 1945; Stan Arneil, 'Aerodrome at Changi Point', 1945; C.P. Tracey, 'Singapore working party', 1944, AWM 3DRL/369 50/7/14.

27   Brian MacArthur, *Surviving the Sword: Prisoners of the Japanese 1942–45*, London: Time Warner, 2005, p. 93.

28   Peter Davies, *The Man Behind the Bridge: Colonel Toosey and the River Kwai*, Exeter: Athlone Press, 2000, pp. 126–28.

29   Edward E. Dunlop, *The War Diaries of Weary Dunlop: Java and the Burma–Thailand Railway 1942–1945*, pp. 252, 341.

30   Barrett, papers, 1942–45.

31   Ian Denys Peek, *One Fourteenth of an Elephant*, Sydney: Macmillan, 2003, p. 8. Peek was a British soldier, though this episode is consistent with Australian experiences.

32   Nelson, '"The Nips are going for the parker": The Prisoners Face Freedom', *War & Society*, vol. 3, no. 2, 1985, p. 129. As a source of protein, eggs were an important and much valued supplement to the prisoners' diet if they could be acquired.

33   'Unsung hero helped POWs', *The Age*, 29 June 2009; Sheila Ross, *And Tomorrow Freedom: Australian Guerrillas in the Philippines*, Sydney: Allen & Unwin, 1989, pp. 144–45.

34   Jack Kerr, PR86/191, diary, 31 August 1945.

35   *Salt*, vol. 11. no. 5, 5 November 1945.

36   *Argus*, 17, 18 and 20 September 1945.

37   Rivett, *Behind Bamboo*, p. 323.

38   David Nathan, radio broadcast, c. September 1945, AWM S04844.

39   Of course, the workings of the mateship ethos were far more complex and far more dynamic. See: Gavan Daws, *Prisoners of the Japanese: POWs of World War II in the Pacific*, New York: William Morrow and Company, 1994; Joan Beaumont, *Gull Force: Survival and Leadership in Captivity 1941–1945*, Sydney: Allen & Unwin, 1988.

40   Hank Nelson, 'Travelling in memories', *Journal of the Australian War Memorial*, no. 3, October 1983.

41   *Australian Women's Weekly*, 29 March 1947.

42   *News Bulletin: The Official Organ of the Australian Ex-Prisoners of War and Relatives Association of Victoria*, August 1997.

43   For pre-war attitudes, see: Pam Oliver, *Raids on Australia: 1942 and Japan's plans for Australia*, Melbourne: ASP, 2010; Steven Bullard, *Blankets on the Wire: The Cowra Breakout and its Aftermath*, Canberra: Australian War Memorial, 2006, p. 42.

44   John Dower, *War without Mercy: Race and Power in the Pacific War*, New York: Pantheon Books, 1986, p. 11.

45   Johnston, *Fighting the Enemy*, p. 86–89; Karl James, *The Hard Slog: Australians in the Bougainville Campaign, 1944–45*, Melbourne: Cambridge University Press, 2012, p. 258.

46 George Johnston, *New Guinea Diary*, Sydney: Angus & Robertson, 1943, p. 225.

47 *Army News*, 27 December 1942.

48 *New York Times*, 9 January 1943.

49 Johnston, *Fighting the Enemy*, p. 88.

50 Barret, *We Were There*, 309–12.

51 Gerster, *Big-Noting*, p. 223.

52 Hank Nelson, 'Beyond slogans: assessing the experiences and the history of Australian prisoners of war of the Japanese', Hack and Blackburn (eds), *Forgotten Captives in Japanese Occupied Asia*, p. 31.

53 Blackburn, *The Sportsmen of Changi*, pp. 4, 167–80.

54 <www.powresearch.jp/en/index.html>, accessed 29 November 2013.

55 John Nevell, diary, 25 October 1944, AWM PR00257.

56 Alexander Dandie (ed.), *The Story of J Force*, Sydney: self-published, 1985, pp. 61–64.

57 Richard B. Frank, *Downfall: The End of the Imperial Japanese Empire*, New York: Penguin, 1999, pp. 81–82.

58 Cited in Hugh V. Clarke, *Twilight to Liberation*, Sydney: Allen & Unwin, 1985, p. 65.

59 Colin Filkins, papers, AWM PR01064.

60 Nevell, diary, 25 October 1944; Hugh V. Clarke, *Last Stop Nagasaki!*, Sydney: Allen & Unwin, 1984, p. 69.

61 Dandie, *The Story of J Force*, p. 65.

62 Miggins, diary, 20 September 1944.

63 Ryoko Adachi and Andrew McKay (eds), *Echoes of War: Australians Voice Their Feelings about Japan*, Melbourne: Mirai Books, 2009, p. 19.

64 Dandie, *The Story of J Force*, p. 77.

65 Clarke, *Twilight Liberation*, p. 27; percentage for Kobe cited in Frank, *Downfall*, pp. 76–77.

66 Tom Uren, 'Journeys in captivity', in Gavin McCormack and Hank Nelson (eds.), *The Burma–Thailand Railway: Memory and History*, St Leonards: Allen & Unwin, 1993, p. 56; 'Tom Uren – back on the Burma Railway', *Dateline*, Broadcast 21 April 2004; <tomuren/compassionateWarrior/tomUrenCompassionateWarrior.html>, accessed 29 March 2010.

67 Hiroki's speech is among the papers of James Moore, AWM PR91/043.

68 <www.powresearch.jp/en/index.html>, accessed 29 November 2013.

69 Lattimer and Dandie cited in Dandie, *The Story of J Force*, p. 59.

70 Kenneth Munro, papers, p. 95, AWM PR01687.

71 <www.abc.net.au/news/2013-11-11/an-former-australian-pow-returns-to-hiroshima-prison-camp/5082186>, accessed 21 November 2013.

72 Ichiji Inoue, letter, 1 August 1951, AWM PR04859.

73 Unknown author, 'The peace comes to X Party', 1945, AWM 3DRL/369 50/7/14.

74 Tuckey, diary, 1945.

75 Thomas Mitchell, papers, AWM PR87/134.

76 Long, *The Final Campaigns*, p. 569.

77 Masuto Hirano, letter, 19 August 1945, AWM PR00736.

78 James, *The Hard Slog*, p. 259.

79 Torney-Parlicki, *Somewhere in Asia*, p. 77; Christina Twomey, 'Emaciation of emasculation: photographic images, white masculinity and captivity by the Japanese in World War Two', *The Journal of Men's Studies*, vol. 15, no. 3, 2007, pp. 295–310.

80 Robert Fitsimons, letter cited in *The Age*, 18 November 2008.

81 Holt, 'A banker at sea'.
82 Torney-Parlicki, *Somewhere in Asia*, p. 60; Peter Stanley, *Invading Australia: Japan and the Battle for Australia, 1942*, Melbourne: Viking, 2008, pp. 117–19.
83 Johnston, *Fighting the Enemy*, p. 88.
84 Nevell, diary, 20 July 1945.
85 Adachi and Mckay, *Echoes of War*, pp. 121–72.
86 Munro, papers, AWM PR01687.
87 Adachi and Mckay, *Echoes of War*, p. 23.
88 Allan Chick, letter, 23 July 1946, AWM PR85/189.

7 At war's end: Facing the new Asia

1   Cited in Clarke, *Last Stop Nagasaki!*, p. 100.
2   Peter McGrath-Kerr, AWM S02898.
3   Nelson, *POW*, p. 189.
4   *Canberra Times*, 4 August 1984.
5   Nevell, papers, AWM PR00257.
6   Cited in Clarke, *Last Stop Nagasaki!*, p. 104.
7   Clarke, *Twilight to Liberation*, p. 59.
8   Nelson, *POW*, p. 201.
9   Nelson, '"The Nips are going for the parker"', p. 137.
10 Burrey, diary, 4 September 1945.
11 Arthur Frederick Shepard, diary, 1942–1945, AWM PR91/049. Others included Harry Ryan, also of the 2/29th Battalion, and R.M. McClure of the 2/4th Anti-Tank Regiment: John Lack, *No Lost Battalion: An Oral History of the 2/29th Battalion*, Melbourne: Slouch Hat Publications, 2005, p. 227.
12 Nelson, *POW*, p. 202.
13 Clarke, *Twilight Liberation*, p. 152.
14 Rodwell, letter, 22 September 1945.
15 *Launceston Examiner*, 26 September 1945; NX68387 Edwin Lloyd Jenkins.
16 Nelson, *POW*, p. 202; A similar scene was described in Pat Darling, *Portrait of a Nurse*, p. 32.
17 William Marshall, *The Western Australian*, 8 November 1945. Marshall signed this letter to the editor under his nickname 'Bacca Bill'.
18 Anthony Reid, 'The Australian discovery of Indonesia, 1945', *Journal of the Australian War Memorial*, no. 17, October 1990, p. 31.
19 Other duties included the repatriation of prisoners of war and internees, and investigating war crimes.
20 Anthony Reid, 'Australia's hundred days in South Sulawesi', in David P. Chandler and M.C. Ricklefs (eds), *Nineteenth and Twentieth Century Indonesia*, Clayton: Monash University Centre of South East Asian Studies, 1986, p. 211.
21 Long, *The Final Campaigns*, p. 567.
22 As an example, see: AWM67, 3/109, I.N. Dougherty, 'Report by Comd Makforce', 28 September 1945; and I.N. Dougherty, 'Speech to Youth Leaders', 16 October 1945. In some places Japanese work parties were on occasion permitted to carry arms for self-protection; W.B. Russell, *The 2/14 Battalion: A History of an Australian Infantry Battalion in the Second World War*, Sydney: Angus & Robertson, 1948.
23 7th Division War Diary, November–December 1945, 'Appendix B to 7 Div. Operational Instr. 6/45'.
24 7th Division War Diary, October 1945, 'Implementation of Surrender – 7 Aust. Div. Daily Bulletin 6', 11 October 1945.
25 7th Division War Diary, 14 and 15 November 1945. Gavin Long notes in the

official history that Robertson's orders were followed (Long, *The Final Campaigns*, p. 568). The unit diary suggests otherwise.

26 Brigadier Fred Chilton took over from Dougherty for a period while Dougherty was on leave. Chilton shared Dougherty's skill in handling the situation.
27 AWM67, 3/109, I.N. Dougherty, 'Speech to youth leaders', 16 October 1945.
28 AWM67, 3/109, I.N. Dougherty, 'Speech to village chieftains', 9 October 1945.
29 2/14th Battalion War Diary, 14 October 1945.
30 Gerke is cited in Reid, 'The Australian discovery of Indonesia, 1945', p. 37; Peter Post (ed.), *The Encyclopaedia of Indonesia in the Pacific War*, Leiden: Brill, 2010, p. 48–49.
31 Long, *The Final Campaigns*, p. 573.
32 Reid, 'The Australian discovery of Indonesia, 1945', p. 35.
33 7th Division War Diary, November 1945.
34 John Burns, *The Brown and Blue Diamond at War: The Story of the 2/27th Battalion*, Adelaide: 2/27 Association, 1960, p. 227.
35 AWM52 8/2/21, 21st Brigade, November 1945.
36 AWM67, 3/109. I.N. Dougherty correspondence with Gavin Long.
37 21st Brigade, November 1945.
38 AWM52, 8/3/27, 2/27th Battalion, 29 October 1945.
39 Reid, 'Australia's hundred days in South Sulawesi', p. 215.
40 21st Brigade War Diary, October 1945.
41 21st Brigade, 'Notes on discussion between Comd Makassar Force and Dr Ratu Langie, 2 Nov 45', November 1945.
42 AWM67, 3/109. I.N. Dougherty correspondence with Gavin Long.
43 AWM67, 3/109. I.N. Dougherty, 'Report by Comd Makforce', 28 September 1945.
44 AWM67, 3/109. I.N. Dougherty correspondence with Gavin Long. It should be noted that such attitudes by the Dutch were also observed elsewhere in Indonesia: Bayly and Harper, *Forgotten Wars*, pp. 168–71.
45 Reid, 'The Australian discovery of Indonesia, 1945', p. 35.
46 This was a view expressed among POWs who had encountered the Dutch as well: Nelson, *POW*, p. 63; Daws, *Prisoners of the Japanese*, p. 92.
47 Robert Lockwood, *Black Armada: Australia and the Struggle for Indonesian Independence 1942–1949*, Sydney: Hale & Ironmonger, 1982, pp. 240–41.
48 Peter Stanley, *Tarakan: An Australian Tragedy*, Sydney: Allen & Unwin, 1997, p. 193.
49 AWM67 2/88, Gavin Long, diary, 15 August 1945.
50 AWM67, 3/109, 'Gantaran, Bonthain, Sindjai, Bikeore letter to Dougherty/Chilton', 18 October 1945.
51 Reid, 'The Australian discovery of Indonesia', p. 35.
52 Lockwood, *Black Armada*, p. 243.
53 Long, *The Final Campaigns*, p. 569. The incident is cited in the 7th Division War Diary 14 and 15 November 1945. Reid and Lockwood have both suggested that it was almost certain that these men were members of the Communist Party of Australia.
54 Stanley, *Tarakan*, pp. 192–93.
55 John Cohen's story is featured in Reid, 'The Australian discovery of Indonesia', p. 38.
56 AWM67, 3/109. I.N. Dougherty, 'Notes on meeting with General Blamey', 18 October 1945.
57 Cited in Long, *The Final Campaign*, p. 575.
58 Reid, 'The Australian discovery of Indonesia, 1945', p. 38; Lockwood, *Black*

Armada, pp. 243–45; Alec Little, AWM S00927.

59   21st Brigade War Diary, November 1945.
60   Lockwood, *Black Armada*, p. 236.
61   Lockwood, *Black Armada*, pp. 144–47.
62   Heather Goodall, 'Port politics: Indian seamen, Australian unions and Indonesian independence 1945–47', *Labour History*, no. 94, May 2008, pp. 43–68; David Lee 'Indonesia's independence', in Goldsworthy (ed.), *Facing North*, pp. 140–47.
63   Lockwood, *Black Armada*, p. 165. Still photos from *Indonesia Calling* depicting Australian soldiers and airmen participating in the protests can be seen in Lockwood opposite page 184 and page 216. *Indonesia Calling*, (dir.) Joris Ivens, Waterside Workers Federation of Australia, 1948.
64   Cited in Martin O'Hare and Anthony Reid, *Australia Dan Perjuangan Kemerdekaan Indonesia – Australia & Indonesia's Struggle for Independence*, Jakarta: Gramedia Pustaka Utama, 1995, p. 15.
65   21st Brigade War Diary, November 1945.
66   Tom Allard, 'Indonesia's consummate diplomat dies', *The Age*, 12 December 2008, p. 12.
67   Awang Maulana Effendi, cited in Reid, 'The Australian discovery of Indonesia, 1945', p. 35.
68   Cited in Long, *The Final Campaigns*, p. 575.
69   Lockwood, *Black Armada*, p. 240.
70   Reid, 'Australia's hundred days in South Sulawesi', pp. 208–209.
71   *Sydney Morning Herald*, 10 November, 1945.
72   Reid, 'Australia's hundred days in South Sulawesi', p. 209.
73   The only two deaths by members of the 21st Brigade during this period of the occupation (October–December) are Private Ivor Sydney Ezzy (NX148169) of the 2/14th Battalion, who died in a jeep accident on 25 December, and Private Eric Nelson Fairall (NX107980) of the 2/27th Battalion, who died of illness on 30 December. There appear to be no deaths recorded for the 2/16th Battalion during this time. The 2/27th was the only unit to report a member wounded. The circumstances of this incident have been described earlier in this chapter.
74   Reid, 'Australia's hundred days in South Sulawesi', p. 209.
75   *The West Australian*, 7 November 1945.
76   27th Battalion War Diary, October 1945.
77   Reid, 'Australia's hundred days in South Sulawesi', p. 220.

8   'Good neighbours' or 'police dogs of imperialism'? Attitudes to empire

1   7th Division War Diary, September 1945, part 1, 17 and 18 September 1945.
2   The program for the event can be located in the War Diary of Kuching Force. Joint Allied Victory and Chinese National Day (Double Ten) Celebrations: Chinese Community, Kuching Sarawak 1945 in Kuching Force War Diary, September–December 1945.
3   Cited in interview with Corey, in 'Australian veterans make journey back to Brunei', *7:30 Report*, ABC, broadcast 10 December 2008.
4   Jack Reddin, 'Memoir', p. 3. AWM PR00902.
5   RELAWM20254; RELAWM32543.
6   Peter Stanley, *Invading Australia*, illustration caption opp., p. 111.
7   *The Age*, 5 August 2008; Tom O'Lincoln, 'Whose liberty? Australian imperialism and the Pacific War', *Marxists Interventions*, vol. 1, 2009, pp. 83–105; Tom O'Lincoln, 'Battles over the war', *Overland*, no. 193, 2008, p. 83.

8   Joan Davis, 'Salt: The journal of the Australian Army Education Service in the Second World War', *Journal of the Australian War Memorial*, no. 17, October 1999, p. 24.

9   Letter published (under the pseudonym 'Anti-Fascist') in *Salt*, vol. 3, no. 3, 20 April 1942, p. 38.

10   D.E. Moffit, letter published in *Salt*, vol. 3, no. 11, 22 June 1942, p. 36.

11   M.D. McGrath, letter published in *Salt*, vol. 9, no. 7, 4 December 1944, pp. 45–46.

12   A.B.E. Harris, letter published in *Salt*, vol. 10, no. 3, 9 April 1945, pp. 50–51.

13   B.H. Evans, letter published in *Salt*, vol. 10, no. 9, 2 July 1945, p. 55.

14   G.S. Brett, letter published in *Salt*, vol. 10, no. 3, 9 April 1945, pp. 50–51.

15   A.J. Taylor, letter published in *Salt*, vol. 10, no. 12, 13 August 1945, p. 46.

16   A.J. Taylor, letter published in *Salt*.

17   Waters, 'War, decolonisation and postwar security', pp. 128–31.

18   Ian Copland, *India, 1885–1947: The Unmaking of an Empire*, New York: Longman, 2001.

19   Noonan, *The Surprising Battalion*, p. 189.

20   Noonan, *The Surprising Battalion*, p. 194. Noonan also observed political unrest and anti-British feeling on the streets of Rangoon while he was in Burma in 1941: 'At that time Burma was going through great unrest. British soldiers were often stabbed in quiet streets and a regulation was introduced compelling them to move about in parties', p. 37.

21   Kelly, diary, 7 June 1942.

22   Wigmore, *The Japanese Thrust*, p. 524; Nelson, 'Turning north', p. 34.

23   Mitchell, papers, 1940–84. Australian imperial ambition is discussed in Lowe, 'Australia in the world', pp. 175–76.

24   Malaya was absent from discussions for three reasons. The independence movement in India and the NEI were topical issues that received wide press coverage during this period. The 'Malayan Emergency' of the postwar period, beginning in 1948, involved small numbers of ethnic Chinese, members of the Malayan Communist Party. This front for independence was not popular among the wider communities of Malaya. Malaysia gained its independence in 1957 during the conflict with communist insurgents, but independence did not arrive because of the insurgency. Unlike in Indonesia or Vietnam, independence was not announced in the power vacuum created by the sudden end of the war. India and debates on Indian independence were not new at this time, and had in fact been given more urgency in the course of the war. Lastly, where Australian troops had encountered India, the NEI and New Guinea they were discussing these issues from as early as 1942, but due to the nature of the fate of members of the 8th Division, the voices of soldiers stationed in Malaya were somewhat lost from these debates.

25   R. Saunders, letter published in *Salt*, vol. 5, no. 4, 26 October 1942, pp. 36–37.

26   P.F. Mortimer, 'It's not too late to win India', *Salt*, vol. 6, no. 1, pp. 40–41.

27   *Salt*, vol. 6, no. 2, 29 March 1943, pp. 40–41.

28   B. Harwood, letter published in *Salt*, vol. 10, no. 7, 4 June 1945, p. 54.

29   Barrett, *We Were There*, pp. 304–305.

30   Braddon, *The Naked Island*, p. 60.

31   Bennett, *Why Singapore Fell*, p. 17; Wigmore, *The Japanese Thrust*, p. 103.

32   Warren, *Singapore 1942*, p. 292.

33   Turner, papers, 1944–45. For a discussion on the experiences of these Indian POWs and the question of their 'loyalty', see: Peter Stanley, '"A disgrace to the Japanese Army": Indian soldiers in NG, 1944–1945', in Toyoda and Nelson

(eds), *The Pacific War in Papua New Guinea: Memories and Realities*, pp. 396–405;
Kaori Maekawa, 'Forgotten soldiers in the Japanese army: Asian POWs in
Papua New Guinea', in Toyoda and Nelson (eds), *The Pacific War in Papua New
Guinea: Memories and Realities*, pp. 362–76; Peter Stanley, '"Great in adversity":
Indian prisoners of war in New Guinea', *Journal of the Australian War Memorial*,
no. 37, 2002; G.J. Douds, 'Indian POWs in the Pacific, 1941–45', in Hack and
Blackburn (eds), *Forgotten Captives in Japanese Occupied Asia*, London: Routledge,
2008, pp. 73–93.

34   Officer quoted in Long, *The Final Campaigns*, p. 340.

35   Text of Singh's farewell address on AWM photograph 101095.

36   *Salt*, vol. 11, no. 4, 22 October 1945, pp. 18–21.

37   W.B. Buchanen, letter published in *Salt*, vol. 10, no. 10, 16 July 1945, p. 49.

38   R. Lewis, letter published in *Salt*, vol. 11, no. 3, 8 October 1945, p. 50.

39   P.L. Smith, letter published in *Salt*, vol. 11, no. 7, 2 December 1945.

40   C.G. Mathews, letter published in *Salt*, vol. 11, no. 4, 22 October 1945, p. 43.

41   F.G. Lynch, letter published in *Salt*, vol. 11, no. 4, 22 October 1945, p. 43.
      Also supporting the view that Indonesia was central to Australian security were
      Sergeant Ross, letter published in *Salt*, vol. 11, no. 9, 31 December 1945,
      p. 49, and Private L.G. Morris, letter published in *Salt*, vol. 11, no. 11,
      28 January 1946, p. 48.

42   J.L. Brown, letter published in *Salt*, vol. 11, no. 4, 22 October 1945, p. 43.

43   G. Steele, letter published in *Salt*, vol. 11, no. 5, 5 November 1945, pp. 51–52.

44   N.L. Rosser, letter published in *Salt*, vol. 11, no. 5, 5 November 1945, pp. 51–
      52. Rosser also proclaimed it would be 'a denial of the statement by President
      Roosevelt that: "We know that the day of exploitation of the resources and
      the people of one country for the benefit of any group in another country is
      definitely over."' The last point made by Rosser is also in reference to the re-
      arming of Japanese soldiers in Indonesia and French Indochina in order to assist
      the return of European control.

45   E.E. Taylor, letter published in *Salt*, vol. 11, no. 12, 11 February 1946, p. 50.

46   Stanley, *Tarakan*, p. 190.

47   Alexander Downer, 'POW politics', 1945, AWM 3DRL/369 50/7/14.

48   'Salute to boong' in *Salt*, vol. 5, no. 13, 1 March 1943, p. 7.

49   NX78467, letter published in *Salt*, vol. 6, no. 4, 16 April 1943, pp. 41–42.
      The author's use of the term 'paternal friends' suggests that the attitudes and
      relations between Australians and Papuans were not entirely equal. Further
      research has identified NX78467 as Captain Ian Bryan Aird. Captain Aird was
      Mentioned in Despatches.

50   J.F. White, letter published in *Salt*, vol. 6, no. 6, 24 May 1943, p. 34.

51   *Salt*, vol. 6, no. 9, 5 August 1943, p. 35.

52   E.J. Johnston, letter published in *Salt*, vol. 8, no. 2, 27 March 1944, pp. 45–46.

53   E.J. Johnston, letter published in *Salt*, vol. 8, no. 2, 27 March 1944, pp. 45–46.

54   H.W. Forster, letter published in *Salt*, vol. 8, no. 5, 8 May 1944, p. 42.

55   W.M. Nicholls, letter published in *Salt*, vol. 8, no. 6, 22 May 1944.

56   Donald Thomson, cited in *Salt*, vol. 11, no. 5, 5 November 1945, pp. 21–22.

57   V504093 (Lieutenant Geoffrey Dean), 'Fuzzy wuzzy fetish', in *Salt*, vol. 6,
      no. 12, 16 September 1943, p. 48.

58   F.G.T. Place, letter published in *Salt*, vol. 10, no. 12, 13 August 1945, p. 48.

59   Results for the Postwar Reconstruction and Democratic Rights Referendum,
      1944, available in *1301.0 – Year Book Australia, 1944–45*, online at:
      <www.abs.gov.au>, accessed 28 March 2010.

60   Lee, 'Indonesia's Independence', pp. 169–70.
61   Lee, 'Indonesia's Independence', p. 170.

Conclusion
1   Paul Keating, 'Anzac Day – 25 April 1992, Port Moresby', <www.keating.org.
au>, accessed 23 October 2007.